D1456489

Reprint editor Jeanne M. Sexton
Cover design Linda McKnight

Library of Congress Cataloging-in-Publication Data

Fredette, Raymond H.
    The sky on fire : the first battle of Britain, 1917–1918 and the
birth of the Royal Air Force / Raymond H. Fredette; foreword by
Hanson W. Baldwin; afterword by Sir John Slessor; introduction by
Tom D. Crouch.
        p.   cm.
    Reprint. Originally published: New York : Harcourt Brace
Jovanovich, 1976.
    Includes bibliographical references and index.
    ISBN 1-56098-016-8
    1. London (England)—History—Bombardment, 1917–1918.   2. World
War, 1914–1918—Aerial operations, German.   3. World War, 1914–1918—
Aerial operations, British.   4. Great Britain. Royal Air Force.
I. Title
D547.8.L7F73   1991
940.4'4943—dc20   90-45774

⊗ The paper used in this publication meets the minimum requirements of the American
National Standard for Permanence of Paper for Printed Library Materials Z39.48-1984.

A Smithsonian reprint of the Harcourt Brace Jovanovich
1976 edition

For permission to reproduce illustrations appearing in this book, please correspond
directly with the owners of the works, as listed in the illustrations list, pp. xi–xii. The
Smithsonian Institution Press does not retain reproduction rights for these illustrations
individually or maintain a file of addresses for photo sources.

00 99 98 97   5 4 3 2

FIRE

the Sky on

Raymond H. Fredette

The First Battle of
Britain 1917–1918
and the Birth of
the Royal Air Force

Introduction by Tom D. Crouch
Foreword by Hanson W. Baldwin
Afterword by Marshal of the Royal Air Force
    Sir John Slessor *G.C.B., D.S.O., M.C.*

Smithsonian Institution Press
Washington, D.C.

To the memory of my father,
who served at sea
in the First World War

Contents

Maps

Illustrations

8a. The plywood forward section of the Staaken R.VI
(*Archiv fuer Fluggeschichte*)

8b. The nacelle of the Staaken R.VI (*Archiv fuer Fluggeschichte*)

9a. Pilot's position in the Staaken R.VI (*Peter M. Grosz*)

9b. The port-gunner-mechanic of R.12 (*Peter M. Grosz*)

10a. The flight engineer's compartment of R.12 (*Peter M. Grosz*)

10b. A flight mechanic rides outside the port nacelle of R.12
(*Peter M. Grosz*)

11a. A gunner-mechanic of R.13 (*Egon Krueger*)

11b. R.13's two pilots (*Egon Krueger*)

12a. The crew of Lo-Ri 3 (*Dr. Kurt Küppers*)

12b. 'Lori 2 before the Grave' (*Harold Fischer*)

13a. A German airman captured in the early hours of 6 December
1917 (*Syndication International: Daily Mirror*)

13b. Wreckage of a Gotha bomber shot down on 28 January 1918
(*The Times*)

14a. The North Pavilion of the Royal Hospital, Chelsea, struck by
the first German one-ton bomb (*Imperial War Museum*)

14b. The wreckage of a Gotha which fell on a farmhouse while
making a night landing approach (*Harold Fischer*)

15a. R.13 (*Egon Krueger*)

15b. The 'indestructible' R.12 (*Dr. Walter Georgii*)

16a. Lord Weir, British Secretary of State for Air
(*Imperial War Museum*)

16b. Twin-engined Handley Page 0/400s of the Royal Air Force
(*Imperial War Museum*)

Introduction to the
Smithsonian Edition
by Tom D. Crouch

Not long after the opening of the new National Air and Space Museum in 1976, Melvin B. Zisfein, then deputy director of the museum, invited me to join him at a luncheon with Barbara Tuchman. Zisfein was particularly anxious to hear what the author of *The Guns of August*, *Proud Tower*, and *The Zimmerman Telegram* thought about our exhibition on the First World War in the Air. In the kindest possible way, Tuchman remarked that we had perhaps blown things a bit out of proportion, considering the limited impact of the airplane on the course of World War I. With all the temerity of a newly minted Ph.D. addressing one of our greatest writers of narrative history, I asked our eminent guest if she had considered the enormous impact of the German bombing campaigns of 1917–1918 on postwar policy, and suggested that she might enjoy reading *The Sky on Fire: The First Battle of Britain*, a book on the subject by Raymond Fredette.

Barbara Tuchman was in very good company. With their vision focused on events of 1900–1918, very few historians of the First World War have paused to consider the long-term psychological and political consequences of aerial operations conducted during that war. As a result, the book that you hold in your hands is one that I have recommended to a good many readers over the years.

More than two decades after its first publication, *The Sky on Fire* remains a genuine classic in the historiography of air power. There is, of course, no dearth of books on aviation in World War I. Most of those volumes offer general overviews of the subject, almost invariably concentrating on the glamor of the single seat fighter planes and the brave young men who flew them. While often enormously readable, such books usually offer only limited insight into the roots of modern air power.

Fredette's approach is very different. He provides a detailed account of the first sustained strategic bombing campaign aimed at a population of urban civilians. More important, he explains the way in which a relative handful of German bombers helped to reshape both popular and official attitudes toward the potential of air power. In immediate terms, the air attacks on English cities during the last two years of World War I led to a much heavier emphasis on home defense and, ultimately, to the creation of the Royal Air Force.

But the real impact of these events was felt during the years after the armistice. The patron saints of air power doctrine—Douhet, Mitchell, Trenchard, and others—based their thinking on the perceived lessons extrapolated from the limited experience with strategic bombing during World War I. The fearful image of Gotha bombers in the sky over London haunted politicians, as well. "I think it well . . . for the man in the street to realize that there is no power on earth that can protect him from bombing," Prime Minister Stanley Baldwin warned the Parliament on November 10, 1932. "The bomber will always get through."

That thought became the cornerstone of strategic thinking among the leaders of the Royal Air Force and the U.S. Army Air Corps during the years between the wars. While experience of World War II demonstrated that the bombers usually required a great deal of assistance in order to "get through," the success of the great aerial campaigns waged against Festung Europa and the Japanese home islands confirmed the role of the airplane as the basic strategic weapon for the postwar world.

In *The Sky on Fire*, Raymond Fredette tells us how it all began. This is a book that should be of interest and value to every student of the military history of the twentieth century. We are proud to include it in the Smithsonian History of Aviation Series.

Foreword

by Hanson W. Baldwin

This book fills a gap in history; Major Fredette has resurrected the facts and the memorabilia of yesterday, with vivid phrase and pointed quotation, to illuminate today.

Alfred, Lord Tennyson, was prophetic when he wrote (in 'Locksley Hall', 1842) that he

> Heard the heavens fill with shouting, and there rain'd a ghastly dew
> From the nations' airy navies grappling in the central blue.

To most laymen, Tennyson's poetic fantasy seems to have been fulfilled with the great bombardments of World War II, London and Berlin, Coventry and Hamburg, Dresden and Tokyo and, most awesome, Hiroshima, that rubbled monument to the birth of the atomic age.

In popular hagiography Guilio Douhet, the great Italian theorist of air-power; Lord Trenchard, the 'father' of the Royal Air Force in England; and General 'Billy' Mitchell and Alexander de Seversky in the United States have appeared to be the true prophets of the 'central blue'. These men, many have argued, were to air-power what Clausewitz was to ground-power and Mahan to sea-power—philosophical theorists, articulators for a new doctrine of military power, prophetic historians of a new age, polemical pamphleteers whose faith in 'airy navies' was unbounded.

They enunciated the doctrine of 'independent' action by air-power, of separate air forces, of so-called strategic bombardment, of attacks directed not primarily at the enemy's military forces, but upon his economic capability and psychological will to resist. Air-power alone, they claimed, could surmount terrain barriers, leap above fortified frontiers, span broad oceans and win wars. And today—in the age of nuclear plenty—their predictions may, at long last, be accurate.

Yet the pilots of World War II did not originate strategic bombing, and well before Douhet wrote, or Trenchard spoke, a few Germans—little known to history—had provided the hard data, the operational experiments, the fundamental basis for the strategic bombing doctrines that have played so large a part for fifty years in the life of twentieth-century man.

For it was the Germans with their Zeppelin, and far lesser known but far more important, Gotha and Giant raids against Britain in the First World War who first attempted strategic bombing with consequences still unended. It was the Germans—not the British, not the Italians, not the Americans—who evolved the concept, the theory, the strategy and the general tactics and some of the techniques of a new form of 'independent' air war.

The German Giant bomber of the First World War had a wing span only three feet shorter than that of the B-29 Superfortress of World War II; it dropped 2,200-pound bombs on London in 1918. For a year in World War I, London was under aerial attack in squadron strength on an average of once every two weeks. In the Fall of 1917, the crump of bombs sounded in London six out of eight consecutive nights. Not even the incendiary bombs of World War II were new; the Germans had developed by 1918 a magnesium 'Elektron' bomb, never used for political and psychological, rather than military, reasons.

To meet the threat of the German heavy bomber—far more deadly than the famous Zeppelins, which were destined like the mastodon to evolutionary extinction—the British, for their part, evolved in World War I all the complex paraphernalia of defence later used in the second war: guns, fighters, barrage balloons, detections nets, listening posts, searchlights, shelters, communications.

Speed, scale, numbers and technology spelled the only major differences between the German raids of World War I and the raids of World War II. That—plus an historically ironic and militarily portentous difference in concept.

Towards the end of World War I it might have been said (as Jean Paul Richter is quoted by Thomas Carlyle as having said in the *Edinburgh Review* in 1827) that 'providence has given to the French the empire of the land, to the English that of the sea, and to the Germans that of the air'.

For the Germans unquestionably had first developed the concept of 'independent' air operations; they far more than any other combatant had tested the theory of striking directly at populated urban areas, at industries, at the will of the enemy to resist.

But, to their mind, the military results in World War I had not been worth the military effort; the ends did not justify the means. Partly—and importantly—because of their assessments of their World War I experience (and partly because they lost the war, in which air-power admittedly played an auxiliary role), the Germans built a different kind of air force for World War II—one that started with no four-engined bombers, one geared primarily to the support of surface forces. And it was this air force that was thrown into the climactic Battle of Britain in 1940; it was this air force that failed to win decision.

But the scars of World War I's bombings were never healed in the British mind. The bombings, though minor as an attrition factor compared to the inferno of the Western Front, left traumatic memories in 'the tight little isle'. For the first time since John Paul Jones landed his 'pirates' on the coast of Scotland, Britain had been 'invaded'; the Channel moat had been crossed. Militarily, strategically, geo-politically Britain, in the dawning age of air-power, was now virtually a part of the continent of Europe.

The memories of shattered homes and broken bodies lingered on, fed between the wars by the ever new achievements of the aeroplane, by the over-enthusiastic proponents of air-power, and by a spate of lurid books and articles, which embellished, in horrid detail, Tennyson's 'ghastly dew'. Prophets of doom forecast millions poisoned by gas laid from the air, whole cities burning, holocausts unending, and this trauma of ancient memories and vivid expectations played a major role in British history, and in that of the world.

The name of Prime Minister Neville Chamberlain has become, along with Munich, a symbol of appeasement. He and Stanley Baldwin and their contemporaries in power in the pre-World War II years, must undoubtedly share the blame of history for Britain's weaknesses at a time of Britain's need, but no Prime Minister of England, facing the horrid military facts of 1938, could have done other at Munich than to seek delay. For Chamberlain was faced with unanimous and emphatic recommendations of his Chiefs of Staff who insisted in detailed and definite terms upon peace for a time. War with Germany in 1938 would mean disaster, they warned.

They were thinking then, as they were in 1939 when war actually came and millions of British women, children and the old were evacuated from British cities, of an aerial blitz, not of the Blitzkrieg tactics, geared to ground armies, which Hitler actually used. Their vision of millions slaughtered, of whole cities burning, was—despite the heavy casualties from strategic bombing that were yet to come in World War II—one war ahead of time.

It was, thus, the British—not the Germans—who nourished and developed the doctrine of independent air action the Germans first introduced; it was the British, not the Germans, who had 'a bomber obsession' prior to and during World War II; it was Lloyd George who first said, in 1917, that the bomber would always get through.

The German strategic bombing of the First World War left therefore, as Major Fredette puts it, a 'fearsome legacy' for the second war. By 1940, the British had feverishly built up their air defences and their radar chain, and even more feverishly they had built big bombers and were preparing to implement plan W.A.8—a night attack upon Germany 'to produce an immediate dislocation of German war industry'.

The British predictions and expectations, like our own, were highly exaggerated; neither London nor Washington anticipated that the numbers of aircraft and bombs required to crush by independent action an enemy's capability and will to resist were astronomical. And no combatant fully anticipated the amazing physical and psychological resilience of the human being under stress, and his ability to carry on amidst disaster. As it was, World War II was not a victory through air-power, though it can be said that strategic bombardment was the final straw that—added to the insupportable strain of land and sea attrition—ultimately broke Berlin and Tokyo.

But the parallels of history go farther than World War II. The Gotha and the Giant bombers of World War I were too little and too late to save Germany from defeat, but they were a portent of what was to come in World War II. Similarly, the V1s and V2s of World War II, and above all the atomic weapons that devastated Hiroshima and Nagasaki were perhaps portents of World War III.

The prophecies of Douhet, the expectations of Trenchard, the claims of Mitchell and de Seversky and the hopes of those obscure German theorists and pilots who are rescued in this book from military oblivion, were never fully realized—probably never could have been realized—until the dawn of the atomic age. Victory through air-power only, through independent strategic operations without the assistance of surface forces, was never possible until the atomic age began in August 1945. Today the strategic concept first tested in the 1917–18 German raids against Britain has come to full maturity; intercontinental ballistic missiles and hydrogen warheads permit the destruction of nations and perhaps of civilization itself.

Yet—again ironically—the immense power of modern aircraft and missiles with nuclear arms is so great that it invokes built-in limitations against its use. Politically and psychologically, as Vietnam and the wars and crises since World War II have shown, strategic nuclear bombardment has become a kind of strategy of terror, a threat that neither side—hopefully—dares to invoke. Thus history has come full circle; the trauma left in England by the bombings of 1917–18, which so affected history between the wars and during World War II, is as nothing compared to today's traumatic memories of Hiroshima. Perhaps, in the end, a recollection of history may preserve us; perhaps, in the end, the edict of the Hague Convention of Jurists of 1923 may become a cornerstone of international law:

Bombardment from the air is legitimate only when directed at a military objective, the destruction or injury of which would constitute a distinct military disadvantage to the belligerent.

It is of this historic episode, the real beginnings of strategic bombing, for far too long neglected by most historians, that Major Fredette writes. He describes in graphic but succinct prose the German bombing of Britain in World War I, the results it achieved, the failures it experienced, and above all the effects—military, political, psychological—it had then, yesterday and today.

This book goes to the grass roots of history. It is the product of intensive research. It fills a gap; it corrects many mistaken assumptions and tendentious interpretations, and it provides a new window to the past and hence, as always with history, a link to the future.

HANSON W. BALDWIN

xix

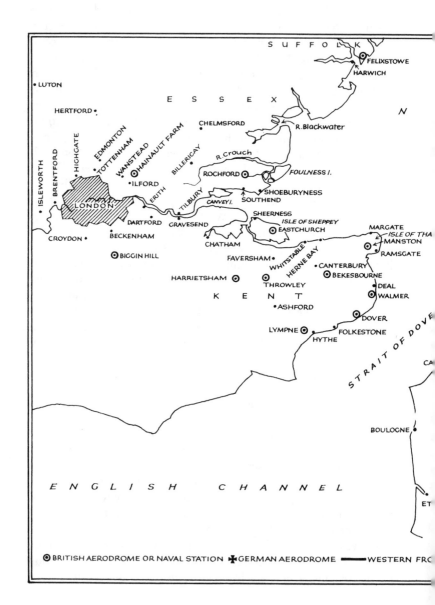

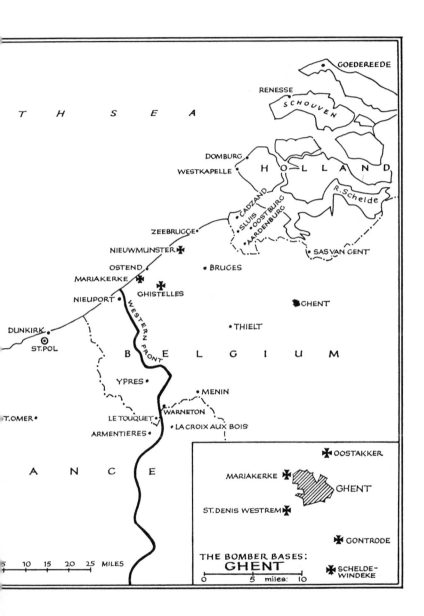

GOEDEREEDE

RENESSE

SCHOUVEN

T H S E A

HOLLAND

DOMBURG
WESTKAPELLE

CADZAND
SLUIS
OOSTBURG
AARDENBURG

R. Schelde

ZEEBRUGGE

NIEUWMUNSTER

OSTEND
MARIAKERKE
GHISTELLES

NIEUPORT

BRUGES

SAS VAN GENT

GHENT

THIELT

DUNKIRK
ST.POL

WESTERN FRONT

B E L G I U M

YPRES

MENIN

ST.OMER

LE TOUQUET
WARNETON
LA CROIX AUX BOIS
ARMENTIERES

A N C E

OOSTAKKER

MARIAKERKE

GHENT

ST. DENIS WESTREM

GONTRODE

THE BOMBER BASES:
GHENT

0   5   miles: 10

SCHELDE-
WINDEKE

5   10   15   20   25   MILES

xxi

A new day is dawning, but the clouds are blood-red over the coming sunrise.

Lord Montagu of Beaulieu (1916)

The Sky on Fire

CHAPTER ONE

'A Single German Aeroplane'

World War I, 'the dreadful tragedy that was turning the world into hell', was at its anguishing mid-point in late 1916. The dead and the wounded already numbered millions. The spectacle of huge armies deadlocked in battle along hundreds of miles of front seemed incapable of producing any new horror or surprise. The machine-gun, massed artillery, poison gas, the tank and the flamethrower had all been tried with deadly but indecisive effect.

Few illusions remained, except possibly in America. President Woodrow Wilson, his campaign aided by the slogan, 'He kept us out of war', was barely re-elected for a second term in November. Aged Franz Josef I of Austria-Hungary died a few weeks later. His death ended a reign longer than that of Queen Victoria, one of sixty-seven years, and foreshadowed the doom of a polyglot empire. The French were at an ebb, their *élan* drained by the bloodletting of Verdun. In December they forsook 'Papa' Joffre, their stolid commander-in-chief who had turned defeat into a 'miracle' at the Marne in 1914, and replaced him with the bombastic General Nivelle.

The Germans occupied a vast area stretching from the coast of Flanders to the plains and marshes of eastern Russia. General Brusilov's spectacular summer offensive, 'the greatest Russian victory of the war', had spent itself by September. Pushed to their limit, the long-suffering armies of the Czar had little more to give for a cause that was about to be engulfed by revolution. The Italians, bitterly engaged against the Austrians high in the Alps since early 1915, had gone to war with the Germans only that August. The Romanians joined the Allies that same month, hoping to profit from the death struggle of their neighbours. The Germans, Austrians, and Bulgarians overran the hapless nation before year's end, as they had little Serbia in 1915.

Great Britain was fighting on 'in the shadows'. Herbert Asquith, who had been Prime Minister for nearly a decade, and his wobbly coalition Government fell in the first days of December. The Battle of the Somme had just ended, at least officially, if not for the troops in the line. The sacrifice of that cataclysmic clash was still too fresh, too numbing, to be fully grasped. At sea, German U-boats were sinking British ships at an alarming rate, and a serious food shortage threatened the country. Harassed at home by night-bombing Zeppelins, the British people had to turn to the air for some sign that the Germans could be bested.

In that autumn of 1916, the raiders were being brought down in flames, their incandescent death-throes setting the sky on fire for miles around London. Courageous pilots of the Royal Flying Corps flying slow but steady aeroplanes were shooting down the hydrogen-filled monsters with incendiary and explosive bullets. The Germans, stunned by the agonizing end befalling some of their best crews, called the devices 'an invention of the devil'.

A reprieve from the raids seemed as certain as the sure-fire defences after 28 November 1916. In the early morning darkness two Zeppelins were destroyed, not on the outskirts of London, but at the coast. England's dimmed-out cities were jubilant. But the date of the double victory over the airships, the first such triumph on one single night, was to be remembered for a far more foreboding reason. In broad daylight, barely six hours after Luftschiff 21 of the German Imperial Navy disappeared with no survivors beneath a black oily scum on the sea off Lowestoft, a series of small explosions gently shook London's busy West End.

Unannounced and unheard beyond a few streets, the feeble blasts inflicted some damage between the Brompton Road and Victoria Station. Quite suddenly, as if struck by lightning, a baker's shop lost its chimney. A stable was wrecked and the roof of a rear addition to a house collapsed. The business office of a large dairy was mysteriously ventilated, its files and furniture scattered. A dressing-room was gutted in a noisy impromptu performance at the Palace of Varieties, a music hall near the station. 'One cobblestone was cracked in Eccleston Mews, opposite No. 23,' noted one meticulous report.

The detonations gave rise to some astonishment, if not alarm, in the immediate area. Rumours abounded as to what had caused them. In all London only two people could be found who were certain that they had seen an aeroplane. The others read about it in the evening newspapers.

4

'Between 11.50 and noon this morning six bombs were dropped on London by a hostile aeroplane flying at a great height above the haze,' announced a brief, matter-of-fact bulletin from the Horse Guards, Home Forces Headquarters. 'The material damage is slight,' the statement reassured, as if such an intrusion was nothing unusual.[1]* First given as four injured, the casualties were later revised to ten wounded.

Quite regularly since 1914, single-engined German aeroplanes had braved the Channel, one or two at a time, to drop a few small bombs along the coast. Their favourite target was Dover Harbour. After more than twenty such 'tip-and-run' attacks, the British had come to accept them as a routine nuisance. It was the cheek of this latest incursion that surprised most people. Certainly, no enemy pilot had been so foolhardy as to fly over London before.

The first Germans to do so were Lieutenant Walter Ilges and Deck Officer Paul Brandt, two young naval airmen. With Brandt at the controls, they had taken off from Mariakerke, an airfield near the Belgian coast, in a single-engined L.V.G. (Luft-Verkehrs-Gesellschaft) biplane. Used primarily for reconnaissance, the machine could easily reach London and return to its base.

Although Ilges had often photographed installations along the English coast, he had never flown very far inland before. With the eagerness of a schoolboy on a summer outing, he took scores of pictures of aerodromes, factories, docks, and other choice targets along his meandering course over Essex and up the Thames. Once over the capital he took more pictures and released the six twenty-pound bombs. Hopefully aimed from 13,000 feet at the Admiralty buildings in Whitehall, all missed the target by at least a mile.

The midday raider left the city from the south, and again escaped detection by flying a wide arc around the British squadrons based at Dover and Dunkirk. Over the Channel the L.V.G. developed engine trouble. Ilges had to toss his precious camera overboard to lighten the load. The pair reached the French coast in a long gliding descent, but without hope of regaining their own lines. Shortly after two o'clock that afternoon they made a forced landing at Boulogne.

The two Germans hastily set fire to their aeroplane, and tried to

---

*Superior figures refer to the sources, a complete list of which can be found at the back of the book, commencing on page 271.

escape on foot. The French soon captured them with a large-scale map of London still in their possession. Even as prisoners-of-war Ilges and Brandt may have sought recognition for their rather startling flight. Its import, only seven years after Louis Blériot blazed the way across the English Channel in a tiny monoplane, was lost to the British. They were too busy exulting over the two Zeppelins.

'London generally was quite undisturbed by the audacious visit,' reported *The Times* with some concern. The paper was part of the politically powerful Northcliffe press, then publishing half the dailies sold in London. Even before the war, it had been a policy of the newspaper chain to boom aviation as having 'revolutionized the art of warfare'. The force behind this stand was the brilliant but capricious Lord Northcliffe.

When, in the autumn of 1906, Alberto Santos-Dumont made the first public flight in Europe with a heavier-than-air machine, the colourful 'Napoleon of Fleet Street' was said to have been riled at the way a night sub-editor of his *Daily Mail* covered the event. 'Don't you realize, man,' scolded Northcliffe, 'that England is no longer an island?'[2]

On the day after London's first aeroplane raid, *The Times* responded with a warning editorial entitled 'Two Airships and an Aeroplane'. The aeroplane, being 'relatively cheap and elusive', was seen to have 'far more dangerous possibilities than the large and costly Zeppelin'. The newspaper reminded its readers 'that, like all fresh portents of the kind, this isolated visit is by no means to be ignored. . . . It is wise to regard it as a prelude to further visits on an extended scale and to lay our plans accordingly'.[3]

Even less tolerant of the general apathy over the attack was pugnacious Charles G. Grey, a 'promoter of decided opinions' who 'did not hesitate to prophesy'. Perceptive and prolific, he had written on aeronautics since 1909. He was also the founder of *The Aeroplane*, a periodical he was to edit for nearly three decades. Not quite forty when the war began, and physically unfit for active service, Grey was undoubtedly the most caustic critic of British air policy then in print. His lively writings prickled with the barbs he aimed at any official he deemed guilty of 'two-dimensional' thinking.

'When the aeroplane raids start, and prove more damaging than the airship raids, the authorities cannot say that they have not had a fair warning of what to expect,' he lectured in his weekly editorial. Grey added his fond and facetious hope that 'the London shop-keeper' would now 'realize that there is a serious chance of proper war being carried into the very heart of his sacred city'.[4]

That danger was far better understood the following summer when German bombers came to London in formation. Nearly every-one recalled then that lone aeroplane which practically no one had seen. And a thoughtful few, ever looking ahead, seemed to have been awe-stricken by a vision of modern warfare. Among them was Lovat Fraser, a *Times* leader-writer.

'If I were asked what event of the last year has been of most significance to the future of humanity,' he wrote in July 1917, 'I should reply that it is not the Russian Revolution, nor even the stern intervention of the United States in a sacred cause, but the appear-ance of a single German aeroplane flying at high noon over London last November.'[5]

Among the fateful turns of 1917, a pivotal year of this century, was the début of the heavy bomber in warfare. The nightmare dig-nified with the name of combat by professional soldiers at the front would henceforth come to the cities; and warfare, once so waged, would quickly lose whatever dignity one could still claim for it in an age of modern weapons.

World War I in the air is popularly recalled as a romance of dawn patrols, a tale of chivalrous duels between Spads and Fokkers. Strategic bombing is not commonly associated with that war. This notion ignores the co-ordinated Allied bombing effort directed against Germany in 1918. It also neglects the earlier bomber raids made by the Germans against England.

Obscured by defeat and disbanded after the Armistice, the airmen who flew for the Kaiser have long served as foils for the air successes of the Allies. The beginnings of strategic bombing are invariably recounted in terms of British achievements. Lord Trenchard is cited as 'the architect of air power', and Sir Frederick Handley Page is widely recognized as 'the father of the heavy bomber'. Their con-tribution, however important, is only part of the story.

While limited and indecisive, the German raids on England during World War I are significant as the first systematic strategic air campaign in history. Besides the notorious Zeppelins, two distinct types of bombers were used in these raids—the twin-engined Gotha and the much larger Riesenflugzeug or Giant aeroplane. Depending on the weather and other factors such as crew replacements, these aircraft attacked Britain in squadron strength on an average of once every two weeks for an entire year.

In October 1917, London was raided on six of eight consecutive nights. The German concept of attack incorporated the idea of 'round-the-clock' bombing. This goal could have been achieved if the Army High Command had been willing to commit the bombing squadrons it would have required. Fire raids were also attempted, first with the Zeppelins and later the bombers, only to fail because of defective incendiary materials. A much improved 'Elektron' magnesium bomb was available in quantity in the summer of 1918. Political reasons alone deterred the High Command from permitting its use against London in the last months of the war.

The German raids caused considerable unrest. Unlike World War II, the British people were not expecting to be bombed by enemy aircraft. Faced with severe political repercussions at home, an 'enlightened' Government headed by David Lloyd George hastily legislated the world's first independent air force in 1917. The British, as a consequence, are credited with providing the lead in a 'revolution of arms'. But the maze of circumstances from which the Royal Air Force emerged as a third Service in 1918 is all but forgotten today. Least remembered of all is the way in which nascent German air-power spurred the British to establish that independent Air Force in the first place.

Britain's indisputable pioneering claims lie more in the field of air defence. During the first Battle of Britain, a complex network was installed around London combining anti-aircraft guns, fighters, barrage balloons, observer and listening posts, and a direct-line telephone communications net. A marvel of ingenuity and organization, the London Air Defence Area finally prevailed against the German bombers in 1918. Except for some technological refinements, notably radar, it was essentially the same air defence system which was to serve Britain so well in 1940.

All this happened several years before General Giulio Douhet, the Italian air prophet, published his first book, and his American counterpart, General William Mitchell, sank his first battleship off the Virginia Capes. That the strategy of bombing cities far from the battle lines should have been born of the Teutonic mind should come as no surprise. In two World Wars the Germans seemed capable of bridging all obstacles save one—the English Channel.

The Gothas and the Giants were, in a sense, the V2s of World War I. These early bombers and the first rockets in warfare traversed the same skies to strike at the same target—London. Both came too late to stave off a German defeat. And though they were without decisive effect on the war in which they were first used, both portended as much for the next conflict.

Since the first aeroplanes were mere contraptions, and civilian ones at that, few early air enthusiasts of any country were to be found among the higher ranks of the military and political leaders. It remained for inspired tinkerers to improve the flying machine and proclaim its potential in warfare. A small group of aeroplane manufacturers, seeking orders for their product, hopefully approached the British War Office as early as 1908. Colonel J. E. B. Seely, Haldane's Parliamentary Private Secretary, dismissed them, saying that 'we do not consider that aeroplanes will be of any possible use for war purposes'.[6]

British officials were also reluctant to promote 'a means of warfare which tends to reduce the value of our insular position and the protection of our sea power'.[7] But air developments abroad could not long be ignored. In 1912, a Royal Flying Corps consisting of a Military Wing and a Naval Wing was created. Seely had since become Under-Secretary for War, upon Haldane's elevation to the House of Lords. His was the task of discussing the Cabinet decision with Brigadier David Henderson, the officer who was to head the new arm.

'What is the best method to pursue,' he asked Henderson, 'in order to do in a week what is generally done in a year?' Seely explained that the Army had 'about eleven actual flying men'. There were 'about eight' in the Royal Navy. 'France has about two hundred and sixty-three, so we are what you might call behind. . . .'[8]

The enthusiasm of the French for the aeroplane was imbued with a national pride much like that with which the Zeppelin was being advanced as a symbol of Teutonic might. General Helmuth von

Moltke, the Chief of the German General Staff, reminded his superiors in Berlin at every turn of 'the progressive achievements of France'. Anxious that Germany should not trail behind, Moltke pleaded for a large air force. He even urged its 'complete independence', a step which 'should be taken now'.[9]

A more conservative German War Ministry authorized, also in 1912, a flying corps to be organized as a component of the Imperial Army's transportation service, the Verkehrstruppen. Despite this modest beginning the Germans mobilized 180 aeroplanes in the West at the outbreak of the war. This force was nearly equal to that of the opposing French and British air units combined.

The Royal Flying Corps had but four squadrons of twelve machines each to send to France in 1914. The War Office was charged with home defence, but the only military aircraft left behind were those which the departing squadrons had discarded as unserviceable. Lord Kitchener, whose name inspired such faith that he became Secretary for War on the very day hostilities began, asked Winston Churchill, then First Lord of the Admiralty, to take on the protection of Britain in the air. Churchill agreed with characteristic eagerness, fully expecting that 'at any moment, half a dozen Zeppelins might arrive to bomb London'.

Churchill, who was not quite forty years old, had foreseen just such a threat. Speaking at the Lord Mayor's Banquet at the Guildhall in 1913, he had declared: 'The needs of the national safety demand the best possible measures for aerial defence.'[10] The First Lord, resorting to what he termed 'various shifts and devices', had taken it upon himself to provide the funds for the expansion of the Naval Wing into a well-equipped and virtually autonomous Royal Naval Air Service. As Churchill had anticipated, its aircraft, seventy-one in all, and its air stations favourably sited along the coast were Britain's only line of defence against aerial raiders when war came.

Once officially saddled with this added responsibility, Churchill turned to it as one 'of the highest urgency'. With amazing insight and attention to detail, he personally drafted a series of memoranda dealing with the deployment of aircraft, the installation of searchlights and guns, and the lighting of landing fields. 'Instructions must be prepared for the guidance of the police, Fire Brigade, and civil population under bombardment,' he directed in September 1914. 'This will have to be sustained with composure.'[11]

Across the Channel a German airship bombed Antwerp shortly before the Belgian port fell to the invading 'grey hordes'. The London press published vivid accounts of the attack, describing it 'in all its ghastliness'. Britain shuddered expectantly, but no Zeppelins appeared over the island that year. The first bomb to fall on British soil was dropped by an aeroplane, not an airship, on the morning of 24 December 1914. The projectile, a small one, made a crater in Tommy Terson's garden near the Castle at Dover.

The Royal Naval Air Service did not wait for that harmless but historic bomb to be delivered. The war was only weeks old when its Director, Commodore Murray Sueter, proposed the bombing of the Zeppelin sheds in Germany proper, targets 'bigger than a battleship and more vulnerable than the Crystal Palace'. The audacity of the scheme appealed greatly to Churchill. With his enthusiastic support the preparations for the long-range attacks moved swiftly.

On 8 October 1914 a British naval aircraft flew from Antwerp to Düsseldorf, and scored a direct hit on a hangar with two twenty-pound bombs. Flames rising several hundred feet into the air consumed an airship inside. Further attacks from Antwerp were frustrated when the city was abandoned to the Germans that same day. The British bombing unit was forced back out of range.

For the next raid four Avro aeroplanes were secretly shipped, still in their crates, straight from a factory in Manchester to Belfort in eastern France. Much to the consternation of the Germans, their Zeppelin works at Friedrichshafen on Lake Constance were bombed late in November. Two of three attacking aircraft returned safely to complete an epic round-trip flight of 250 miles. These British raids were the first strategic aeroplane strikes of the war.

This visionary use of air-power so energetically fostered by Churchill was also short-lived. A prime-mover of the disastrous Gallipoli campaign, he was compelled to resign as First Lord in May 1915. His departure led to policy changes which saw 'air efficiency sacrificed on the high altar of Admiralty tradition'. Many years later Lord Trenchard, Britain's first Chief of the Air Staff, said of Churchill: 'If the Admiralty had grasped his view of what aviation could do to help, the history of air-power might have taken a different turning.'[12]

What aviation could do early in the war was not so much a matter of foresight as it was one of the limited capabilities of the aeroplane itself. None of the armies which went into battle in 1914 expected much more of their air squadrons than surveillance of the enemy. The men who went up in flimsy machines for this purpose were often regarded as having more courage than sense. Their reports, consequently, were not always taken seriously. But after 'the race to the sea', and the anchoring of the Western Front on the coast at Nieuport, observation from the air was virtually the only means of reconnaissance.

Aerial photography quickly developed as the maze of trenches became too complex to be described verbally. With the armies dug in, there was also ample time for pictures to be taken and studied. Fixed ground positions also accelerated the techniques of directing artillery fire from aircraft, with which the French had experimented before the war. Fighting in the air, though not completely antici-pated, became a feature of modern warfare with the arming of aeroplanes in 1915.

The first trials in aerial bombing made in support of the fighting on the ground were discouragingly unrewarding. At the battles of Neuve-Chapelle and Loos in 1915, the Royal Flying Corps bombed railway stations to impede the movement of German reinforcements. Between March and July of that year, 141 such targets were attacked. A close analysis of the results revealed that only three of the bomb-ings had been successful. By early 1916, British air squadrons in France were restricted to bombing no farther 'than a few miles from our front lines unless the results obtained . . . are commen-surate with the possible losses in pilots and machines'.[13]

The Royal Flying Corps did prove its worth with the launching of the Somme offensive in July. The British Fourth Army alone was supported by a first-line force of over a hundred aircraft. The drive in the air was as relentless as the 'big push' was expected to be on the ground. British airmen flew 'contact patrols' over the slowly advancing troops, attacked German billets and supply dumps, and bombed railway junctions farther to the rear.

The Battle of the Somme has been called 'the climax of the initial growth of the air forces into one of the indispensable arms of war-fare'. John R. Cuneo, a painstaking student of that early develop-ment, concludes that when the offensive in the air 'was extended to include raids against all establishments contributing to the main-tenance of the enemy air force, the Allies had the basic strategy which brought them victory in 1944-45'. He discounts the influence of 'the widely publicized air prophets', and writes that 'the air triumph of World War II is owed to anonymous staff officers at the R.F.C. Headquarters in 1916'.[14]

While Cuneo is only referring to the methods the British developed for 'securing and maintaining air superiority', his sweeping accolade seems to imply much more. Many of the staff officers who forged the basic concepts of aerial warfare in the war of 1914-18 do share a common anonymity, but they did not all come from the same headquarters.

The Germans recovered swiftly from the aerial onslaught of the Somme. Even before that terrible battle ended, they reorganized their military aviation and redressed the balance in the air with superior new fighters. And, by the spring of 1917, German airmen were ready to do battle with the British over their own capital. In the light of what happened in World War II, that German challenge may well go down as one of the most devastating boomerangs in history.

A Vision of Modern Warfare

The time will come, when thou shalt lift thine eyes
To watch a long-drawn battle in the skies,
While aged peasants, too amazed for words,
Stare at the flying fleets of wond'rous birds.
England, so long the mistress of the sea,
Where winds and waves confess her sovereignty,
Her ancient triumphs yet on high shall bear,
And reign, the sovereign of the conquered air.

Translated from Gray's *Luna Habitabilis* (1737)

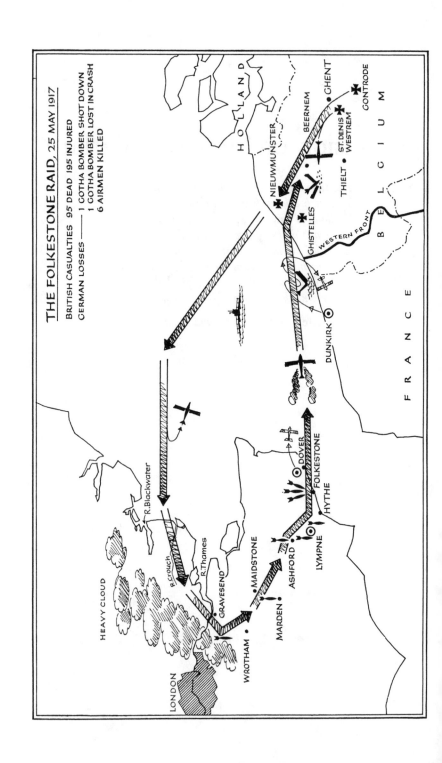

THE FOLKESTONE RAID, 25 MAY 1917

BRITISH CASUALTIES 95 DEAD 195 INJURED
GERMAN LOSSES ——— 1 GOTHA BOMBER SHOT DOWN
                    1 GOTHA BOMBER LOST IN CRASH
                    6 AIRMEN KILLED

HOLLAND

NIEUWMUNSTER

BEERNEM

GHENT

CONTRODE

THIELT

ST. DENIS
WESTREM

GHISTELLES

WESTERN FRONT

BELGIUM

DUNKIRK

FRANCE

R. Blackwater

R. Crouch

R. Thames

HEAVY CLOUD

LONDON

WROTHAM

GRAVESEND

MAIDSTONE

MARDEN

ASHFORD

DOVER

FOLKESTONE

HYTHE

LYMPNE

CHAPTER TWO

The Coming of the 'Wong-Wongs'

In the lazy warmth of late afternoon the air hung heavy over the south of England. Clouds drifting in from the west had covered London and much of the area. But the sky over the south-east coast was clear. The chalk cliffs of Dover and Folkestone stood out sharply against the grey-blue sea.

A Friday, it was pay day for the people of Folkestone. Tontine Street, which runs up from the harbour into the poorer section of the town, bustled with shoppers. Housewives, loaded down with purchases for the Whitsun week-end, shepherded their children through the throng. Customers jammed a draper's shop on the street. A queue formed quickly outside a vegetable market, as people heard that a delivery of potatoes had just been received. A man entering an off-licence nearby was asked if he would like to sample a bottle of wine from some new stock. He agreed, and the proprietor went to the rear of the shop for some glasses.

A policeman impassively watching the jostling crowd added a touch of calm and order to the busy scene. Though the war was raging just across the Channel, there seemed to be little reason for concern. True, Zeppelins had prowled over East Anglia the night before; but they had been foiled by high winds, snow, hail, and even lightning streaking the skies at higher altitudes. Most of their bombs had fallen in open country or off shore. Only one death had been reported. The last really damaging attack had occurred eight months before to the day. Since that raid on the Midlands the number of people killed by German air action had averaged less than one per month.

The increasing confidence radiating from London that spring of 1917 was evident in many ways. Guns ordered for air defence were being diverted to the Merchant Navy for the arming of ships against the U-boats. Other guns already in place in the capital were being moved to outlying areas. London had even brightened its lights at

17

the turn of the year. Later, it was decided to dim them again. The reason was not the fear of air raids, but to save coal. An 'Advertisement Lights Order' prohibiting outdoor illumination at places of amusement and in shop windows after business hours, was to go into effect that following Tuesday.

In view of the 'diminished risk' many combat-ready pilots kept at home to fly patrols were being sent to squadrons at the front. This action stirred no protest in Government circles until mid-March when the Zeppelins reappeared over England. Even then, the only dissenting voice was that of Lord French, the Commander-in-Chief of the Home Forces.

Elevated to the peerage not long before, he was better known as Sir John French, commander of the B.E.F. in France during the first year of the war. He had come home late in 1915, after being relieved and replaced by a subordinate, Sir Douglas Haig. French's career was a casualty of what he called the 'modern appliances of war'. The honours showered on the stocky, bandy-legged field-marshal on his return did little to soothe the 'acute pain' of that humbling experience. A hero of the Boer War, he was considered at one time to be the best cavalry commander in the British Army.

As commander of the Home Forces, French inspected troops, visited hospitals, and made speeches, duties which were largely ceremonial. But much to his apprehension, they also included control of Britain's air defences after that function was returned to the War Office early in 1916.

The March raid, though bloodless, revived French's misgivings. The home defence squadrons, he complained, were being 'reduced to a dangerously low point'. French recommended that at least a hundred trained night pilots should be kept in England. The War Office disagreed, replying that 'the shortage at home was not disproportionate to that existing . . . overseas'.[15]

French's anxiety about Zeppelins gave way to total complacency as far as aeroplanes were concerned. Shortly before warning against the drain on pilots, he had issued a rather astonishing directive. It prohibited all anti-aircraft gunners, except for those along the coast, from firing at 'aeroplanes or seaplanes, even if recognized as hostile'. The restriction was primarily intended to reduce the need for gunners by day, but it was to apply 'either by day or night'.[16]

The order was especially frustrating to the commander of the London artillery defences, Lieutenant-Colonel M. St. L. Simon. A 'painstaking and competent officer', he had been summoned from France for this particular post over a year before. Anticipating aeroplane raids, Simon was already hard at work on a new firing scheme to counter the threat. Receiving 'neither encouragement nor assistance', the artillery commander nonetheless persisted until a detailed plan was completed. The gunners of London at least would be ready whenever French decided to cancel his order.

The ban remained in effect even after a 'nocturnal Albatros' flew to London in early May, the first German aeroplane to do so by night. Five bombs fell between Hackney and Holloway. The only fatality was a man killed in his bed. Observing that one of the bombs had gone 'through an outhouse into a bathroom and wrecked the fittings', one report estimated that 'the whole damage' of the attack 'could be repaired for a sum well under 100 pounds'.[17]

The British again dismissed the incident as a daring but futile stunt. As the nights grew shorter, even the prospect of Zeppelin raids seemed remote. The people of England trustingly turned their thoughts to more pleasant things, such as the coming of summer and the approaching Whitsun holiday.

This supreme but misguided sense of security was completely shattered when German bombs tumbled down on Tontine Street in Folkestone late in the afternoon of 25 May 1917. The shoppers in the crowded street were given no warning. Earsplitting explosions smashed shop windows, splintered beams, and sent bricks and rubble cascading into the roadway. Then all was quiet except for the cries and moans of the injured.

'There is always an uncanny "calm" after a bomb falls,' commented one eyewitness.[18] A choking dust rising from the disembowelled buildings filled the warm air. The flying glass and falling debris had left some people miraculously unharmed. One of them was the policeman who found himself still standing in the midst of prostrated shoppers. The queue outside the vegetable market was now a crumpled heap of grotesque mannequins splattered by the dirt from a large crater.

'I saw an appalling sight which I shall never forget,' testified the town's chief constable. 'Dead and injured persons were lying on the ground. Three or four horses were also lying dead between the shafts of vehicles, and fire had broken out in front of premises which had been demolished.'[19]

Many victims were buried in the shambles of the draper's store. Still another casualty was the customer waiting in the wine shop. The proprietor rushed excitedly back, glasses in hand, to find him decapitated. Others died because of the construction of the old town. One bomb exploded above a narrow, stairlike passage between two buildings; those passing through at that moment were killed by the blast.

Most of the casualties occurred on Tontine Street, but other parts of Folkestone were also hit. Two cabmen and their horses were killed at the Central Railway Station. A direct hit on 'a very nice house' in a residential area reduced it 'to matchwood'. Two maids working in the kitchen were entombed in the rubble. A layer of 'finely broken glass' resembling 'a thin coating of ice on a winter's day' covered the road in Grimston Gardens. All the glass had been blown out of a conservatory, and in a tennis court there was a crater, twenty-five feet across.

Many townspeople, seeing the bombers overhead, were actually fascinated by the rare spectacle of so many aeroplanes in the sky at one time. One of them was a housewife out for a stroll on 'such a perfect evening'.

'Before I got any distance,' she wrote, 'I became interested in a very large flight of about twenty aeroplanes circling and pirouetting over my head. I stopped to watch their graceful antics and thought to myself: at last we are up and doing, fondly imagining that they were our own machines practising.

'I leisurely walked on and as I was crossing Earl's Avenue, I noticed a woman coming towards me carrying a basket. I had hardly time to reach the Olivers' garden gate when a bomb fell behind me, killing the poor woman I had just seen. . . .'[20]

Even when it became apparent that the aircraft were German, many viewers were held spellbound. An American clergyman residing in Folkestone was alerted by cries of 'Zepps! Zepps!' coming from the street. He dashed out of his seaside house to find 'crowds gazing upwards in the direction of the sun'.

'I could see nothing for the glare,' he related. 'Then I saw two aeroplanes, not Zeppelins, emerging from the disc of the sun almost overhead. Then four more, or five, in a line and others, all light bright silver insects hovering against the blue of the sky. . . . There was about a score in all, and we were charmed with the beauty of the sight. I am sure few of us thought seriously of danger.'[21]

For lack of a better name at first, many people referred to the strange machines as 'wong-wongs', a label which approximated their sonorous, double hum. However expressive, the term more accurately reflected British naïveté of the dangers of attack by the aeroplane. But before the summer was over, the word 'Gotha' was a familiar one in every British home within striking range of the new German bombers.

The raiders had valid military reasons for finding their way to Folkestone. The bombs which devastated Tontine Street were probably intended for the nearby harbour. Shorncliffe Camp, a large base with accommodations for several thousand troops, was only a few miles away. The camp was crowded with Canadian troops when the Gothas came. Many of the soldiers were out on the parade ground as bombs fell on the camp and the town at almost the same time.

The attack on Folkestone was not in the original plans of Captain Ernst Brandenburg, the German squadron leader. On this first Gotha raid across the North Sea, he had hoped to reach London. The weather, as observed from Belgium earlier that day, had seemed to favour such a flight. The sky was sunny and there were only a few clouds.

Twenty-three bombers in all took off from two grass aerodromes near Ghent. One of the Gothas failed less than half-way to the coast and came down near Thielt. The others flew on to an airfield at Nieuwmunster where they landed to refuel. The distance covered was less than forty air miles, but refuelling added greatly to the bombers' margin of safety. London was barely within range on the first few flights. Later, a reserve tank installed on the upper wing of the Gotha made this stop unnecessary.

Taking off again, the bombers were almost immediately over the North Sea. As the Belgian coast faded away, the crews settled down for the stretch over the water. The flight was uneventful, yet an anxiety born of uncertainty began to mount. Watchful waiting and the lonely emptiness of the sea were as trying on the airmen's nerves as active combat. Before very long one of the Gothas was obviously in distress. It straggled farther and farther behind as the formation neared England.

Brandenburg had no radio with which to contact the bomber. He could only guess at the cause of the trouble. As for the crew, there was no doubt about its identity. The aeroplane was decorated with large undulating serpents painted from nose to tail on both sides of its sparkling white fuselage. This particular Gotha was known to everyone in the squadron as the 'serpent machine'.

Aboard the ailing bomber, the observer, Lieutenant Walter Aschoff, was much concerned about the dwindling power of the starboard engine. As the other strained heavily, the pilot, Lieutenant Erwin Kollberg, was finding the large aircraft increasingly hard to control. Aschoff finally fired several red flares to notify Brandenburg that he was giving up the flight. Dumping his bombs into the sea, the observer then scribbled a message to be carried back to a coastal station by one of two pigeons on board. Sergeant Mayer, the rear gunner, tossed the bird away from the whirling propellers, and watched it disappear into the haze.

Steadily losing altitude, the crippled Gotha seemed to inch its way back toward the Belgian coast. Aschoff had been anxiously scanning the inhospitable waters for half an hour when suddenly his eyes lit up. On the surface a submarine was approaching from the south-east. The lieutenant stood up in his open nose position to fire a recognition signal. A white ring insignia soon appeared on the deck of the submarine. The worried airmen knew then that the craft was German.

They grinned and waved to each other, greatly relieved by the certainty of prompt rescue should they come down into the water. The submarine followed the bomber faithfully until it reached the coast. An airfield at Ghistelles was but a short distance away. Landing safely at seven in the evening, Aschoff and his crew learned later that their unscheduled visit was due to a clogged fuel line.

The remaining twenty-one Gothas passed from sea to shore north of the River Crouch in Essex at about five in the afternoon. Approaching in a 'rough line abreast' at 12,000 feet, the bombers clustered themselves into two groups so as better to defend themselves against any attacking fighters. The sky had already begun to fill with clouds, and a mist shrouded much of the land below.

Brandenburg was sharply disappointed by the unexpected change in the weather. Reluctant to give up the attack on London, he decided to lead his bombers inland. The raiders headed south-west to reach the Thames near Gravesend, a bare twenty miles away from the capital. Here the Gothas came up against towering clouds which covered everything before them. Since it was useless to go on, Brandenburg turned south in search of some suitable alternative target.

The Gothas ranged over Kent, scattering a few odd bombs along the way. Five British aeroplanes were about to take off from the airfield at Lympne when the formation flew over. The Germans let loose with a shower of small bombs, which destroyed some of the aircraft and damaged the hangars. The coast was regained at Hythe. Changing course at this point, the Gothas followed the shore line to arrive over Folkestone for the main attack.

A haphazard warning system had failed to alert the unfortunate town. But at Dover, the next place up the coast, local officials had been notified of German aircraft over England. Among those who saw the raiders leave the country was an officer of the Dover Patrol whose family lived in Folkestone. He angrily recalled:

'About 6 P.M. we were startled in Dover by the siren sounding and a heavy fire opening simultaneously from every A.A. gun in the place, both from the shore batteries and the ships in harbour. Looking seawards in the direction of the exploding shrapnel, we could see a long line of enemy aeroplanes. . . .

'The explanation of their course and direction was not long in dispute. The dirty dogs had dropped all their bombs on the defenceless town of Folkestone. . . . When we saw them they were merely making a joy-ride home, probably smacking their lips at their unusual success. No wonder the swinehounds did not attack us. . . .'[22]

Apart from the Dover barrage, which brought nothing down, the Germans encountered no opposition over England. Seventy-four British machines rose to the defence, but none was able to press an attack over land. One pilot of the Royal Naval Air Service, Flight-Lieutenant Reginald F. S. Leslie, nearly succeeded in bringing down one raider half-way across the Strait. Taking off from Dover in a 'land machine', Leslie overtook one trailing Gotha at 12,000 feet and opened fire from less than a hundred yards. The bomber went into a 'steep nose-dive, emitting smoke and steam'. Two other

Gothas concentrated their own fire on the British pilot, and drove him off. Though Leslie could not confirm his kill, he was later awarded the Distinguished Service Cross for his gallant effort.

Tipped off by telephone, the British naval air squadron at Dunkirk also went up to harass the Germans on their return flight. The Admiralty later announced the destruction of 'two large twin-engine machines' in a running scrap along the Belgian coast. German records indicate that only one Gotha was lost over the sea. Another crashed at Beernem near Bruges and the crew was killed. There was no apparent cause for the mishap, and it was assumed that the pilot had suffered a sudden heart attack.

London had been spared only because of the weather, a most uncertain ally. A little wary of British defences by day, the Germans were surprised at the ease with which the 'inland' flight had been made. They were not aware that Lord French was co-operating by restricting defensive fire to the coastal areas.

This first blow in a new phase of the air war was far more ominous for the British. Their casualties stood at 290, including ninety-five dead, the highest of any air raid thus far. The worst previous attack, made by Zeppelins in October 1915, had inflicted a toll of 199. After the quiet of several months, the reaction among the people was one of alarm and shock.

The uproar was understandably loudest in Folkestone. At an emergency session of the Town Council that evening, one alderman decried that the Germans should have been allowed to fly overhead for ten minutes 'without interference'. Had they chosen to do so, he protested, the raiders could have destroyed the whole place at their leisure. The residents gathered at a tense public meeting. They passed unanimously a resolution urging the Government to take 'such steps as will prevent further attacks . . . and the wholesale murder of women and children of the town'.[23]

In London, the Chief of the Imperial General Staff, Field-Marshal Sir William Robertson, called a conference of important officials to consider 'the defence of the United Kingdom against attack by aeroplanes'. Sir David Henderson represented the Royal Flying Corps in his capacity as Director-General of Military Aeronautics. Now a lieutenant-general, he sought to revive his earlier project for the development of airborne radiotelephony. Radio contact with pilots in the air was vital for the interception of enemy bombers. The Admiralty again opposed the proposal for fear that such experiments would interfere with its own fleet communications.

An Argyll and Sutherland Highlander, Henderson was one of Britain's first military pilots. He had learned to fly in 1910 at the age of forty-eight, while on leave and at his own expense. The spare, craggy-featured general had 'nursed and reared' the Royal Flying Corps since its creation. During the first year of the war, he had commanded its squadrons at the front. Henderson was truly a pioneer of flight, yet the ultimate use of the aeroplane in war somehow escaped him.

'The command of the air', a concept much discussed at the height of the Zeppelin raids, he dismissed as 'foolish' because it 'never existed—neither command nor mastery'. During the spring of 1914 he had said that the bombing of 'undefended towns' was unlikely in a future war. He reasoned then that 'no enemy would risk the odium such action would involve'.[24]

Such a trusting outlook was typical of Henderson, a capable officer of 'almost excessive calmness and forbearance'. Temperate by nature, he reacted to bureaucratic squabbles with a kindly patience that some regarded as weakness. The wireless dispute was deferred 'for separate discussion'. Though more immediate in effect, the other results of the conference called by Robertson were hardly equal to the appeal from the stunned people of Folkestone.

Twenty-four anti-aircraft observers were recalled from France. Decked out in naval garb, they were assigned as spotters on lightships in the Thames estuary and off the coast. Air training squadrons in England were also re-sited to cover those areas considered most vulnerable to Gotha attacks. This latter action failed to pacify French, whose grumbles against the outflow of pilots were heard anew after the Folkestone raid.

In a letter to the War Office, he testily denounced as an 'impracticality' the expedient of relying 'on such machines and pilots as happen to be any time available at Training Squadrons'. That much, he wrote, 'was recognized by the formation of the Home Defence Wing over a year ago'.[25] Though he warned that 'the present policy may have disastrous results', French did not see fit to revoke his hold-your-fire order of 7 March.

The choleric field-marshal was gibbeted in the House of Commons, as he had been many times before, by Noel Pemberton-Billing.

'We are told that Lord French is in command in England,' clamoured the self-styled 'First Air Member' of Parliament. 'I would like to know what he did on the night of the Folkestone raid, or whether he knew anything about it until all the people were dead.'[26]

With the active support of C. G. Grey and other aviation enthusiasts, Pemberton-Billing had ridden the crest of the fear aroused by the Zeppelins to his seat in the House. Lean and square-jawed, he revelled in controversy. A monocle screwed in his right eye provided an indispensable theatrical touch. Indeed, he had been an actor at one time. His many other occupations included bricklaying, selling motor cars, and inventing such gadgets as a cigarette-making machine. He had even tried his hand at boxing and once invited another M.P., who had accused him of using 'the most offensive, insulting, and caddish language', to 'repeat this outside . . . where I can deal with it'. The police intervened in the 'undignified scuffle' which followed in Palace Yard, 'before any harm was done to either' contestant.[27]

For all his escapades and eccentricity, Pemberton-Billing was not without some understanding of aeronautics. As early as 1908, he began making experimental 'air machines'. At the outbreak of the war he zealously designed and constructed within one week an aeroplane for use as a fighter. Reputedly, it broke all records for aircraft of its power at the time. But the enthusiasm of its maker failed to convince the Admiralty or the War Office. Pemberton-Billing never forgot the official snubbing of his 'seven-day bus'.

As an officer in the Royal Naval Air Service, he organized in 1914 an anti-aircraft unit of armoured Rolls-Royce cars armed with wooden guns for the defence of Windsor Castle. He also helped plan the raid on the Zeppelin works at Friedrichshafen. But his main concern was not so much the war against the Germans as, in his words, to fight 'the great political octopus that was strangling the Air Service'. Obtaining his release from active service, he campaigned for Parliament as an Independent with the avowed purpose of giving 'the Government the benefit of my expert knowledge'.[28]

No sooner seated, Pemberton-Billing charged that British airmen were being 'murdered rather than killed' by the 'dud machines' they were given to fly. The Government soon seized upon the reckless innuendoes to discredit the 'air agitators' who were then pressing,

both in and out of Parliament, for an independent air force. The upshot was a full-blown Air Inquiry, a highly publicized political sideshow, which dragged on for several months in 1916. Disproven for the most part, Pemberton-Billing's accusations were finally dismissed as an intemperate 'abuse of language'.

In the early spring of 1917, he sought to spark a 'second air agitation' with much the same charges, but on a somewhat more ominous tack. 'In the next summer we shall experience raids of a much more serious character than Zeppelin raids,' he predicted. 'Aeroplanes may come over this country or any other country at night, and at 15,000 or 20,000 feet they may drop their bombs and get back before we know where they are.' He argued that the 'only way' to deal with such raids was 'to carry out reprisals; otherwise, we shall have such a wail of indignation if we are raided day and night in the coming months, that it may bring the Government down. . . .'[29]

By this time, he was better known for his 'failure as a parliamentarian', than he was for his 'expert knowledge'. Many derided him as the 'hot air-man' or the 'bogey man'. On this occasion, he failed to excite the slightest stir in the House of Commons.

Feeling himself vindicated by the Folkestone raid, he followed up his blast against French with the demand that the control of the air defences be given to 'a capable man of aeronautical experience and training, and not too senior in age'. The Parliamentary Under-Secretary for War, Ian Macpherson, replied that 'everyone is satisfied . . . with Lord French, who is one of the most distinguished of living generals'.[30]

The next day, Macpherson had to contend with Sir Frederick Banbury, who represented the City of London. Was the Government aware, Banbury asked in the House, that the military were cutting down the trees on Kenley Common, 'some of which are eighty years old?' Macpherson retorted that the trees were being sacrificed because of 'urgent national necessity'. The Royal Flying Corps planned to use the Common as an aerodrome in the defence 'against hostile daylight raids'.[30]

Complaints of another kind were aroused when the press was subjected to strict censorhip in reporting the attack on Folkestone. Although 'all Fleet Street knew the facts that same evening', newspapers were not permitted to mention the places hit or details of the damage. This was intended to inconvenience German intelligence, but it also caused complications at home. Rumours of a heavy toll in 'a coastal town to the south-east' alarmed everyone with relatives in that general area. Thousands of telephone calls and telegrams jammed the communications lines, as people sought to confirm the safety of loved ones.

The 'town in Kent' was identified as Folkestone a few days later. After one or two such raids, the places bombed were reported without delay. The Gothas, unlike the night-blind Zeppelins, knew what cities and towns they were attacking by day. The British had defeated the airship only to be confronted by a far superior and deadlier weapon.

CHAPTER THREE

Air War and Baby-Killing

Mass burials in Folkestone cast a pall of sorrow over the entire south-east coast. Long lines of silent mourners, and schoolgirls laying flowers on the fresh graves of their slaughtered classmates, even when seen only in the lifeless grey tones of news photographs, had a searing effect. Yet, despite the grief and the anxiety, there flickered a newborn spirit of defiance, one that would burn brightly one day to light the darkness of Britain's 'finest hour'.

'We in this corner of England on the Kentish coast,' affirmed the Archbishop of Canterbury at a memorial service, 'have the trust —would it be an exaggeration to say the solemn privilege?—of being the bit of England nearest the enemy.'[31]

Few residents of the area doubted that the bombing was a brutal, fiendish act. But in still calm London some press commentators were able to maintain a remarkable objectivity. It was not quite right, they wrote, to think of the Germans as 'mad dogs', or that the attack was the work of 'baby-killers'. *The Times* observed with begrudging admiration that the 'principal objectives were essentially of military importance and the plan for attaining them was most carefully conceived and carried out'.[32]

Strategic bombing, as it became known, found a quick and ready place in the German mode of warfare. The Prussian military mind was nurtured on the Clausewitzian dictum of 'unlimited war'. The bombing of cities was clearly in keeping with the Teutonic idea of Schrecklichkeit which held that acts of 'frightfulness' served to paralyse an enemy's will to resist. Air war against his military potential was also an obvious complement to an equally new type of strategic attack waged far from the clash of armies with the submarine. In either instance, there seemed to be no way of avoiding innocent people.

The real horror of the 'great war' was that it established new patterns for an old game. The rules which nations had tried to spell out in times of peace so that reason and moderation might prevail in war were swiftly swept aside. This tragic turn in warfare was more a consequence of modern machines than it was of human depravity.

'You must not suppose that we set out to kill women and children,' the first Zeppelin commander to fall in British hands alive had tried to explain. 'We have higher military aims. You would not find one officer in the German Army or Navy who would go to war to kill women and children. Such things happen accidentally in war.'[33]

The British were less understanding of 'higher military aims'. Juries holding inquests over air raid victims often returned a verdict of 'wilful murder' against the Kaiser and the Crown Prince. Such a finding was duly recorded on at least one occasion despite the coroner's objection that it was useless 'against persons who could not be brought to trial in this country'.[34]

Kaiser Wilhelm, though propagandized as an ogre worse than Attila, actually had some deep-seated qualms about bombing England. The son of an English mother, and the eldest grandson of Queen Victoria, 'Willy' brooded over the safety of his royal cousins and the damage which might be done to the ancient landmarks of London. In higher imperial circles, the Kaiser's sentiments were shared by at least the Chancellor, Theobald von Bethmann-Hollweg.

Tall and distinguished with his well-trimmed beard, Bethmann-Hollweg spoke fluent English. He had served at the German Embassy in London before the war, and lived for a year in a country house at Walton-on-Thames. Local officials knew him well for refusing to pay the taxes on the property on the grounds of his diplomatic status. To the world, Bethmann-Hollweg is better remembered for his angry 'scrap of paper' utterance when Britain entered the war over the German invasion of Belgium.

Though he sought to justify the violation of Belgian neutrality by saying that 'necessity knows no law', the Chancellor was no iron-fisted worshipper of Thor. The crockery breaking of total war was repugnant to him. His Christian outlook and legal bent of mind inclined him to favour a more gentlemanly recourse to 'understanding', especially with the British whom he regarded as a 'kindred nation'.

The Chancellor's insistence on moderation strongly reinforced the 'humane' attitude of the Kaiser, a situation which exasperated the

German military from the first days of the war. The admirals, in particular, were bent on a hasty fulfilment of the boast that 'England shall be destroyed by fire'. One of the most vocal among them was Rear-Admiral Paul Behncke, the Deputy Chief of the Naval Staff.

Behncke, who stayed behind in Berlin when the war broke out, was greatly stirred by the news of the swift German advance in Belgium. In mid-August 1914, he dashed off a letter to his superior, Admiral Hugo von Pohl, to suggest the bombing of London 'with aeroplanes and airships from the Belgian and French coasts'. Behncke was highly optimistic, adding that 'the panic in the population may possibly render it doubtful that the war can be continued'.[35]

Pohl, the Chief of the Naval Staff, was attached to Imperial Headquarters in Luxembourg. Suspecting the Kaiser's feelings, he was not prepared to propose air-raids on England. He was satisfied to remind his deputy at home that the services of all available aircraft were needed by the High Seas Fleet for reconnaissance. Though given to indecision under the best of circumstances, Pohl did have a point. The Imperial Navy's air fleet at the time consisted of only two airships and nine operational seaplanes.

But finally the hesitant naval chief yielded to the prodding of his subordinates. At the turn of the year he petitioned the Kaiser for permission to launch air attacks across the Channel. The Supreme War Lord relented a bit after being assured that 'historic buildings and private property will be spared as much as possible'. He agreed to the bombing of docks, shipyards, and other military facilities in the lower Thames and along the English coast. But London remained strictly out of bounds to the raiders.

The High Seas Fleet was notified of the Kaiser's approval of limited raids on 10 January 1915. Only days later, the news of an airship attack on the Norfolk coast was received with 'the wildest enthusiasm throughout Germany'. Bethmann-Hollweg was not in a congratulatory mood however. In a curt letter to Pohl, he scolded the Admiral to the effect that the dropping of 'bombs on apparently undefended places makes a very unfavourable impression on foreign neutrals, particularly in America'.[36]

An Imperial Order issued a short time later again prohibited attacks on 'the residential areas of London, and, above all, on royal palaces'. Airship commanders were instructed to return with their bombs if they could not release them on military objectives. But the order also listed for the first time the docks of London as a permissible target.

The Army was now anxious to outdo the Navy over England with its own airships. The generals boldly interpreted the reference to 'the London docks' to mean the entire metropolitan area east of Charing Cross Station. The Navy, which looked upon England as the prime enemy, quickly adopted an equally liberal view of the Kaiser's order. The airships of both Services then made one attempt to reach London only to fail because of the weather.

On hearing of this, the Kaiser vetoed, in March 1915, the Army interpretation of his directive 'as going beyond his wishes and desires'. Bombing the London docks apparently did not mean bombing London. The stand taken by the Supreme War Lord puzzled the generals and the admirals more than ever, but they were determined to bring the full weight of air attacks to bear on the British capital. They were convinced that to go on sparing London would only be regarded as a sign of German weakness.

Early in May, the order permitting attacks on the London docks was amplified to include all military targets found to the east of the Tower of London. This change made a good third of London vulnerable to air raids. Wilhelm mulled over the new directive for three weeks before he begrudgingly made up his mind to sign it.

Within twenty-four hours London's eastern suburbs were bombed for the first time, on 31 May 1915. Once again, the German public revelled in the exploits of 'our airship heroes'. Their newspapers publicized the attack in the most intemperate language. 'The City of London, the heart which pumps the life-blood into the arteries of the brutal huckster nation, has been sown with bombs by German airships,' announced the *Neueste Nachrichten* of Leipzig. 'At last, the long yearned for punishment has fallen on England, this people of liars and hypocrites. . . .'[37]

Much to the annoyance of the admirals, the raid had been made by an Army airship. The new Imperial Order which had been so promptly acted upon made them even more unhappy. Targets 'of direct service to the war effort' which the Navy had painstakingly catalogued months before—the War Office, the Bank of England, the Stock Exchange, the main railway stations, and especially the British Admiralty—were still outside the revised bombing zone.

Pohl, who was to die of cancer before the end of the war, had since been replaced by Admiral Bachmann. The new Chief of the Naval Staff set out to have all restrictions removed. He was given a convenient and timely pretext when the French made a particularly murderous raid on Karlsruhe in June 1915. Bachmann first consulted Bethmann-Hollweg. The Chancellor reluctantly agreed to unrestricted attacks on London, provided they were conducted on weekends when many of the people were out of the city. The Navy rejected this condition as totally impractical, 'because of the dependence of airships on the weather'.

His patience wearing thin, Bachmann finally appealed to the Kaiser directly on 20 July. The naval chief argued that air attacks could be 'really effective only if the City, the heart of London's commercial life, is bombed'. He pointed out that the capital emptied itself of people not only on weekends, but every night. To clinch his argument he reminded the Supreme War Lord that the enemy was showing 'no regard for humanitarian behaviour in attacks on Karlsruhe and elsewhere'.[38]

The Kaiser capitulated completely at this, and agreed to the bombing of all London. But he still insisted that the raiders were to avoid the royal residences and national shrines, such as the Tower and St. Paul's Cathedral. Such a prohibition was unworkable. The Zeppelins, which could hardly fix their own positions with any accuracy at night, could not bomb the city with any such precision.

To Kaiser Wilhelm must go the final credit for the often overlooked fact that London was not attacked freely until the autumn of 1915. But after that time, the hub of the British Empire was wide open to the Zeppelins and the bombers which came after them.

CHAPTER FOUR

The England Squadron

The Germans are sometimes said to have been so obsessed with their vaunted Zeppelins that they completely neglected the aeroplane as an air weapon. A legacy of wartime propaganda, many such notions die hard. In a fairly recent account of World War I in the air, for example, one reads: 'It is almost incomprehensible that the German High Command, so thorough in studying military treatises by experts of all nations, should have completely ignored Douhet's theories of total warfare. . . . The Germans . . . just dismissed the whole concept of an aeroplane being anything but an observation outpost, and a rather unreliable one, at that.'[39]

The Douhet 'theories of total warfare' became known only after the war. It is all the more striking, therefore, that the German Army High Command, or Oberste Heeresleitung (hereafter OHL), should have seriously entertained the idea of systematic raids on England with bomb-carrying aeroplanes as early as October 1914.

One of the first officers in the German Army to suggest such attacks was Wilhelm Siegert, a hawk-nosed major with greying close-cropped hair and a mangled right hand. He had suffered the mutilation at an air exhibition before the war when he threw himself against a runaway aeroplane to keep it from bolting into a crowd. Siegert did not readily conform to the choke-collar discipline of the Kaiser's Army. He believed that the airman had to be a 'true revolutionary to rise to the stars'.[40]

Prone to act as he felt, Siegert's own rise was somewhat more modest. Though 'full of ideas', and 'close to being a genius', he finished the war as a lieutenant-colonel. But when he died in 1929, scores of top-hatted dignitaries were in attendance as his body was carried up the stone steps of the domed crematorium at Berlin-Wilmersdorf. And nine ancient biplanes, the only type available for the Germans no longer had an air force, noisily flew overhead in a grey January sky in final salute to the oldest of the 'Old Eagles'.

A one-time balloon pilot, Siegert was one of the oldest German flying officers even in 1914. The year before, he had initiated night flying training for his air battalion at Metz. The reaction to such an innovation at the time was perhaps best expressed by Siegert's own adjutant. On receiving the written order, he scribbled the comment: 'Downright ridiculous!'

Much to everyone's surprise there were few accidents, as night and cross-country flights were made by as many as forty aeroplanes. Formation flying proved more difficult because of the different types flown and the varying power of their engines. Siegert encouraged his airmen by giving them bronze medals. Since he had no authority to grant such awards, he explained that he only 'lent' them.

Siegert's novel plan to carry the war directly to the British homeland with the aeroplane in the autumn of 1914 had considerable appeal. The OHL, unlike the Imperial Navy, never saw fit to put all of its eggs in the frail basket that was the airship. The scheme was promptly approved, and Siegert was given the task of organizing a special squadron for raids across the Channel.

Only the best observers and pilots were selected for what was considered to be a highly hazardous undertaking. Within a month, they were dispatched with their aircraft to recently occupied Belgium. A temporary airfield was improvised for them at Ghistelles, a village near Ostend on the North Sea coast. Because the project was a closely guarded secret, the unit was given an innocuous cover name. Officially, it was known as the Carrier-Pigeon Detachment of Ostend (Brieftauben-Abteilung Ostende).

Calais, separated from Dover by only twenty-two miles of water, was expected to serve as a permanent base. Since Siegert was as short on range as he was long on ambition, this location was critical to the success of the operation. His 'pigeons' were powered by a single 100 h.p. engine. Besides the observer and his pilot, each machine could carry only three or four bombs. Small and pear-shaped, each weighed about twenty pounds. The aeroplanes were unarmed except for whatever weapons the airmen themselves took along. Later, Mauser automatic rifles were issued to them. The water-cooled machine-guns then available were far too heavy to be taken aloft.

The prospects for routine bombing flights against England were

35

quashed late in 1914. The German troops sweeping down from Antwerp were stopped short of the Channel ports. Stranded at Ghistelles, Siegert and his airmen had to be content with bombing Dunkirk, Nieuport, and other points behind the Allied front. Calais became a target, but never a base. The following spring, the squadron was transferred to Metz. With this move all immediate plans to bomb England, except with the Zeppelin, were abandoned.

Though premature, Siegert's hopes were not stillborn. Even before his squadron had left Ghistelles, the best aeronautical brains in Germany had designed and flight-tested an aircraft with two 100 h.p. engines. This was the beginning of the G-type 'battle aeroplane', the Grosskampfflugzeug. The earlier models of what was to become the most successful German bomber of the war required months of tedious trials to develop. By the end of 1915 there were less than twenty G.I and G.II machines at the front.

Apart from the technical difficulties, there were other problems to distract the Germans from any serious bombing of England from aeroplanes. In the spring of 1916 all available air squadrons had to be thrown into the boiling cauldron of Verdun. And the 'thunderbolt' struck by the British on the Somme that summer all but drove the black cross from the sky.

The reorganization of the German military aviation in the midst of that crisis clearly established its new status as a fully fledged fighting arm of the Army. Renaming it the Luftstreitkräfte, or Combatant Air Forces, the OHL decreed for the first time that these forces would be commanded by a general officer.

The general summoned to provide the leadership this 'branch of the future' so badly needed was Ernst von Hoeppner. Slim-waisted and sharp-featured, he had not acquired the 'von' by birth, but through long years of loyal service on the General Staff. The son of a major, he had left his home on the Baltic island of Wollin at the age of twelve to enter the Military Academy at Potsdam. Seven years later he became a lieutenant in a dragoon regiment.

Now nearly sixty, Hoeppner acted with the energy and enthusiasm of a far younger man, but he was without experience as an airman. When he was later given the Pour le Mérite, Imperial Germany's highest military decoration, there were many raised eyebrows among flying officers. Among them was Siegert, who had since become chairborne as Inspector-General of the Flying Corps. Crotchety as ever, he reportedly carried his own medals in his trouser pocket thereafter in disdain of such an award for headquarters heroics.

Hoeppner did revive, however, the Army's dream of raiding England with aeroplanes. Siegert's old plan of 1914 was no longer impractical as improved G-type bombers went into production. Soon after he was appointed Kogenluft (Kommandierender General der Luftstreitkräfte), Hoeppner advised OHL that, since 'an airship raid on London has become impossible', aeroplane attacks should be carried out 'as soon as practicable'.

He proposed the creation of a new squadron equipped with thirty G.IVs for such raids. The big twin-engined aircraft were to be delivered by 1 February 1917. Hoeppner estimated that eighteen of the bombers, each carrying 660 pounds of explosives, could be as destructive as three Zeppelins. 'Up to now,' he added, 'three airships have never reached London at one time.' He also mentioned a second squadron flying the R-type Giant airplanes, the Riesenflugzeugen. These much larger multi-engined machines were expected to be ready for use over England 'in the near future'.[41]

Following OHL approval of Hoeppner's memorandum the projected bomber campaign was given the code name 'Turk's Cross'. Siegert's original squadron was called upon to provide three of its six Staffeln, or flights, as a nucleus for the new unit. Regrouped several times, the Ostend squadron was now called Kampfgeschwader I of the OHL (hereafter Kagohl 1). Several of these 'battle squadrons' were flying the large, single-engined C-type biplanes at the front. Though the primary task of the Kagohls was tactical bombing, they were also used for barrage patrols, long-range reconnaissance, and as escorts for the aeroplanes spotting for the artillery.

The three flights selected for raids on England continued to operate in Flanders, pending the arrival of the Gothas. As if to erase the frustration of Siegert's failure, they were again assigned to the airfield at Ghistelles. Three permanent aerodromes were in the meantime being made ready for them on the outskirts of Ghent, approximately 170 air miles from London.

The return to Ghistelles was a nostalgic one for the surviving veterans of Siegert's old squadron. They were back amidst the sand dunes, smelling the sea air. During their off-duty hours, the airmen tramped the streets and piers of Ostend. They happily revisited familiar seaside cafés where they had earlier acquired a taste for oysters and other sea food. Almost nightly, they attacked their old targets of Dunkirk, Calais, and St. Pol. Everything, in fact, was much the same as two years before.

Although they were not told immediately why they were back at Ghistelles, the airmen soon sensed that their return was more than mere coincidence. From the large tents on the edge of the field, where mechanics worked on the machines, to the officers' mess in the village, there was again talk of flying against England. Rumours persisted that the squadron would soon be receiving 'big battle aeroplanes' capable of flying all the way to London.

The secret of Operation 'Turk's Cross' became an open one when selected groups received orders to return home for special training. Hoeppner had specified in his memorandum that 'especially good crews' were to be indoctrinated 'in flying over wide expanses of water'. In the last months of 1916, battle-wise pilots and observers boarded trains for a long journey to the German North Sea coast.

At the naval stations on Heligoland, and at Westerland on the isle of Sylt, the Army airmen were initiated into the perils of flying over the sea. Though its own fliers were old hands at this, the Imperial Navy had no aircraft suitable for mass raids across the Channel. Naval aircraft were too slow and vulnerable with their heavy floats, and the bomb loads they could have carried were too small. The Army, then, would bomb London with the Gothas.

Lieutenant Aschoff, who was to miss the raid on Folkestone because of an ailing engine, was among the Kagohl airmen who spent Christmas on the drab, wind-swept island of Heligoland. As an observer, he received intensive instruction on how to navigate over the trackless sea, and in the recognition of British ships. He had much to learn. Less than a year before the lieutenant had commanded an infantry company at the front.

By the time Aschoff rejoined the squadron at Ghistelles, the trees in Flanders were budding. He returned to find only a few lonely Gothas tethered on the airfield. Hoeppner's delivery schedule had not been met because of production problems at home. But even a few of the towering bombers were an exciting sight to the restless crews.

An angular biplane, the Gotha G.IV was larger than any aeroplane they had ever seen before. Its long slender fuselage stretched for over forty feet, and ended with a high monoplane-type tail. The longer upper wing measured nearly seventy-eight feet, a span greater than that of any German aircraft sent against England in World War II.

Mounted on the lower wing were two Mercedes six-cylinder engines, which together generated 520 h.p. Although the Gotha cruised at only 80 m.p.h., it was anything but a sitting duck with its armament of three machine-guns. Truly a remarkable aircraft for its time, the bomber was named after the firm which made it, the Gothaer Waggonfabrik. The company's principal peacetime product had been railway carriages.

Shortly after the first Gothas arrived in March 1917, the squadron was officially designated as Kagohl 3. Its original strength of three flights soon increased to four as new crews were assigned to it. Because of its unique mission the unit was quickly dubbed the England Geschwader, or the England Squadron. Clearly the élite of the Kaiser's bombing squadrons, Kagohl 3 was the first to be given a strictly strategic bombing function. The squadron was attached to the German Fourth Army in Flanders, but it operated independently of the war at the front. Brandenburg received his orders directly from OHL.

Arriving with the Gothas to assume command, the captain was a striking figure with dark intelligent eyes and a massive brow. Quite bald, his large head was made to appear all the bigger by the tight broad collar of his officer's tunic. A devoted chess player, and an avid student of philosophy, he impressed some as having 'an inner urge to raise himself above the limits set for a soldier'.

If not a soldier by instinct, Brandenburg was one through training and a strong sense of duty. He had marched off to war in 1914 as a regular officer in the infantry. Wounded severely that same year, he was declared unfit for the trenches. Like many other German officers disabled in ground battle, Brandenburg became an air observer flying over the front in a two-seater. A natural leader, he easily gained the admiration and confidence of his men. Brandenburg was also a capable organizer and administrator. Hoeppner had personally selected him to lead the raids on England.

Only thirty-four, Brandenburg was facing his toughest challenge of the war. With a few dozen bombers of very limited capabilities, he was expected to provide 'a basis for peace' by intimidating 'the morale of the English people' and crushing their 'will to fight'.

Materially, his raids were 'to disrupt the British war industry, dis-organize the communications between coastal ports and London, attack the supply dumps of the coastal ports, and hinder the transport of war materials across the Channel'.[42] The Germans were also hopeful of a large-scale diversion of British squadrons and guns from the front.

Brandenburg had no manuals to consult, no previous air 'blitz' to guide or inspire him. No air force, much less a single squadron, had ever considered such a military *tour de force* before. In attempting it against the largest city in the world, Brandenburg had only the open sky, an agile mind, and the courage of his crews. Nearly fifty years later one of the pilots still remembers 'the somewhat depressing feeling of having to solve a difficult problem with inadequate means. This had to be compensated for with our youthful enthusiasm. And so it was!'[43]

The difficulty of obtaining accurate weather data was never com-pletely overcome. As they took off from their Belgian bases, the Germans never knew for certain what storm was brewing beyond the North Sea. Unfortunately for them, the weather on the Continent was generally that of England's several hours before. If head winds were encountered, and they proved stronger than anticipated, there was a good chance that the whole squadron would go down into the sea on the way home from fuel exhaustion.

Brandenburg ordered long trial flights with maximum bomb and fuel loads. He concluded that the capacity of the Gotha's tanks, as delivered, was barely sufficient for the flights to London. Refuelling en route between Ghent and the coast could only be a temporary expedient. Auxiliary tanks were speedily installed to provide for an additional two hours of flight.

This permitted the Germans to deviate slightly from the straightest course to London. Gun defences had to be avoided as much as possible, particularly in daylight. German intelligence about anti-aircraft installations was very limited at first, and the British had mobile guns mounted on lorries. Considerable protection was afforded the Gotha by its attack altitude of over 14,000 feet. The aircraft, once unburdened of its bombs, could climb even higher for the hazardous return journey when British fighters were most likely to be encountered.

To keep the crews alert at such heights, each bomber was equipped with two small cylinders of compressed oxygen. The system worked much like an Oriental smoking pipe. The flow of oxygen was regulated by a valve and inhaled by means of a mouthpiece at the end of a hose. The discomfort of having to breathe into a soggy rubber mask, a familiar one to World War II airmen, was unknown to the Gotha fliers. Their complaint was that direct inhalation produced 'a disagreeably dry throat'. The oxygen equipment had to be taken along, but it was not always used. 'We rather preferred,' writes one pilot, 'to restore our body warmth and energy with an occasional gulp of cognac.'[43]

The cold at the higher altitudes had not been overlooked in equipping the crews. Each airman was issued a heavy pair of gloves, high boots reaching up to the thighs, and a thick half-length coat, all fur-lined, for wear over his field uniform. A crash helmet was also provided, but the standard leather headgear was often preferred for its greater warmth and comfort.

The lack of parachutes did not particularly worry the Kagohl airmen for such equipment was not in general use at the time. Even if they had been available, the crews would have seen little advantage in using them over water. Though accustomed to the dangers of aerial combat at the front, many of the airmen were squeamish about venturing over the North Sea.

Crews in distress, it was felt, should have some means of sending word back when forced down at sea. The Gothas, unlike the Zeppelins, carried no radios. The weight of such equipment was prohibitive. When the use of carrier pigeons was suggested, some of the airmen were amused, if not downright reluctant, at having to rely on the birds' homing instincts for rescue. Brandenburg nonetheless decided that they would be provided, two to a crew. Even then, the airmen grumbled that pigeons would be of little use if their aircraft sank soon after coming down into the water.

Actually, much inventive effort had gone into the Gotha to make it seaworthy. According to the manufacturer's specifications, the bomber was capable of remaining afloat for at least eight hours. Vents and other openings in the fuselage were to close tightly. Water brakes were installed to lessen the chances of damage as the aeroplane struck the water. The crews were even given air bags to inflate on the descent. Many of these innovations were later abandoned as they proved impractical. But, at first, they were of much comfort to the water-shy land fliers. A system of sea patrols by torpedo boats and submarines, to coincide with the Gotha flights, was also arranged with the Navy for the prompt recovery of the crews.

Despite the many hours spent on practise flying, crash landings were tragically frequent. Another difficult training problem arose when it was agreed that flying over England in battle formation was the best defence against fighters. Unfamiliar as they were with the unwieldy bombers, pilots had to be trained to assemble and fly together like geese. And, as the leader of the flock, Brandenburg had to be able to communicate in the air with his flight leaders and other crews. Because the possible signal combinations were too limited, the firing of coloured flares was an obvious but not very satisfactory way of doing this.

In preparing his crews for combat, Brandenburg had little air space in which to fly. Occupied Belgium was but a narrow strip wedged between neutral Holland and the guns of the Western Front. The crews had strict orders to avoid the battle lines. If a single Gotha fell prematurely into enemy hands, London and all England could be alerted to the coming blow.

The lagging construction of the bases at Ghent was another cause for concern. Kagohl 3 was literally being assembled under the noses of the British. Ghistelles was barely fifteen miles from the front in Flanders. The airfield became dangerously crowded as more Gothas were flown in. Proof of Brandenburg's amazing luck in keeping the British in the dark was amply shown later at Folkestone.

The chances of arousing British curiosity were lessened in April, when the England Squadron finally left Ghistelles to occupy its permanent aerodromes. Brandenburg assigned Staffeln 13 and 14 to the field at St. Denis-Westrem. Gontrode, which had a large airship hangar, was taken over by Staffeln 15 and 16. Two additional flights, 17 and 18, were organized later with the delivery of more bombers and the completion of a third base at Mariakerke.

Led by a Staffel Führer, each flight was equipped with six Gothas. The Kagohl headquarters at Gontrode had its own aircraft. Once at full strength, the Geschwader was expected to attack England with forty or more bombers. Each Gotha was flown by a three-man crew which was commanded by the observer rather than the pilot.

Aschoff, who was assigned to Staffel 15, was given a bomber and a crew soon after the transfer to Gontrode. As navigator and bombardier, he occupied the Gotha's box-like nose. This commanding position, which sat high off the ground, was quickly nicknamed the 'pulpit' by the crew. Though his open berth was quite spacious, Aschoff found it crammed with equipment. The oxygen cylinder was installed inside, and he had a movable Parabellum machine-gun. The weapon was affixed to a geared ring lining the edge of the circular turret.

Aschoff was also cramped by the large Goerz bombsight. Its principal component was a vertically mounted telescope which was over three feet long. The bombsight was the best German instrument of its type produced during the war. The bombs themselves could be loaded either internally or externally. Smaller bombs were placed in two racks located within the fuselage between the pilot and the rear gunner. Bombs weighing 110 pounds or more were shackled underneath the wings and fuselage between the twin-wheel landing gear.

Aschoff's pilot, Lieutenant Kollberg, was only nineteen years old. He still wore the spurs and full uniform of the Uhlan regiment in which he had been commissioned. Imbued with the old dash of the fading cavalry, Kollberg had hoped to find an outlet for this spirit in the Flying Corps. He was not at all keen on piloting a slow bomber, even if it did take him all the way to London. His ambition was to fly a fighter and become an ace. The great Richthofen had started his meteoric career in the same regiment. But as a Gotha pilot, Kollberg had his hands full simply keeping the big aeroplane on a straight and level course. There was not even a gun for him to fire.

Mayer, the third man of the crew, was a reserve sergeant. A sturdy man of lesser ambitions, he was much more enthusiastic about his assignment. His job as rear gunner was to defend the bomber's tail with two machine-guns. The 'tunnel' in the underside of the fuselage, a unique feature of the Gotha, particularly intrigued him. Fighters attacking from the rear and below, the blind spot of bombers, could be fired at through this open, inverted U-shaped depression. Mayer was eager to try his luck against some unsuspecting British pilot.

Soon after they were united as a crew, the trio decided upon the bizarre design which won for their Gotha the title of 'serpent machine'. Most of the bombers were emblazoned in one fashion or another to suit the taste of the individual crews. The usual markings consisted of the oversized initials of the observer and his pilot, but others were more decorative. One Gotha had large herringbone stripes painted down the whole length of its fuselage. Apart from crew morale, the markings served the very practical purpose of identifying the crews in flight.

Kollberg spent much of his time flying the 'serpent machine' on his own, while Aschoff and Mayer were occupied with gunnery and other ground training. Each new bomber was test flown for at least twenty-five hours before it was considered ready for combat. Brandenburg was intent on checking the reliability of the Gothas' Mercedes engines. Many were sent back to the factory as defective, but the German home industries were already using substandard materials because of shortages. Engine failure continued to plague the crews on nearly all their raids.

Because of the many difficulties, Brandenburg was unable to report to OHL that his squadron was ready for the first attack on England until the middle of May 1917. A few days later, Field-Marshal Paul von Hindenburg, the Chief of the General Staff, arrived at Ghent to give Kagohl 3 an appropriate send-off.

The revered Feldmarschall was ceremoniously driven out onto the airfield in a large open car. Waiting to receive him, Brandenburg and his officers stood stiffly along a sandy road which ran across the landing strip. Beyond, over twenty Gothas were lined up, wing-tip to wing-tip, in a neat precise row. Brandenburg's own aircraft and those of his flight leaders were drawn up in front of this solid line.

Snow-white except for their crew markings, and the bold black crosses on their tails and fuselages, the Gothas glistened in the glare of a brilliant sun. The day could not have been more perfect, nor the setting more peaceful, for the display of the martial birds. In the midst of this pastoral calm in the third spring of the war, Siegert's vision of a German squadron capable of bombing England had finally come true.

A hundred booted feet trampled the tall grass as Hindenburg and his spike-helmeted staff were led to one of the waiting Gothas. The bomber was battle-ready with its polished guns in position and bombs buckled to its belly. A tall incongruous ladder had been placed at its front, so that the distinguished visitor might have a closer look. But the portly, seventy-year-old field-marshal declined, leaving that pleasure to his younger staff officers. Brandenburg stepped forward to explain the bomber's capabilities. Hindenburg, looking very much like a hoary lion, blinked intently at the white hulk and nodded his approval.

The horse-and-sabre memories of the stern old Junker went back even before the Franco-Prussian War. As he stood there, dwarfed by the looming nose of a Gotha, war's past was momentarily linked with its future. The crew of one bomber farther down the line had decorated their machine with an odd twisted cross. The strange device was nothing more than a little known sun symbol of some ancient tribe. It was a swastika.

CHAPTER FIVE

Gotha in the Sea

The elation and high spirits aroused by Hindenburg's visit began to fade with the coming of June. Days passed, and the promise of an early attack on London, so confidently given to the Feldmarschall, went unfulfilled. The weather, which had co-operated so beautifully that day, now seemed to be conspiring against Brandenburg at every turn.

His first attempt to fly to London had ended at Nieuwmunster, the refuelling stop on the coast. Informed of sudden storm warnings, he had ordered the Gothas to return to Ghent. The second try resulted in the roundabout raid on Folkestone. Though the bombs had been delivered, it had cost him the element of surprise.

Brandenburg had wanted the shock of that attack to fall on London. It was now reasonable to assume that the British were feverishly at work on the defences of their capital, making them stronger day by day. Had Brandenburg known that the authorities in London were not unduly alarmed, he could have rested easier.

Until the weather favoured such a flight, there was little he could do except to placate Hoeppner. Kogenluft's inquiries as to when OHL could expect an attack on London were becoming increasingly anxious. Brandenburg, meanwhile, resolved to raid the English coast. Since he had already tipped his hand, there was little to lose in attacking secondary targets.

Shortly after six on the evening of 5 June, Brandenburg flew in over Essex just north of the River Crouch. The approach was the same as that of his first visit made eleven days before. Behind him followed twenty-one Gothas carrying nearly six tons of explosives. Brandenburg's bombers had been fairly fortunate up to this point. None had fallen behind because of mechanical trouble.

Four British naval machines out on patrol from Dunkirk had spotted them earlier, but the bristling formation was already well out over the sea. The official British communiqué later noted the chance encounter. After 'indecisive engagements,' it announced, 'the enemy were chased to England', which was hardly in the right direction. If anything had driven the Gothas to the English shore, it was a strong east wind.

Standing in his 'pulpit', Brandenburg signalled his pilot with a wave of the arm and fired a flare. The lead bomber banked to the left, and the entire formation turned due south towards the Thames estuary. Two militarily important objectives were directly ahead. Munitions were manufactured at Shoeburyness on the north shore. Many of its isolated barren acres served as a proving ground for all kinds of weapons and projectiles. On the opposite bank, five miles to the south, lay Sheerness on the Isle of Sheppey, with its extensive Admiralty docks.

Although it was early in the week, the heat had attracted a good crowd to the Sheerness seaside front. It was a relaxed, gay throng made up mostly of women and children. Except for the wounded soldiers home from the front, who were being entertained with boat trips, one could have forgotten the war. The people on the beach were not the least bit alarmed when the shore batteries began to rumble. The gunners often practised. Those who did bother to look skyward saw nothing unusual at first. Only a little later did a cluster of aeroplanes suddenly break through the haze.

The crowds watched with expectant fascination as the crackling shells tracked the formation across the estuary. Crippled by a near burst, one of the bombers began to roll erratically. Then, as it tumbled downward, loud cheers arose from the shore. The Gotha splattered into the sea a few thousand yards north of Barton's Point. With great excitement, the owners of motor-boats and other small craft took to the water in a rush to reach the downed bomber.

British fighters were roaring out over the estuary by this time, trying to reach the German formation. Their enthusiasm was that of a bucket brigade summoned to a fire, and they were just about as effective in their confused and unco-ordinated attacks. Only a few of the sixty-six British pilots in the air that early evening actually managed to get within machine-gun range of the enemy. One naval pilot, who landed later at Dunkirk, claimed to have shot down two Gothas off the coast. But this could not be confirmed.

The guns and aeroplanes did not prevent Brandenburg from reaching Sheerness, which was briefly but sharply bombarded. One

47

rocking explosion tossed debris several hundred feet into the air. The crews reported several hits on the arsenal and dock facilities. A few small ships were also believed to have been sunk.

Because of the good visibility, the bombing was quite accurate. Damage was limited only because many well placed bombs had failed to explode. Brandenburg's preoccupation with military installations was reflected by the casualties. Of the forty-five people killed or wounded, only twelve were civilians. At Shoeburyness, the effects were practically nil. Most of the bombs fell on empty wasteland or exploded harmlessly deep down in the estuary mud. Casualties were limited to two soldiers killed.

For the Gothas, the most serious threat came as they approached the Belgian coast on their homeward flight. The tiring crews were already within sight of Ostend when they observed dark, ominous specks bobbing on the western horizon. These turned out to be ten machines of the Royal Naval Air Service at Dunkirk.

The British aeroplanes pounced angrily on the slow-moving formation from the rear. One Sopwith pilot, possibly attracted by the serpents on Aschoff's bomber, dived to within fifty yeards of it. The Gotha shuddered under a spray of bullets which punched holes in the wings and fuselage. The main fuel tank was hit and punctured. As the fighter zoomed beneath, Mayer twisted under his seat to reach the lower gun. Before he could fire more than a few shots, the attacker was out of range.

Just as it would seem that the whole formation might be wiped out, other German aircraft suddenly appeared to join in the uneven battle. After the flight to Folkestone, Brandenburg had arranged for escorts from German fighter squadrons in Flanders to meet the returning bombers. As fighter engaged fighter in an aerial free-for-all over the sea, the Gothas regained the coast and struck a course for Ghent.

The 'serpent machine', its fuel all but gone because of the leak in the main tank, approached Gontrode with sputtering engines. A Gotha had crashed on the northern edge of the field. Closer below, another was burning on the landing strip. Ashcoff fired a flare to indicate an emergency landing. Gliding skilfully, Kollberg managed to bring the giant aeroplane safely down.

Once on the ground, Aschoff and his crew hurriedly inspected their Gotha. The wings and fuselage were well riddled, and one of the propellers had been nicked. Aschoff's pulse quickened when he found a phosphorous bullet embedded in the tail. It had failed to ignite. The only really serious damage was the punctured tank.

The 'serpent machine' had survived its first air battle. Even before Aschoff and the other airmen left, the men of the ground crew were busy with an old custom. They quickly painted coloured circles around the numerous holes, and inscribed the date of the damage. They too wanted to share in the narrow escape. But, most of all, they were relieved and happy that their 'bird' had returned to its roost.

Thrilled by rousing accounts of scrambling air duels over the Thames estuary, many in England were given to believe that the German raiders had received a sound thrashing. The London newspapers, in particular, expressed their satisfaction with gusto in their news columns and editorials.

The *Daily Express* of 7 June, for example, crowed that only ten of twenty attacking bombers had escaped. Pointing out that the destruction of German airmen and their machines hastened the end of the war, the newspaper commented that 'England hopes such attacks will be repeated often'.

But the British had definite evidence of only one Gotha having gone down into the sea. The Germans themselves reported no other losses. In their anxiety for a close look at the new bomber, the British probed the waters off Sheerness until the wreckage was found. The sinister Gotha looked more like some lifeless sea monster than an aeroplane, as it was hauled up with its crumpled wings and broken landing gear dangling limply.

Two of the Germans had been rescued that evening. One, the pilot, died soon afterward, but the other was able to give the British their first positive information on Kagohl 3. This intelligence had its greatest effect on Lord French in London. Two days after the attack, he cancelled his order prohibiting the anti-aircraft guns, except in certain coastal areas such as Sheerness and Dover, from firing at enemy aeroplanes. The ban had been in effect for ninety days and through two Gotha raids.

To save time, the cancellation was made verbally. It came only six days before a formation of German bombers roared over London.

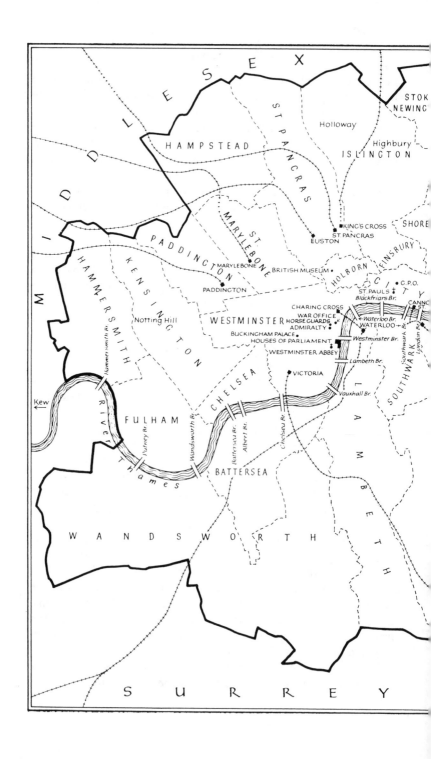

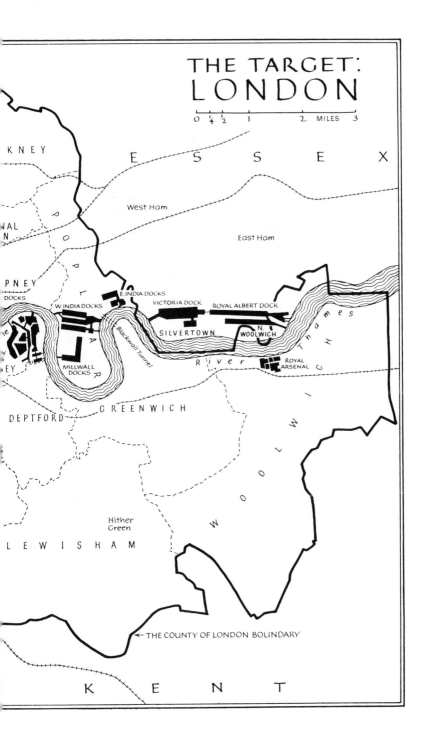

THE TARGET:
LONDON

0 ¼ ½ 1   2 MILES 3

K N E Y

E   S   S   E   X

West Ham

East Ham

NAL
N

PNEY
DOCKS

P
O
P
L
A
R

E. INDIA DOCKS

W. INDIA DOCKS

VICTORIA DOCK

ROYAL ALBERT DOCK

Thames

SILVERTOWN

N.
WOOLWICH

Blackwall Tunnel

River

EY

MILLWALL
DOCKS

ROYAL
ARSENAL

W
O
O
L
W
I
C
H

GREENWICH

DEPTFORD

W
O
O
L
W
I
C
H

Hither
Green

L E W I S H A M

← THE COUNTY OF LONDON BOUNDARY

K   E   N   T

London by Day

But what would be the security of the good, if the bad could at pleasure invade them from the sky? Against an army sailing through the clouds neither walls, nor mountains, nor seas, could afford them any security. A flight of northern savages might hover in the wind, and light upon the capital of a fruitful region that was rolling under them.

Samuel Johnson (1759)

CHAPTER SIX

A Grand but Deadly Show

At St. Denis-Westrem and Gontrode, a feverish activity had been set off by the studied forecast of one man. Clear skies, informed Lieutenant Cloessner, the squadron weather officer, would prevail over England for at least two days. Brandenburg was delighted by the report. More anxious than ever for his first real look down the British lion's throat, he promptly alerted his four flight leaders.

A new day, 13 June 1917, was breaking. The Gothas were rolled out in the half-light of dawn and lined up on the dewy grass. Straining ground crews hung up the heavy bombs and installed the machine-guns. Mechanics revved up the engines and manipulated the controls. The sun was well up when the crews themselves began to arrive. Among them were Aschoff, Kollberg, and Mayer. As he inspected the loaded Gotha, Aschoff had a battered oak cane tucked under one arm. A good luck charm, it had seen him safely through months of patrols over the Somme. He never would have thought of flying to London without his walking stick.

The flight leader passed from machine to machine for one last word with the crews. He reviewed the targets assigned and the course headings to be flown. The latest estimates of the winds aloft could not have been more favourable. A tail wind was expected up to 13,000 feet on the flight out. Another was anticipated above 14,000 for the return journey.

To make the most of these winds, the squadron was to depart at 10 A.M. Then, at the last minute, Brandenburg decided to delay the take-off. Several planes needing only minor adjustments were not yet ready. Cloessner insisted that the bombers should leave as planned, so as to be back on the ground by three o'clock in the afternoon. Severe thunderstorms, he warned, were expected shortly after that time. Not a foolhardy man, Brandenburg reverted to his original schedule, and settled for an attacking force of twenty Gothas.

At the appointed hour of ten the air was filled with the roar of engines. The bombers vibrated and shook, as if anticipating the straining effort that would be needed to lift their heavy loads. At each wave of a red flag from the 'start' officer, an aircraft lurched forward from its place in the line. The bombers successively bounced down the strip at precisely timed intervals, and rose hesitantly into the air.

The three lead aircraft headed straight for the coast, flying at reduced speeds to allow the others to catch up. By the time the Gothas had reached the coast, all but two had taken their place in the formation. These two had been forced to land soon after taking off owing to faltering engines. The long concrete mole arching out into the sea at Zeebrugge was clearly visible from 10,000 feet. German gunboats, spouting dense black smoke, were standing by to speed out to the rescue should any of the bombers come down into the water.

The Gothas left this comforting sight behind to fly on over the unfriendly North Sea. About half-way out, Brandenburg turned on a south-westerly heading to keep the formation on course for the Thames estuary. The bombers had no sooner changed their heading when a solid cloud bank slipped in below and blotted out the sea. The crews watched and wondered if the flight to London might not be frustrated once more. A little later, the clouds began to loosen. Brandenburg, peering into the hazy atmosphere, was relieved to see the English coastline taking shape ahead.

When all seemed well again, another Gotha indicated engine trouble and broke away. The British reported later that the raiders had made a diversionary attack on Margate to draw attention from their main force. Five bombs dropped on the seaside resort were from this same Gotha, whose crew was determined to hit something before going home.

Brandenburg saw his formation dwindle still further over Foulness Island. Three aircraft abandoned him this time, firing red flares. At least one raided Shoeburyness without doing any damage. Another headed up the Thames, and dumped its load at Greenwich, also without effect. By now, Brandenburg very likely regretted having taken Cloessner's advice. While still over the Essex coast, he had but fourteen bombers left.

The sky over the Thames resounded with the distinctive throb of the Mercedes engines. In many villages and towns the reaction was more of wonderment than fear. The distant drone could be heard long before the aircraft were seen. As they came into view, the people peered from their windows or ran out into their gardens to stare at a diamond-shaped formation flying three miles up. Few realized that the aircraft were German, and that they were on their way to London.

The raiders, despite their great height, did not escape a lively barrage from the city's outer defences. An observer aboard one of the Gothas sketches the scene: 'Suddenly there stand as if by magic, here and there in our course, little clouds of cotton, the greeting of enemy guns. They multiply with astonishing rapidity. We fly through them and leave the suburbs behind us. It is the heart of London that must be hit. . . .'[44]

Yet, at 11.35 A.M., some bombs were dropped on the eastern suburbs. They fell in a cluster between the Royal Albert Docks and the borough of East Ham, north of the Thames. Eight men were killed at the docks, and some sheds, offices, and railway stock were damaged. But most of the raiders reserved their bombs for the centre of the city.

Brandenburg and his crews were awed at the breath-taking expanse of London stretching out in all directions below them like a vast sea. The airmen could see Tower Bridge casting its shadow on the Thames, the grey-walled Tower, the majestic dome of St. Paul's —all 'sharply outlined in the glaring sunlight'. And on the Thames there were ships 'that looked like toys'.

The sight of the white Gothas high in the sky no less fascinated the populace of London. The novelty of it caused many people to ignore the danger of an air-raid, while not a few seemed to have been positively dazzled. A correspondent for *The New York Times* observed the grand but deadly show from the top of one of London's open buses. In describing how 'wonderstruck eyes watched the drama of the skies', his dispatch was almost poetical:

'In the gracious loveliness of a perfect summer's day when the sky was blue and gold and clear, enemy aeroplanes journeyed through the clouds like little silver birds and their passage was watched by thousands of men and women who had but dimly seen the Zeppelins of other days. . . .

'It was amazing because it was so beautiful. It was not easy to believe that those little silver specks far up in the heaven had

55

the power to bring death and destruction and unendurable suffering. . . .

'I saw no quick searching for shelter, no taking cover. If it had been an exhibition of flying at Hendon, the attitude of the people would not have been very different, except in the immediately affected streets. Men and women . . . stood watching vastly interested, a little excited, but not in the least frightened. . . .

'It all happened in a quarter of an hour. . . .'[45]

Those gazing skywards saw a white flare fired from the lead machine. At this signal, the Gothas scattered to drop their bombs individually. The target of the main attack was Liverpool Street Station. Observers crouched intently over their sights until the appropriate sighting angle for the altitude and speed was reached.

'With my telescope in one hand,' relates one German, 'I signal with the other to my pilot. Slowly long rows of streets pass the small orbit of the sight. At last it is time to drop. I give a signal and in less time than it takes to tell, I have pushed the levers and anxiously follow the flight of the released bombs. With a tremendous crash they strike the heart of England. It is a magnificently terrific spectacle seen from mid-air. Projectiles from hostile batteries are sputtering and exploding beneath and all around us, while below the earth seems to be rocking. . . .'[46]

In a two-minute period, beginning at 11.40 A.M., seventy-two bombs fell within one mile of the railway terminus. Only three hit the station itself. Two bombs came crashing through the high arched roof; one was a dud but the other exploded on a platform. The third scored a direct hit on a passenger train about to leave for Hunstanton. A dining-car was wrecked and two coaches were set afire with some of the victims trapped inside.

Many of the bombs were quite large, weighing more than one hundred pounds. On Charlotte Street, running parallel to the Tottenham Court Road, a factory was burnt out. Where no fire resulted, structural damage was largely confined to the upper floors. Fifteen people died and fourteen were hurt when the three top stories of a building in Fenchurch Street were demolished. One dud bomb buried itself in the dry moat around the Tower of London. Working perfectly, another bomb caused thirty-four casualties as it blasted a mechanic's shop at the Royal Mint.

Some Londoners found themselves in awkward spots when the

bombs came swishing down. One man was repairing a flagpole atop a building when he saw 'something like a stick falling'. Then he heard an explosion close by. 'Never came off a roof quicker in my life,' he exclaimed. Many of the victims were struck down in cafés and restaurants which were crowded for the noon meal. At one such place, a man had his arm blown off 'as he was raising a cup of tea to his lips'.

General John J. Pershing, the commander of the American Expeditionary Force, missed the first Gotha raid on London by only a few hours. The United States had been at war little more than sixty days. Pershing and his staff had arrived in Liverpool three days before to consult with the British, and arrange for the coming of the A.E.F. to Europe. At a state dinner given for the American commander in London the previous evening the talk had not been of air-raids, but U-boat losses 'spoken of almost in whispers'. Very early that morning, Pershing had quietly boarded a special train for Folkestone where he sailed for France. The general disembarked at Boulogne as the Gothas were leaving Ghent. Some American correspondents immediately suggested that the attack was intended as a special welcome to Pershing which came too late.

After rocking the Liverpool Street area, the raiders split into two groups. Six Gothas flew across the Thames near Tower Bridge to bomb the railway stations in the Southwark district. The warehouses along the river absorbed the brunt of the bursts. Fire broke out and heavy smoke began to rise in the sunny sky. The other wing of Gothas headed north to strike at rail targets in Dalston. Following this attack the bombers wheeled about to rejoin the other group. As they neared the Thames, the Gothas passed over Poplar, the scene of the raid's most tragic incident.

In that East End borough, a 110-pound bomb struck the Upper North Street Schools, attended at the time by six hundred pupils. The projectile broke in two as it hit the roof, but did not immediately explode. Killing two pupils in its passage, one piece of the bomb pierced three floors to reach an infants' class in the basement. Classes were being conducted there for sixty-four very young children in a large partitioned room with an earthen floor. The teachers saw the ceiling come crashing down along with one child from the floor above. Then, with a sudden sharp clack, the bomb fragment blasted the room. Sixteen children were killed almost outright, and thirty others were injured. Only two of the dead infants were over five years old.

In a street nearby a soldier was talking to a policeman when the disaster occurred. Recalling the 'terrible sight' he said: 'I dashed around to the school as the policeman advised, and there I found the school mistress, who had got the uninjured children into a passage. . . .

'We both went into the classroom where the bomb had sunk into the earth when it exploded. . . . Many of the little ones were lying across their desks apparently dead and with terrible wounds on heads and limbs, and scores of others were writhing with pain and moaning pitifully. . . .

'Many of the bodies were mutilated, but our first thought was to get the injured. . . . We packed the little souls on the lorries as gently as we could . . . and so at last we got them to the hospital. . . .'[45]

The neighbourhood was in an uproar. Distraught mothers converged on the school and tore at the gathering crowd. Those who could not find their children ran inside, and 'rushed through the bodies looking for them'. Five gruff sailors helping in the rescue emerged from the building weeping. But most of the people were too dazed to show any emotion. The 'silvery specks in the sky' were all but forgotten for the moment. Reflection as to what this kind of warfare meant, and the anger it provoked, came only after the streets had been cleared of the crowds and the clanging vehicles.

A week later, the tiny victims were buried in a common grave in an East End cemetery. High government officials attended the service conducted by the Bishop of London. Condolences were received from the King and Queen. Many of the messages on the floral offerings poignantly expressed the mood of the people. They read simply: 'To our children murdered by German aircraft.'

The Germans had been able to reach central London in broad daylight without any fighter opposition. The circling Gothas had closed up into a formation again, and were withdrawing from the city, before they had to deal with some plucky but vain attacks by a few odd aeroplanes.

'As we reach the suburbs,' recounts one raider, 'the first three English fliers suddenly appear in front of us, seeking to block our flight. At a hundred or two hundred metres' distance both sides open fire, striving to get each other's weak spots. Two hostile pilots turn and do not come back. But a third is a brave and tenacious fellow. 'For ten minutes we fire at each other almost incessantly, my opponent looking for an opening. Suddenly he makes for us and showers his bullets on our machine. I can see or feel that the bullets have struck our craft, but I know I've got him. I send a whole sheaf of fire into his body. His machine rears up in the air like a wounded animal, turns a somersault, and disappears in the depths. This is the first enemy I have defeated over British soil. Three cheers!'[46]

The repulsed aircraft may have been a Bristol Fighter from 35 Training Squadron. Badly battered, the 'Brisfit' touched down at Northolt aerodrome with its observer-gunner, Captain C. H. C. Keevil, slumped dead behind his guns in the rear cockpit. The pilot, Captain C. W. E. Cole-Hamilton, said that Keevil had been hit as they took on 'three Gothas straggling over Ilford'. When his own gun jammed, Cole-Hamilton gave up the fight and sped home with his dying gunner.

Flying over an alerted and vengeful England, the Germans were hellbent for the coast. As they passed over airfields, still more fighters were rising to take up the chase. Aschoff's heart sank when he saw a triplane coming from the direction of Southend. Though a deadly threat to the slow bombers, the 'Tripe' was apparently flown by an inexperienced pilot. He failed to press his attack, limiting himself to a few bursts at long range. The Gothas left the half-hearted defender behind, and flew on over the North Sea.

Hardly believing that they had bombed London without losing a single machine, the wearying crews were lulled into a happy stupor by the vibrating roar of their engines. Time itself became blurred after several hours at higher altitudes. The early morning preparations, the risky take-off, and the flight across the sea now seemed vague and unreal. Huddled in their wind-lashed cockpits, the airmen were almost insensitive to the cold and the swelling stiffness of their limbs. They felt nothing but a wooden numbness.

After nearly two hours, which seemed much longer, the airfields near Ghent were reached at last. Buildings and trees loomed larger as Aschoff's Gotha descended for a landing. The machine coasted smoothly over the open meadow until Kollberg set it down with a bump. Aschoff tore off his uncomfortably warm helmet and goggles, and waved to the mechanics running out to meet the returning crews. It was three o'clock in the afternoon, and the five-hour flight was over.

Half an hour later the sky darkened and a violent thunderstorm broke out. Hailstones 'the size of dove eggs' pelted the aerodrome. 'Had this weather developed sooner, it easily would have led to the destruction of the entire squadron,' Brandenburg observed in his report. 'Thanks to Lt. Cloessner, that did not happen in this instance.'[47]

Aschoff submitted his own report and hurried to his quarters. There he changed before going to the newly built Officers' Kasino where food, drink, and good cheer awaited the airmen. Endless toasts would be drunk later that evening to the Kaiser, Brandenburg, and the success of the first Gotha strike on the British capital.

The spectacular raid would swell German pride everywhere. Up and down the front, and to the war-weary people at home, the official German communiqué would announce triumphantly, 'Today our airmen dropped bombs on the Fortress of London. . . .'

Brandenburg was acclaimed a hero overnight. 'For years,' congratulated Hoeppner in a long-distance call to Ghent, 'a squadron attack on London has been the goal of our airmen and our technology. By carrying out this raid Kampfgeschwader 3 has provided a new basis for air attacks. . . . Good luck for further successes under the slogan: Brandenburg over London!'[48]

The Gotha commander was summoned to Supreme Headquarters. He took off for Kreuznach the next day with his pilot, Oberleutnant Freiherr von Trotha, in an Albatross two-seater. The German war lords listened almost enraptured as Brandenburg told them of the raid. Hindenburg's shrewd and calculating right-hand man, General Erich Ludendorff, was particularly attentive and full of questions. With the ground war at a hopeless stalemate, what did this blow on distant London portend?

Brandenburg judged that 'the effect must have been great'. Seventeen Gothas had reached the target under conditions of 'exceptionally good' visibility. The gunfire 'over London was not particularly strong and was badly directed'. Brandenburg estimated that thirty enemy fighters had risen to oppose him, but the crews had counted only sixteen. The bombing had been conducted 'with no hurry or trouble'. The majority of the bombs 'fell among the docks, and among the city warehouses'. Brandenburg was certain that 'a station in the City, and a Thames bridge, probably Tower Bridge, were hit'. The new Gothas had flown well, and all had 'landed safely on their aerodrome'.[49]

The Kaiser thanked the captain and decorated him with the eight-pointed blue and gold cross of the Pour le Mérite. After spending the weekend at Kreuznach, the exuberant Brandenburg left early the following Tuesday for Ghent. As he took off, the engine of his Albatross sputtered and the aeroplane crashed. Brandenburg was pulled out of the wreckage with severe injuries, including a shattered leg. Trotha was dead.

The airmen of Kagohl 3, still flushed with success, were stunned by the irony of the accident. Ill luck had achieved what the guns of London and British fighters had not been able to do to Brandenburg. Trotha, one of the most experienced fliers in the German Army, had survived countless flights. He had qualified as a pilot in 1912, exactly five years less one day before his death. The Kaiser attended the funeral, and Trotha was buried at Kreuznach.

CHAPTER SEVEN

'Send over . . . One or Two Squadrons'

Although the first Gotha raid on London had been more spectacular than crippling, an oppressive uneasiness gripped the city. Many workers, fearful that the bombers would soon return, stayed away from the East End factories. And the average citizen turned angrily to the authorities for the safety of his home and family with almost unreasonable expectations. The officials, in turn, were appalled by the statistics being tabulated from incoming reports.

The final figures showed that 162 people had been killed, and 432 had been injured. No previous raid, either by aeroplane or airship, had claimed such a human toll. The loss was greater than three-quarters of all casualties from some twenty-three Zeppelin raids in 1915, the worst year for that type of attack. Unlike airships gingerly probing by night, the Gothas had struck directly at densely populated areas, and dropped improved bombs with an accuracy possible only in daylight. The raid was to go down as the deadliest of the war in Britain.

The next day, the furore rose to a high pitch in Parliament. Banbury, the M.P. for the City of London, now had other concerns besides the trees on Kenley Common. He proposed the tolling of the bells of St. Paul's Cathedral as a warning of an air attack. Bank clerks would then have time, he explained, to return large sums of exposed cash safely back to the vaults. The suggestion visibly angered Bonar Law, then a member of the War Council. He snapped back that 'we are more interested in the lives of the people than in the money in the banks'.[50]

Pemberton-Billing reminded the House that he had 'prophesied what was going to occur'. He moved that business be set aside to permit discussion of the raid. The Speaker denied the request. Pemberton-Billing kept insisting until he was silenced by loud cries of 'Order! Order!' and 'Sit down'. The boisterous M.P. repeated his performance the following day. This time, he was called upon to leave for failing 'to respect the authority of the Chair'. While still trying to speak, Pemberton-Billing was led out through the doors of the Chamber 'amid laughter and ironical cheers'.

A more sedate House of Lords was told by the War Minister, the heavy-jowled Earl of Derby, that the bombing was of no military significance. He confided triumphantly that 'not a single soldier' had been killed. Not only incorrect, the revelation was also not altogether reassuring to civilians. A question raised by Lord Gainford was more to the point.

'Were any aeroplanes brought down yesterday?' he asked bluntly.

'I am afraid not,' replied Derby. 'There are some doubts about one, but I would not like to say for certain. . . . Lord French is doing all in his power to secure this city. . . .'[51]

The vague reply brought to the fore the real reason for the deep anxiety aroused by the daylight raid. The defences were evidently unable to cope with the bombers, despite the presence of air defence squadrons in Britain. By the end of 1916, there were twelve such units deployed against the airship raiders at thirty aerodromes strategically located from the Thames estuary to Scotland.

The undoing of the thin-skinned 'gasbags' was dramatically proven again soon after the Gotha attack on London. During the night of 16 June, four airships prowled along England's east coast. One of them, L48, was set aflame by a British pilot and fell, 'a red ball of fire', near Leiston. Commander Viktor Schütze, the chief of the German Naval Airship Division, was one of the fourteen men who died in the fiery disaster.

But hunting a flock of Gothas was quite a different matter. The challenge now facing the British was like having to switch overnight from whale harpooning to mosquito swatting. The London raid, in which ninety-two aircraft had actually gone up from airfields in England alone, amply demonstrated that it was no easy task to find the raiders.

Taking off from widely scattered fields, the fighter pilots were entirely on their own. On the ground, the German bombers could be heard for miles around. But the pilots searching for them in the air heard nothing but the sound of their own engines. Without contact with ground observers, they received no information as to the whereabouts of the enemy. Those pilots who did come upon the

Gothas usually attacked singly. Such piecemeal attacks were obviously no great threat to a heavily armed bomber formation.

On reaching England, the Germans also had the distinct advantage of being two or three miles up. Robertson, the Chief of the Imperial General Staff, explained that 'the distance in time from the coast to important places like London is less than the time required by most of the machines we have got to ascend to the necessary height. Consequently, before they can get up the enemy has done his job and is on his way home again'.[52]

Most of the defence squadrons were equipped with the early B.E. aeroplanes. 'A delightful touring machine, beautifully made', the type was good enough to fight the Zeppelin. But it was hopeless against the Gothas because of its crawling speed and slow rate of climb. The latest fighter aircraft that were necessary to intercept the German bombers were to be found only at the front.

Less than a week before, Field-Marshal Sir Douglas Haig had asked that 'every possible man, aeroplane, and gun be sent to France'. The B.E.F. commander was convinced that Germany was wavering, and now was the time to end the war with an all-out effort. Despite this urgent plea, Lloyd George and his War Cabinet felt that some priority had to be given to soothing an aroused citizenry at home. Meeting in emergency session on the day after the London raid, they agreed to call back two fighter squadrons.

In communicating the Cabinet's decision on 15 June, 'Wully' Robertson took great pains to placate Haig. 'There is no panic here and no desire to play the enemy's game . . . but at the same time it is thought that the raiders must be given one or two sharp lessons,' he wrote. Adding that 'to do this we have not enough of the right sort of machines in this country', Robertson finally informed Haig 'that you should send over for a week or two one or two squadrons so as to give the enemy a warm reception and the machines would then return to you. . . .'[52]

The offensive-minded field commander was pained at having to spare even a few squadrons. The air situation in France was precarious. Major-General Hugh Trenchard, who commanded the Royal Flying Corps at the front, had advised his brigade commanders on 10 June 'to avoid wastage in both pilots and machines'. Trenchard had indicated that 'my reserve at present is dangerously low, in fact, in some cases it barely exists at all'.[53] Haig very reluctantly released two squadrons with the stipulation that they were 'urgently required to be back by the 5th July'.

Crack 56 Squadron, still mourning the recent loss of its renowned Captain Albert Ball, was sent to England. The combat-weary pilots did not exactly share Haig's concern over the loss of their services in France.

'The squadron arrived at Bekesbourne without incident, vastly elated,' gloated one of them, a nineteen-year-old. 'Machines were put away and the men, who had been rushed home, took charge of them. Needless to say, all the musicians were among them. The defence of London was quite a secondary affair. The things of real importance were squadron dances. To fight Hun bombers over London would have been a picnic for us after a month of gruelling Offensive Patrols. Good old Jerry! Good old Lloyd George!'[54]

Based near Canterbury, the squadron was in a good position to raise havoc with enemy bombers flying in and out of London. Its S.E.5s were more than a match for the lumbering Gothas. This first-rate fighter was armed with two forward-firing machine-guns. Powered by a 150 h.p. Hispano-Suiza engine, it could climb to nearly 10,000 feet in twelve minutes and fly at about 120 miles an hour.

No. 66 Squadron had fallen back to Calais a few days before. Its one-gun Sopwith Pups had an endurance of three hours, and a service ceiling of over 17,000 feet. They were ideal for flying high altitude patrols over the Channel. The Germans would receive a 'nasty knock' indeed, provided they returned within the prescribed time of two weeks.

More lasting protection for the British capital was also considered. The War Cabinet called in military experts and other officials to draft an anti-Gotha strategy. Robertson submitted that there must be a rapid increase in aircraft production. Concurring readily, the Cabinet charged the Air Board, in consultation with the War Office and the Ministry of Munitions, with preparing a plan for increasing the output. These agencies conferred one week later. Lord Derby, who presided as the Secretary of State for War, restated his earlier position that the strength of the Royal Flying Corps should be doubled. If necessary, he maintained, even the production of the 'tanks' and motor transport should be curtailed to this end.

The War Minister's views were developed by a committee which

65

held its final meeting on 2 July. This group sweepingly recommended the expansion of the Royal Flying Corps from 108 to 200 squadrons, to include all necessary aerodrome facilities and supporting equipment. The Cabinet not only approved this proposal, but provided for an increase of the Royal Naval Air Service as well.

All this had been instigated by some fifty German airmen hovering over England for a few hours. True, they had claimed nearly 600 victims. But this was a trifle when weighed against the 2,500 casualties the British were suffering every day during this period at the front. According to one dispassionate observer in *The New York Times*, the military effect of the raid 'would not amount to as much as a before-breakfast skirmish almost any morning on the Somme'. He concluded that, 'from the war point of view, not one ounce of strength should be taken from the real fighting to make security more safe for Londoners'.[55]

But 'the war point of view' overlooked the psychological impact of the raid. Its victims were not soldiers, but civilians. As they had set out about their business that June morning, they had no expectations of becoming war casualties before noon. The impelling thing was not the number killed and injured, but that this could happen at all, suddenly and unexpectedly, far away from the trenches.

British grand strategy was heatedly being debated when the Gothas appeared over London. Heartened by Plumer's limited but spectacular success at Messines Ridge earlier that month, Haig was planning a general offensive in the Ypres sector. His objective was to roll up the German-held Belgian coast and push the enemy inland beyond Ghent. Since this would eliminate the German submarine bases at Ostend and other places along the coast, the Admiralty fully supported Haig.

The Prime Minister, on the other hand, favoured joining forces with the Italians against Austria. He felt that a combined effort could bring about the collapse of Germany's first ally. But to the professionals, Lloyd George was a 'protagonist of eccentric warfare' whose military judgment was suspect. There was much sniggering over his remark that Trieste should be taken because it was nearer to the front than Ostend.

At the request of the 'little Welshman', Robertson rendered his 'official opinion' on 23 June. Concealing his contempt, the Chief of the Imperial General Staff expressed his 'deep regret' that he could not 'advise the adoption of a policy so greatly desired by the Prime Minister'. In arguing for the 'Flanders Project', Robertson cited the added 'necessity for breaking up the hostile air bases in Belgium'.[56]

Haig had already stated that 'the most effective step of all' against the Gotha raids was 'the capture by us of the Belgian coast'. Haig had his way. Over three months and at least a quarter of a million British casualties later, the offensive was halted. The front was not pierced, and the Gotha bases at Ghent remained undisturbed except for frequent raids made by the Royal Naval Air Service.

CHAPTER EIGHT

'The Hammer is in Our Hands'

'The Germans had a perfect right to bomb London,' Lord Montagu of Beaulieu told the House of Lords late in June 1917. 'London was defended by guns and aeroplanes, and it was the chief centre for the production of munitions,' he pointed out in his usual candid and outspoken manner. 'We were, therefore, but deluding ourselves in talking about London being an undefended city and about the Germans in attacking it being guilty of an act unworthy of a civilized nation.'[57]

Montagu was roundly denounced for 'justifying the killing of civilians', a charge he heatedly denied. Few credited the far-seeing peer for his longstanding warnings of such a danger. A modern among Victorians, he had often expounded on what he called 'sky power'. As early as 1911, Montagu had predicted that air attacks 'would be more nerve-shattering and would do more to shake the confidence of a people than a definite threat on sea or land'. Claiming then that Britain was 'behind other great Continental Powers' in the air, Montagu had urged 'an adequate air force for defence.'[58]

Some still found it easier to accuse the Germans of 'scientific barbarism' than to admit that British unpreparedness had contributed in some measure to the daylight spectacle of the Gothas flying over London. Time, somehow, still seemed to favour debate. Despite the clear sunny weather, the raiders had not returned. For 56 Squadron, temporarily installed at Bekesbourne, the passing days were ones of peace and the airmen made the most of them.

Flooring was laid down in the large field tent used as a squadron mess. A dance was held one night with girls coming in from Canterbury and other nearby towns. The event was a gay candlelit affair with wine and music. Even an impromptu flying exhibition was held for the ladies before dinner. Days of grim battle in Flanders' skies would return soon enough. For the time being, it was up to the

Germans to decide whether the pilots of 56 would have to fight at home as well.

More specifically, the next raid on England was up to Captain Rudolf Kleine, who arrived at Gontrode at the end of June to replace Brandenburg. To the flight leaders and staff officers who greeted him, he emphasized that OHL wanted the attacks on London continued. A thin-lipped man with deep brooding eyes, Kleine was never to gain the affection that Brandenburg had enjoyed of his crews. But, from the start, he commanded no less respect.

Kleine's drive and dedication had impressed Hoeppner's chief of staff, Lieutenant-Colonel Hermann Thomsen. The young captain seemed highly qualified to lead Kagohl 3 in its raids against England. Though only thirty, he had been an officer twelve years. The son of an infantry colonel, he had earned two Iron Crosses and the Order of Hohenzollern. The latter, a high decoration, was awarded him when his report following a flight over the Champagne front alerted OHL that the French were preparing an attack. Kleine commanded a reconnaissance squadron at the time. Previously, in 1915, he had made many bombing missions as a flight leader in Siegert's old squadron, Kagohl 1.

Kleine also wore the oval silver badge of a fully qualified German military pilot, a distinction among Kagohl commanders, who were usually observers. He had been sent to the flying school at Gotha in 1913, and then assigned to an air battalion at Cologne. In August 1914, Kleine participated in the first battle of the war by flying reconnaissance for the German brigades charged with the capture of the Belgian fortress city of Liége. Twice wounded in the air, Kleine had only recently recovered from his latest injuries when Brandenburg crashed at Kreuznach. At Thomsen's suggestion, Hoeppner quickly approved his transfer to Ghent.

Soon after Kleine's arrival, a raid was set for 4 July. The weather reports of the night before were uncertain, and there were other distractions. The British bombed the airfields at Ghistelles and Nieuwmunster, but no bombs fell on St. Denis-Westrem and Gontrode. With the weather remaining unsettled, Kleine had to be satisfied with some coastal target for his first raid. He chose to bomb the naval base at Harwich.

Well before six o'clock that morning, twenty-five Gothas were aloft and heading for the Belgian coast. Flying in the lead machine,

Kleine further damned his luck as this force steadily dwindled away. By the time he reached the sea no less than seven crews had fallen away because of engine breakdowns. The very early take-off seemed to assure at least one advantage. Even if not totally surprised, the British were bound to be less alert at such an hour. But, quite by chance, the Germans were seen long before they reached England.

Captain John Palethorpe of the Royal Flying Corps, and his observer-gunner, Air Mechanic James O. Jessop, had also eaten an unusually early breakfast that morning. Assigned to a Testing Squadron, they were out over the sea flight-testing a D.H.4, a fast single-engined aircraft armed with two guns firing forward and two guns aft. On sighting the flying wedge of German bombers, Palethorpe promptly attacked despite their numbers. Unwisely, he singled out a machine in the centre of the formation and went into a dive. As the D.H.4 came within range of the combined fire of the Gothas' guns, Jessop in the rear cockpit was killed instantly with a bullet in the heart.

The Germans were much surprised to see a fighter suddenly plunging down on them, seemingly out of nowhere. Kleine, apparently expecting other British aircraft to appear, momentarily turned the entire formation eastward. Palethorpe hovered about helplessly for a few minutes, and then hurried home to give the alarm. He landed at Martlesham Heath, and quickly took off again with another gunner to continue the fight. He failed to find the raiders anew, but his wish for battle would be satisfied a few days later.

The bombers struck the Suffolk coast almost in line for Ipswich at about 7 A.M. Though the weather was bright and sunny, only sections of the shore could be seen through the mist. Low-flying clouds obscured much of the landscape beyond the coast. Roaring over Harwich with 'a loud whirring noise', the Gothas were so low that 'the black crosses on the wings could be plainly seen'.

Ignoring the clustered houses of the town itself, the raiders took aim on the naval base where destroyers were berthed. They later reported several hits on the docks and warships, but most of their bombs actually fell in the water. An army camp and the naval air station at nearby Felixstowe were not so fortunate. A hangar was struck, a flying-boat was wrecked, and another was badly damaged. The telephone system at the air station was knocked out. Some near misses slaughtered a flock of sheep grazing in a field. Human casualties among the soldiers, sailors, and civilian workmen were seventeen killed and thirty injured.

The Germans barely crossed the coastline, and within minutes they were heading out to sea again. The gunners of the Harwich defences saw the aeroplanes only at odd moments through breaks in the clouds. Their booming barrage scored no hits. British pilots had even less chance of running down the elusive raiders. Of the eighty-three machines which went up from aerodromes in Essex and Kent, including the S.E.5s from Bekesbourne, none so much as sighted the German bombers.

The pursuit was taken up later by twenty naval pilots from Dunkirk. A furious air battle reportedly took place over the sea when five of the British machines overtook the returning Gothas about thirty-five miles north-west of Ostend. Leading the fray in a Sopwith Pup, Flight Commander Alexander M. Shook pounced on the nearest German. He claimed that the bomber began to smoulder under his fire, and then fell from the formation. Flight Sub-Lieutenant S. E. Ellis reported firing over 300 rounds at another Gotha. He said that the large machine went down, twisting and turning, with heavy smoke coming from the rear gunner's cockpit.

'All our aeroplanes returned undamaged,' Berlin announced the next day. German records indicate six air battles, but no Gotha losses. Shook was given the D.S.C. for his 'victory'. The squadron ordered back to Calais, 66, did not even get into the fight. Due to 'some unexplained muddle in communications', the battle-ready pilots were notified too late.

Brandenburg and Kleine would have been pained, no doubt, to learn that the German Chancellor, of all people, was as unappreciative of their efforts as he had been of the earlier Zeppelin raids. The war, by this time, had dragged on for nearly three years with disillusionment mounting on both sides. In the Allied camp, there was talk of 'peace without victory'. In Germany, the cry was for a 'peace of understanding'. To Bethmann-Hollweg, it seemed highly possible that the Gothas might frighten away the elusive dove.

On 25 June, he wrote Hindenburg that the chances for 'compromise' could be enhanced by 'avoiding anything which could impede England's decision to enter into peace negotiations. . . .'

Bethmann-Hollweg had 'no doubt that the last aerial attack on London has had a disastrous effect in this respect'. Citing 'reliable reports', he cautioned the Chief of the General Staff that 'the anger of the English public has reached a pitch that . . . no English government which was willing to treat with Germany after such an occurrence would be able to withstand the indignation of the nation for a day. As I am unable to believe that such aerial attacks are absolutely necessary . . . may I be allowed to suggest that they be given up. . . .'[59]

The Chancellor had persisted in his stubborn opposition to the German military and their strategy of all-out war. Throughout 1916, he had managed to align the Kaiser against unrestricted submarine warfare. His policy was denounced as 'trying to fight Great Britain with one foot in the grave of chivalry'. But Bethmann-Hollweg's influence had been such that even Grand Admiral Alfred von Tirpitz, who believed in 'war to the knife', had been forced out as Navy Minister.

Early in 1917, Kaiser Wilhelm finally consented to the unlimited use of the U-boats. The hope of such a stroke was a swift victory. But, as Bethmann-Hollweg had warned would happen, it brought about America's entry into the war instead. Though the Chancellor had been proven right by events, it was not likely that his latest rebuke over the Gotha raids would be heeded. His political power, by this time, had been completely undermined by the military. As 'the grey ghost of a man who seemed to portend disaster', his advice on the conduct of the war now counted for little.

Nor was it entirely a matter of weapons and policy. Apart from the yearning for peace, there also prevailed an anger so fierce that the causes which had provoked it were forgotten. This spirit of uncompromising wrath was vented in a semi-official communiqué issued in Berlin towards the end of June. It advised Britain to move her population from the 'neighbourhood of store places of equipment' such as London, if she wanted to spare them from being bombed. 'The German people, under pressure of English starvation and the war, has become a hard race with an iron fist. . . . The hammer is in our hands, and it will fall mercilessly and shatter the places where England is forging weapons against us.'[60]

Hindenburg, for one, certainly did not believe in giving the British any quarter. 'I do not think that England will be ready for a peace of understanding as long as she still hopes that Germany will collapse before herself,' he replied to Bethmann-Hollweg. 'We must, therefore, prosecute the war with all our resources and the greatest intensity. Your Excellency deprecates the aerial attacks on London. . . . The military advantages are great. They keep a large amount of war material away from the French front, and destroy important enemy establishments. . . . I should be glad if you would acquaint me with the facts . . . that the recent attack on London has aroused the passions of the English nation to a disastrous degree. . . .'[61]

Hindenburg did not patiently await a reply. With the support of the Crown Prince and certain political factions, OHL compelled Bethmann-Hollweg to resign as Chancellor less than one week later. The Reichstag quickly approved Ludendorff's choice of a successor. Germany was now unalterably committed to a policy of total war under a virtual military dictatorship.

Hindenburg's letter to Bethmann-Hollweg was written on 7 July, a day better remembered for the second Gotha raid on London.

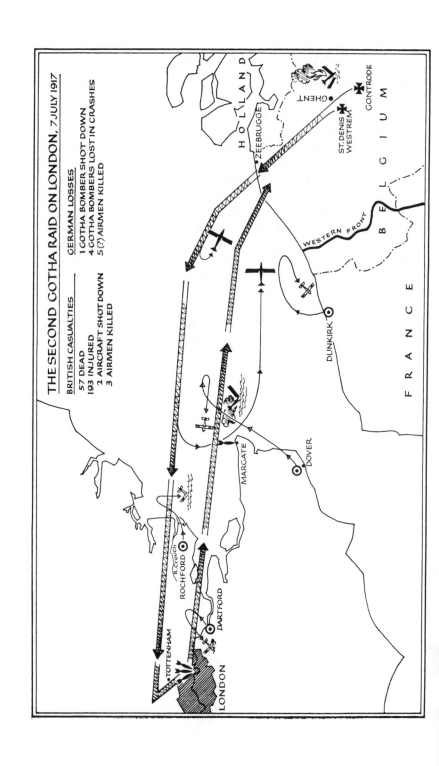

THE SECOND GOTHA RAID ON LONDON, 7 JULY 1917

BRITISH CASUALTIES
57 DEAD
193 INJURED
2 AIRCRAFT SHOT DOWN
3 AIRMEN KILLED

GERMAN LOSSES
1 GOTHA BOMBER SHOT DOWN
4 GOTHA BOMBERS LOST IN CRASHES
5 (?) AIRMEN KILLED

HOLLAND

GHENT

CONTRODE

ST. DENIS
WESTREM

ZEEBRUGGE

BELGIUM

WESTERN FRONT

DUNKIRK

FRANCE

MARGATE

DOVER

TOTTENHAM

LONDON

DARTFORD

ROCHFORD

R. Crouch

CHAPTER NINE

The Raid Heard Round the World

The German bombers returned to London on a Saturday. No horn or siren heralded their approach as they bore down on the city from the north-west. The 'Hun aeroplanes' came on unopposed, 'as if they were in a peacetime parade'. Twenty-one in all, they could be easily counted against a grey fleecy sky which had been blue and sunny a few hours before.

A single aeroplane spearheaded two clusters of eight Gothas each, flying side by side in battle formation. Bringing up the rear were four others which, at times, straggled far behind. The bombers were clearly observed to be biplanes. Unaware of their true dimensions, many people judged them to be flying at 5,000 feet, less than half their actual height. In the eyes of one observer, they were 'so low, their approach was so leisurely, and so well kept was their fan-like formation, that to suppose they were enemies was preposterous'.[62]

Michael MacDonagh, a reporter for *The Times*, was on a bus on his way to work when he first saw the aeroplanes. He tried to reassure a woman passenger who wondered if they were British. Stepping off at his usual stop, he walked the remaining distance to the office without hurrying. He was not due in until eleven o'clock that morning, and the weather was pleasant and warm. As he strolled along, MacDonagh was startled by the sound of gunfire. The aeroplanes were much closer, almost overhead, and no longer in formation. Still staring in puzzlement, he heard a 'weird swish' and then a 'roaring rending explosion'.

'Instantly the scene in the streets was wholly transformed,' noted the newspaperman, who no longer had to worry about a story for that day. 'The policeman standing near the monument of Queen Victoria worked himself into a state of excitement, shouting "Take Cover! Take Cover!" and wildly waving his arms. Everybody ran hither and thither for shelter. I joined in the rush for the Blackfriars Station of the Underground.

'We tumbled down the stairs to the platform of the trains going west, and ran along it to its end. . . . A second terrific explosion had given added swiftness to our feet. The girls of the Lyons' and ABC teashops at the station were in our wake, some of them being helped down, screaming hysterically. . . .

' "The raiders have London at their mercy," I kept saying to myself; "there are no defences against them." '

'For about five minutes more we could hear the uproar of guns and bombs. Then silence fell, and ten minutes later, gathering our scattered senses, we concluded it was safe to emerge from the tunnel into the streets.'[63]

A late morning service was in progress at St. Paul's. Despite the deafening din coming from outside, it continued uninterrupted. Those attending may have felt that there was no better time to pray, nor a better place to do so than under the cathedral's sturdy dome. At the Royal Aero Club, there was no immediate inclination among the members to rush down to the billiard room in the basement. A few 'uncomfortably near' explosions quickly changed this casual mood. 'I think I'll go down for a few minutes,' said one of them, 'as I want to see the next raid too.'[64]

Most of the bombs fell on private houses, a few offices, and some warehouses in the northern and eastern districts of the city. The Central Telegraph Office was the only 'military' objective struck in the raid. A 110-pound bomb shattered a temporary wooden structure atop the large building, hurling debris all over the roof. Falling rubble killed a sentry on duty in the street below. On the Thames, a pier was damaged and a barge was sunk.

One bomb exploded with violent force in the quadrangle of the Ironmongers' Hall, causing considerable havoc to the venerable building. A synagogue and a few churches were slightly scarred in the attack. The congregation of one of them later passed a resolution 'expressing detestation of the wanton destruction . . . of the east window of the Parish Church, one of the most beautiful examples in London'. A vote of thanks would have been equally appropriate, for the detestable bomb had failed to detonate.

On the coast of Kent, Margate was again bombed by a Gotha which could not make it all the way to London. Three 'aerial torpedoes' wrecked two houses, killed three persons, and injured three others. The only survivor in one house was a parrot whose screeches brought about his rescue from the rubble. The constable who released the ungrateful bird from his battered cage was severely bitten.

Several minutes after the attack on the capital had ended, and the last Gotha had disappeared in the haze, a 'solitary aeroplane' was seen scurrying across the London sky. Recognizing it as one of their own, the still frightened crowds jeered and shouted mockingly at this seemingly belated and futile gesture of defence. But the German raiders had not come and gone uncontested.

A mixed assortment of ninety-five British aircraft attempted pursuit. The Royal Flying Corps alone sent up twenty-one different types, from the hopelessly obsolete to the most modern. This emergency force lacked direction and co-ordination, a deficiency which determination and courage alone could not entirely overcome.

Lieutenant John E. R. Young, a bank clerk before he became a pilot, was a heroic example. Steady-eyed and handsome, he looked older than his nineteen years. Posted to 37 Home Defence Squadron, which guarded the northern approaches of the Thames estuary, Young was serving in the 'front lines' of England's air defences. Upon receipt of the first warning shortly after nine o'clock, he took off in a Sopwith two-seater from Rochford aerodrome near Southend.

Striking out to sea, Young sighted the Germans coming in towards the coast. The unwary pilot immediately attacked, flying a collision course against the bombers until he was shredded by their opposing fire. The fighter nosed up for a moment, and then fell into a twisting two-mile descent. A ship reached the sinking machine, but Young's body was so badly entangled that it could not be extricated before the aeroplane went under. His lifeless gunner, Air Mechanic C. C. Taylor, was recovered with six bullets in him.

The dead pilot's father received the customary letter of condolences. Unsparingly descriptive, it included vivid testimony of the terrific firepower of the Gotha bombers:

'The volume of fire to which he was subjected was too awful for words,' informed Young's squadron commander. 'To give you a rough idea—there were twenty-two machines; each machine had four guns; each gun was firing about 400 rounds per minute.

'Your son never hesitated in the slightest. He flew straight on

until, as I should imagine, he must have been riddled with bullets.
. . . I unfortunately had to witness the whole ghastly affair. . . .'[65]

Another Royal Flying Corps lieutenant was killed as he sought to
battle the bristling Gothas not far from London. He came down
near Dartford with a wound in the head, damaged controls, and a
punctured fuel tank. He had fired only fifty-five rounds at the
Germans. Several spectators were arrested at the scene of the crash
for having taken the pilot's goggles, gloves, safety belt, and various
pieces of the aeroplane. They were later fined as 'irrepressible
souvenir maniacs'.

On the way out, the formation was intercepted by Captain Palethorpe whose gunner had been killed in combat with the raiders
three days before. Palethorpe made repeated passes, concentrating
his fire on the lead machine, but he too was beaten off with a bullet
in the hip.

The Germans had already left the Kentish coast when they were
overtaken by still another British two-seater. This one was piloted
by Lieutenant F. A. D. Grace of 50 Squadron from Dover. Lieutenant G. Murray occupied the observer's seat. The pair were engaging
the rearmost bomber in the formation when they spotted another
Gotha straggling far below and behind the others, Grace and Murray pounced on it with guns firing, like hawks diving on an unsuspecting chicken. Before the Germans could react to the sudden
strafing, it was too late.

The Gotha plunged into the water trailing smoke, but it stayed
afloat with its tail rising high above the water. Circling low, the
British airmen saw two of the bomber's three-man crew clamber
out on the broad square wing, apparently to show that they were
still alive and about to sink. Murray fired signal flares to attract some
passing ship, but none appeared on the horizon. Finally, their flares
exhausted and the needle on their fuel gauge dipping dangerously
low, the two airmen had to leave the Germans to their fate. British
ships later searched the area and found nothing. And along the coast
in Belgium, watchers waited in vain for an exhausted pigeon to fly
in from the sea.

Four pilots from the naval air station at Manston pursued the
raiders almost all the way across the North Sea. Three of them each
claimed having shot down a bomber off the Dutch coast, and the
other said he saw one crash. There was immediate satisfaction that

British pilots should have destroyed five Gothas in one afternoon. This total of the raiders' losses turned out to be quite accurate, but it was more a consequence of German misfortune than it was of British marksmanship.

By two o'clock all but two of the Gothas were circling Ghent for a landing. They had been in the air for nearly six hours. Reserve tanks, whose installation had been only recently completed, had allowed them to stay airborne for an extra hour. The bombers had made the return flight much farther north than before, on a course which barely avoided neutral Dutch territory. The raiders thus evaded the Dunkirk naval pilots who were out as usual seeking to intercept them on their way home.

One Gotha had not quite reached its base when the improvised tank ran dry. The pilot made a skilful deadstick landing, but the large machine crumpled as it rolled into a ditch. Another bomber crashed and burned as it circled. Only the rear gunner survived. The Gotha was notoriously nose-heavy, particularly when empty. Setting it down safely was not easy even for an experienced pilot. Strong wind gusts were blowing across the airfields at Gontrode and St. Denis-Westrem that afternoon. Two more bombers crashed on landing but the crews escaped injury.

The bold tactics the raiders had employed under Kleine's leadership produced a profound and lasting psychological effect. Fleet Street deplored the attack as a national shame. Britain, howled the *Daily Mail*, had not been so 'humiliated and disgraced' since the Dutch Fleet ravaged the Medway in 1667. In a leading article entitled 'Humiliating and Incredible', the *Graphic* lamented 'the dishonour of being outfought in the air' after 'so many triumphs on land and sea'. It did not seem to matter that the casualties from the 'Germans' biggest air exploit' (57 killed and 193 wounded) were less than half of those inflicted by the June bombing.

'The air raiders,' commented one report, 'were no dragonflies or fluttering birds. They were huge, sharply defined, mobile magazines of death. . . . Their turning movements were masterly, defiantly precise . . . like ships at a naval review. The manœuvre was a well-rehearsed triumph for the enemy. . . .'[64]

'For fifteen to twenty minutes, they did not appear to move,' seethed Sir Hall Caine, the distinguished author. 'Against the gray banks of clouds they looked precisely like a collection of cholera

FOUR RAIDERS DOWN IN GREATEST LONDON AIR RAID

Fierce Air Battles over Capital in Attack from North-West to South-East.

NAVAL AIRMEN CHASE INVADERS OUT TO SEA

Three Caught and Destroyed 40 Miles from Coast and One off Mouth of Thames.

34 KILLED AND 139 HURT IN LONDON.

Six Enemy Machines Destroyed by British Airmen in Fighting off Dunkirk.

OFFICIAL—FROM LORD FRENCH.

11.45 A.M.—At about 9.30 this morning hostile aircraft in considerable numbers, and probably in two parties, appeared over the Isle of Thanet and the east coast of Essex.

After dropping some bombs in Thanet, the raiders proceeded in the direction of London, moving, roughly, parallel to the north bank of the Thames. They approached London from the north-east, then, changing their course, proceeded north and west and crossed London from north-west to south-east.

Bombs were dropped in various places in the metropolitan area.

The number of raiding aeroplanes is at present uncertain, but was probably about twenty.

They were attacked by artillery and by large numbers of our own aeroplanes, and reports as to the results of the engagements, as to damage and casualties have not yet been received.

6.40 P.M.—The total casualties reported by the police at present are as follow:—

KILLED.

TAUBES' SEARCH FOR "PARTICULAR SPOT."

Air Hawks Hover and Look for Prey.

BIG BUILDING HIT.

From the roof of a building in the heart of London I watched the greatest air raid that has been made on the metropolis, writes a representative of the *Sunday Pictorial*.

The invaders came from the north-east. They came not as single spies, but like a great flock of wonderful birds.

I tried to count them. It seemed such an easy task, for they were flying comparatively low and in steady formation, one large squadron leading and a smaller squadron following close behind. This latter consisted presumably of fighting machines which were escorting bomb-dropping invaders.

Over London all the machines gathered in close V-shape formation and made for the west and north-west. All London could see them.

Then our anti-aircraft guns boomed out their defiant challenge, and bombs carried their messages of death and destruction to those below.

A bomb seemed to fall every second. The hawks of the air hovered over London in a way which suggested that they were seeking some particular prey—some particular spot on which to drop their bombs.

Then up into the air went the British aeroplanes. Their coming disturbed the invaders, who split into sections. They reminded me of a covey of frightened partridges.

A series of desperate air duels followed. It was splendid to watch the way in which our airmen went to the attack.

One man engaged two machines.

SLOW DEFIANCE.

Leisurely Enemy Mistaken by Spectators for British Patrols.

An amazing feature of the raid was that the

SECOND AIR FLEET DRIVEN OFF.

Thrilling Story of Great Sky Battles.

OUR AIRMEN AT GRIPS.

22 Raiders Turn Back 10 Miles from London.

BY A SPECTATOR.

I have just seen the biggest battle in the air ever fought over England.

Between 10 and 11 a.m. a squadron of hostile aircraft were distinctly visible almost above our village.

Twenty-two were counted as the aeroplanes headed towards the north-east of London. They looked like a cluster of rooks, and the hum of the engines could be heard plainly.

Suddenly four of our warplanes emerged from a cloud and opposed the enemy from the front. There was a rattle of guns and the German craft swerved slightly.

Puffs of smoke from bursting projectiles floated in the blue air and our airmen seemed mingled with the raiders.

Presently British aircraft appeared on all sides and two great fights occurred simultaneously. One group of combatants was like a company of angry hawks.

CLOSED AND GRAPPLED.

Aeroplanes hovered, swooped and closed with one another. The larger battle was waged at a great height, but could be seen through field-glasses.

In one cluster I counted thirty-eight combatants, the majority being British. Once or twice the machines almost closed and grappled, and most of the firing was at very short range.

The attackers and defenders were intermingled in a remarkable tangle.

There were moments when the opponents scarcely moved. They seemed to be entirely stationary, like poised kestrels.

The air resounded with the fierce firing, and

One of the enemy machines was brought down by Royal Flying Corps and fell into the sea off the mouth of the Thames.

THE AIR FIGHT OVER THE SEA.

The Secretary of the Admiralty makes the following announcement:

The enemy raiding squadron was chased by Royal Naval Air Service machines from this country and engaged 40 miles out to sea off the East Coast.

Two enemy machines were observed to crash into the sea. A third enemy machine was seen to fall in flames off the mouth of the Scheldt.

All our machines returned safely.

The Secretary of the Admiralty announces:—

Vice-Admiral at Dover reports from Dunkirk, on information being received that enemy aircraft were attacking England, five flights were sent up to intercept them as they returned.

The raiding enemy aircraft were not seen, but three enemy seaplanes were encountered and destroyed, and one enemy aeroplane was driven down into the sea and another enemy aeroplane driven down.

The machines returned to replenish petrol and left again immediately.

In the course of this patrol one enemy aeroplane was brought down in flames and another forced to land on the beach, damaged, near Ostend.

During the course of their operations none of the raiding enemy aeroplanes were encountered, and it is thought highly probable that they returned near the Scheldt and over Dutch territory.

SMOKE CLOUD RUSE?

How Raiders Tried to Hide from Our Guns.

An eye-witness states that when the raiders broke up their formation several of them seemed to disappear in small clouds of smoke, in which it is assumed they enveloped themselves as soon as they were fired at.

These smoke clouds seemed distinct from the puffs which were caused by the bursting of the anti-aircraft shells, and it was obvious that the Germans were making an effort to hide themselves.

Another spectator said that he saw the advance guard of the raiders send up a smoke screen through which bombs were dropped.

WHO WAS THE HERO?

Single British Airman Attacks Whole Enemy Force.

From a little town, in Essex, nineteen miles from London, a solitary British airman rose to attack the sky-raiders.

It seemed a hopeless proposition—a death-seeking task. Yet up he went.

At last he got the whole enemy squadron.

Machine guns were turned on him from all sides, but the intrepid airman and his machine escaped unscathed.

The airman pursued the whole squadron until his stock of ammunition was exhausted, but he chased and worried the enemy all the way to London.

FEARLESS LONDONERS.

Few People Take Shelter and Omnibuses Continue Running.

Great excitement was caused in the West End when the booming of guns was heard. In a few minutes the number of hostile machines were clearly visible.

The absence of panic was very remarkable. The omnibuses continued on their routes and only a comparatively few persons appeared to run for shelter.

If the Germans could have only seen the streets of the City they would have been easily convinced that London has not be terrified, for all the streets were simply filled with people at the first sounds of firing and the roofs and windows of upper stories were framed with faces.

ANTI-GERMAN RIOTS.

Angry Crowd Demolish Shop Fronts at London Fields.

Anti-German riots broke out at London Fields last night. A large body of men and women, the latter forming the majority, paraded the Broadway and attacked the premises of several butchers and pork butchers.

The shop fronts were demolished, and in two instances the goods exposed were strewn about the street.

Other tradesmen in the vicinity closed their shops.

higher haze of the ruin of sky.

"So daringly low did they appear to be, so seemingly slow did they move that one could scarcely credit one's eye-witness, were flying low and travelling very slowly. No guns were firing and they seemed to be coming along so peacefully that practically everyone ridiculed the idea that they were enemy aircraft. Then falling bombs revealed their identity.

There appeared to be thirty-two in the bunch when I first saw them, but the formation resembled that of a fan with the apex due north.

They were in perfect formation and close together, and though it was obvious that shells were bursting all around them they did not seem to be seriously troubled, for it could not be seen that any were altering their course.

The enemy group that intended to wreak its vengeance on London appeared to have the first check in their career as they reached the inner northern districts.

It could then be seen that the gunners had found the range with considerable accuracy, for the machines began to waver and get out of line.

A STEAM PURSUIT.

This section were attacked vigorously from anti-aircraft guns. Their glided with a rapid strike. Amid the rattle of the smaller guns the deep booms of the large explosives could be heard in the distance.

Although several of the invading army had been headed off from London, some of the craft were making their point under a perfect welter of shot.

This fleet was soon out of sight; but the other portion was no more guessed by our aeroplanes that it abandoned its design on the metropolis and turned for the coast.

At least twenty-two of the enemy planes were driven off within about ten miles of London. For about fifteen minutes the battle raged, now nearly over our heads, and then within a mile or two.

It was a circular fight, sometimes almost an indescribable jumble of our own and the enemy's aircraft, and sometimes a combat at rather longer range, though throughout the battle our airmen opposed with extreme boldness and in a well organised fashion.

OVER 100 BOMBS.

Hundreds of Girls Escape Though Building Catches Fire.

Over a hundred bombs, it is computed, were dropped in different parts of London.

An important building was seriously damaged.

Bombs fell on the roof.

There were casualties also on the top floors of the building, where a fire broke out.

One bomb fell close to a square where there were hundreds of girls working.

A building caught fire and was practically burnt out, but a single life, however, was lost, and only one or two people received minor injuries.

"It was a most providential escape," said the manager. "I never heard of a more lucky let-off."

In another street close by two hundred girls were working in a blouse factory when a bomb exploded a few yards away.

The building caught fire, but not a girl received so much as a scratch.

In one street hundreds of women were busy shopping when the raiders began dropping bombs.

Some of the stalls were wrecked, a public-house was badly damaged, and other buildings set on fire.

From beginning to end the raid did not last more than fifteen minutes. It was fifteen minutes, however, of strain and anxiety.

southwards towards the Thames.

The second daylight Gotha raid on London as reported by the *Sunday Pictorial*. The casualties indicated do not include the ten Londoners killed and the fifty-five injured by falling debris from the anti-aircraft fire *(Syndication International: Daily Mirror)* germs on a glass disc. . . . It was an example of the most brutal bullying.'[66]

Flying against the wind, the Gothas had bombed the city with complete indifference to the 'impatient bombardment' of the useless guns. 'Our gunners are not old gunners, but they shoot remarkably well,' one embarrassed official tried to explain. 'It was only hard luck . . . that they did not score a hit. Our own pilots have remarked with what precision the shells were bursting,' he added. without elaborating at whose aeroplanes they had been aimed.[67]

That afternoon a procession of 'big motor-cars' made its way through some of the poorest sections of London's East End. Most of the streets where bombs had struck were barricaded. Wherever the motorcade appeared, policemen hastened to remove the barriers. The cars halted as they came to some devastated place, and a pink-cheeked man with twinkling eyes and long grey hair stepped out. He was flanked by high-ranking officials, some in uniform with gold-laced hats and resplendent ribbons. The shabbily dressed people in the crowd did not readily recognize very many of the distinguished visitors. But they all knew the short broad-shouldered man who spoke to them. He was the Prime Minister.

These Londoners understood the war only in its simplest terms. The bombing of their run-down homes was something which they could not quite understand. It aroused a wrath in them which even a kindly Lloyd George could not quiet. In one street where two 'Germans' were known to live, an unruly mob, nearly all of them women, gathered. The house was ransacked and broken furniture was tossed out into the roadway. The police finally managed to clear the block. But the rioters, disappointed because they had not been able to lay their hands on the occupants of the house, refused to disperse. 'Let us pay those German devils for killing our children,' shrieked the women, almost spitting in the faces of the policeman. 'If this Government won't do it, we will.'[68]

That night, a large throng assembled at London Fields. From there, they marched through the streets of Hackney, smashing store fronts. Several butchers' shops, bearing such names as Strumm and Wenninger, were looted. Breaking into one house, the mob heaped bedding, a piano, and other furniture in the middle of the street and set it ablaze. Harassed constables were rushed to five different places in Tottenham, where the homes and business places of naturalized aliens were attacked. In the Highgate district, two baker's shops were wrecked with stones. Violence flared anew two nights later. The property of foreigners, not always German, was heavily damaged in various districts. At one place, the crowd numbered five thousand.

London and its civilian population, as Lloyd George only too unhappily realized, had become pawns of war. The cost for their security would have to be paid for in the hard currency of front-line air squadrons. And Britain, in the early summer of 1917, could not comfortably afford the price. 'By whose responsibility is it,' many were asking, 'that the Huns can spare machines for attack, whilst we can spare none for defence?'

Anxious for support, the Prime Minister addressed a secret session of the House of Commons two days after the raid. The mood was tense for many of the Members were angry and indignant over the second bombing of the capital. But Lloyd George with his 'dulcet voice' lived up to his reputation as the 'Welsh Wizard' in that evening session. Not only did he 'clear the House of its anxiety, its impatience of the Government, its querulousness', but he also left it with 'a loud cheer of satisfaction' ringing in his ear.[69]

This was no less than amazing for what the Prime Minister said, in effect, was 'that complete protection in the air would never be secured'. He also admitted that there were not enough aircraft for home defence as well as operations at the front. In establishing a priority, he told the House that 'the Army must come first'. Haig and his senior air commander, Trenchard, would certainly have agreed. But Lloyd George could not, for political reasons, strictly comply with his own policy.

By an ironic twist of timing, the two Royal Flying Corps squadrons recalled from the front in June were not on hand when the Gothas reappeared over London. The fighters had left Bekesbourne and Calais only twenty-four hours before to meet Haig's deadline for their return. Lord French was inconsolable. Five days earlier, on 2 July, he had tried to warn the War Office that the departure of the squadrons 'would leave wholly inadequate forces with which to meet an attack on London'. On the eve of the raid, he had written again, this time to Robertson, the C.I.G.S., to put his 'most emphatic opinion on record'.[70]

Famed for his Irish temper, French was not so easily put off at an emergency meeting of the War Cabinet held a few hours after the second attack. 'One would have thought that the world was coming to an end,' Robertson confided to Haig. 'I could not get in a word edgeways. French . . . gave a long story as to his insufficient forces, and made a great protest because the two squadrons you had lent him were taken away.'[71]

French came prepared at the next Cabinet meeting to read his letter of 2 July. Derby, the Minister of War, and Robertson both denied having seen it. The correspondence, it appears, had gone to Henderson, the Director-General of Military Aeronautics, because it included a 'minor point' for his attention. Other Cabinet members joined in the lively debate at this point. They argued that they also should have been consulted before the squadrons were released.

The polemics were outwardly pooh-poohed by Lloyd George. 'We [the Cabinet] do not sit down every day to consider whether a squadron should be sent from here or . . . brought back from there . . . ,' he said publicly.[72] Despite this show of unconcern, that was just about what the Cabinet was trying to do, and not very well at that.

Haig had been tersely directed, within hours after the second attack, to return 'two good squadrons' home for an indefinite period. Both he and Trenchard cursed the levy, but they had no other choice. Haig promptly replied by telegram that the 'squadrons will proceed to England tomorrow as ordered'. But he also shook his finger in a disturbing postscript: 'Fight for air supremacy preparatory to forthcoming operations was definitely commenced by us this morning. . . . Withdrawal of these two squadrons will certainly delay favourable decision in the air and render our victory more difficult. . . .'[73]

Taken aback, the Cabinet's first reaction was to cancel the order. But French was insistent about his own needs. As a compromise, the Cabinet settled for one squadron, and 46 Squadron arrived at Sutton's Farm airfield, near Romford, on 10 July. Its Sopwith Pups were assigned to defending London's eastern approaches until late August. Like the other two squadrons temporarily transferred to home defence, 46 returned to France without once engaging the Gothas over England.

The squabble over aircraft was not limited to the shifting of squadrons. Less than a week after the raid, Trenchard learned that twenty-eight fighters destined for France were to be kept in England for home defence. The notification came from a subordinate directorate in the War Office. Much concerned, Trenchard rushed to Haig with the news. The commander of the B.E.F. was as much upset at not having been informed through the proper channels, as he was about the 'serious reduction' of aircraft for the front.

'I have no information as to the authority on which such an important decision has been arrived at,' Haig wrote tartly to Robertson. 'You will appreciate without explanation from me, the unsatisfactory nature of such a method of procedure, and still more the seriousness of my being deprived suddenly and unexpectedly . . . of forces on which I was counting to carry through an offensive of such great importance. . . .'[74] Haig was stilled, though not quite satisfied, with the reply that the decision had been made by the Cabinet.

Britain learned a lesson in air-power on 7 July 1917. 'The experience of Saturday,' trumpeted *The Times*, 'makes it abundantly clear that . . . all our arrangements in connexion with air campaigning, both offensive and defensive, require fresh investigation. . . . Many people consider that one great defect in the present system is that the air defences are under the dual control of the Army and Navy. . . .'[75]

Lord Syndenham, long an aviation spokesman in the House of Lords, hastened to restate his views in an article on 'Air Raids and Air Power': 'A new arm has arisen which has revolutionized the art of war and brought new psychological conditions into play. Happily for us the new qualities required are well suited to the genius of the British people. . . . But we have yet to learn how air-power must be organised, administered and handled.'[76]

Robertson, Britain's senior soldier in 1917, had watched the raid from a War Office window. A hard-headed, practical man, inclined to direct everything 'to a special and definite end', he was moved to write in a personal letter to Haig: 'I doubt if any real progress will be made until a different organization is established. The Army and the Navy now say what they want, the Air Board considers their wants, and then Addison [Minister of Munitions] makes the machines. I am inclined to think that we need a separate air service but that would be a big business.'[77]

Lloyd George had already decided on how to determine the 'best possible use of the air weapon'. In his view, the perplexing question

called for 'a fresh and able mind, free from departmental pre-
judices'.[77] His choice of a trouble-shooter fell on General Jan
Christiaan Smuts. Now serving Britain's cause, the once Boer rebel
was in London only by a quirk of circumstance. He had come to
London 'with some misgivings' four months before to attend an
Imperial War Conference. He had hoped to return home by May
at the latest. But the astute Smuts was persuaded to stay on as a
member of the War Cabinet, 'so deep was the impression' he made
on Lloyd George.

On 11 July, the War Cabinet agreed to the formation of a 'Prime
Minister's Committee on Air Organization and Home Defence
against Air Raids'. The committee was to consist of Lloyd George
and Smuts, but the Prime Minister did nothing except to give it the
prestige of his title. The work was left entirely to the 'altogether
extraordinary man from the outer marches of the Empire'.

The Gotha raid which cast Smuts into the role of decisive arbiter
was truly one 'heard round the world'. More than any other single
event, it led to the creation of the Royal Air Force in 1918.

CHAPTER TEN

The Fortress of London

When he touched down at Gontrode early in the afternoon of 7 July, Kleine had no way of knowing that his first flight to London was also to be his last by day. But, as his report to OHL indicated, he was quite impressed by the rocking gun barrage and the stubborn fighter attacks. From what he was told by the crews who had made the first raid with Brandenburg, it was clear that the defences of London were now much stronger and better organized.

In the weeks following the attack, Kleine kept an anxious eye on the weather and the number of serviceable Gothas which could be mustered on any one day. The earliest favourable date for a raid was 22 July, a Sunday. Assured of good visibility, at least along the English coast, Kleine again selected Harwich as the target.

The crews were notified that the 'start' time was to be 5.30 in the morning. They went to bed early the night before, but they did not sleep very well. The artillery at the front was firing a barrage which could be heard as far as Ghent, and aircraft were flying over Flanders. The drone of their engines was disturbingly British.

The day broke sunny and bright. Over the North Sea the Gotha formation shook the calm of early morning. Unteroffizier Kurt Delang was more nervous than most pilots, for this was his first mission to England. Flying over a perfectly still sea, there was ample time for thought. Delang had gone home on leave in Silesia less than a month before. Only his sister met him at the railway station, for his father was serving with the Army on the Eastern Front. The young flier's sister greeted him with a telegram ordering him to return immediately to his training squadron at Cologne. That same night he was back on a train on a long journey that was to end at Gontrode.

From above 10,000 feet in the bluish grey void of sky and sea, Delang had the odd sensation that his machine was standing still.

LONDON BY DAY

Other bombers oscillated up and down not far from his wing tips. Now and again, the shadow of one above would darken his cockpit, but he himself had no feeling of motion. Delang listened intently to his engines, as first one Gotha, and then another, fell behind firing emergency flares. He had little confidence in his 'floating suit' which, he had been told, would keep him from drowning if he went down at sea.

A narrow strip, 'white as a cloud', finally appeared on the horizon. It was the coast of England. Delang, a little excited now, reached down for a rod he had brought along to communicate with his observer. Leaning forward, he jabbed Lieutenant Paul Döge up front. Heavily bundled, Döge turned in the open forward turret, his 'hat box', and clumsily waved back. His face, feeling like a stiff mask in the cold wind, wrinkled in a grin. As the coast became more distinct, there was a muffled hammering sound from the back of the bomber. Delang glanced up at his rear-view mirror to see Sergeant Ruhl testing his guns.

The Gothas reached the shore at Hollesley Bay in Suffolk, and turned on a southerly course. It was just after 8 A.M. by the clock in Delang's cockpit. Coming down the coast, the twenty-one bombers were almost immediately within range of the gun batteries protecting Felixstowe and Harwich. From the ground, it appeared that the raiders were reeling under the jarring bursts, their formation swiftly broken up by the deadly black and white puffs. But the Gothas were actually scattering for their individual bombing attacks.

The first bombs splattered along the sandy beach at Felixstowe, 'much to the consternation of the early morning bathers'. A direct hit on a country cottage left only the walls standing. The couple who lived there were outside at the time weeding their garden. Though unhurt, they were not surprisingly taken to hospital to be treated for shock. In Felixstowe itself a hotel and some houses were badly damaged. Some docks at Harwich were also struck. Many bombs actually fell in the harbour, sending small ships scurrying out for the safety of the open sea. One bomb narrowly missed a Harwich church, just as Communion was being given, only to shatter the rectory. But the attack was clearly intended for military facilities. At the naval air station in Felixstowe a hangar was demolished and barracks were hit. All but four of the casualties (13 killed, 26 injured) were soldiers and sailors.

86

Although the attack was over in minutes, the air defences through-out the south of England reacted with amazing energy. No less than 121 aircraft were put up from various aerodromes, two dozen more than on 7 July. But the British pilots saw nothing of the Gothas. Those who flew out to sea in pursuit returned disgruntled, and not a little annoyed, because they had been fired upon by their own gunners along the coast. Two British aeroplanes landed safely with flak damage.

The excitement of the coastal raid was felt as far away as London. For about ten minutes, a series of loud bangs disrupted the peace and quiet of a Sunday morning throughout the capital. Many people dashed about the streets seeking shelter, thinking that it was a German attack. For at least a few Londoners, the shock was fatal. The firing of 'maroons', sound bombs originally developed as a marine distress signal, caused the uproar. Nearly 250 of the rockets had been set off as a raid warning from the roofs of seventy-nine metropolitan London fire stations. The new alert system had been decided upon only the day before. Few people had had time to read the official notices in the morning newspapers. Its somewhat pre-mature use therefore came as a complete surprise.

The Government, up to now, had resisted demands that the general public in London should be warned of approaching bombers. Such warnings, it was feared, would cause panic and bring about work stoppages in critical war industries. Alerts had been issued only to the police, fire brigades, hospitals, and explosives factories. The arrangement was one worked out during the earlier Zeppelin attacks.

The War Cabinet reconsidered its 'perverse' policy after the raid of 7 July. As an 'emergency expedient', it was decided to send police-men cycling through the streets of London with placards reading: 'Police Notice—Take Cover'. The sight of policemen wearing these signs amused some people. 'This fore and aft placard business is somewhat crude in its simplicity, and moreover smacks of the ridicu-lous for the "wearee",' wrote one critic.[78] But women sometimes fainted after being nearly run down by a 'perambulating notice board'.

Warning a city the size of London posed many problems at first. Such ideas as the raising of captive balloons, the lighting of street lights in daytime, the firing of guns, and coloured smoke signals were all turned down as impractical or ineffective. The blowing of factory whistles, and those of ships on the Thames, was tried and rejected because they could not be heard beyond the immediate area. Finally, the 'maroons' were accepted as 'a system of general instantaneous notice', after a test on the Horse Guards parade ground which the Prime Minister himself attended. The policemen were also to continue riding with their placards to spread the news that the Germans were coming.

The false alarm on the morning of the Harwich raid demonstrated that the sound signals were effective. The number of 'maroons' had to be reduced, in fact, because of the many complaints about the noise. Some commercially minded citizens protested that, had it not been a Sunday, the unnecessary warning would have greatly disturbed routine business. As it was, only church attendance suffered that morning. Others, apparently over-excited by the din of the rockets, 'felt cheated at not having their show' when German bombers failed to appear over London. 'While I did not want anyone killed,' groaned one thrill-seeker, 'I shared the general disappointment of not seeing a repetition of the wondrous spectacle of three weeks ago.'[79]

Raid communiqués from Berlin invariably referred to the British capital as the 'fortress of London'. The Germans were intent on proclaiming to the world that the place was not an open city, but a heavily defended military target. It was retorted that 'not even the wildest flight of Prussian imagination' could make it so, because one did not find women and children living in a fortress. Probably the greatest merit of this propaganda duel is that words alone never killed anybody. As for London, the city literally became a bastion by 1918.

British apprehension of air attacks had long remained latent. After the June raid Grey was moved to write with his usual blend of truth and sarcasm that 'if you want to put life into an Englishman, you have to scare him to death'. With the bombing of 7 July, the overtime effort of the clear-headed Smuts was all that was needed to distil anxiety and confusion into sound suggestions for air defence.

'London occupies a peculiar position in the Empire of which it is the nerve centre,' he noted in his report to the War Cabinet.

'Exceptional measures' had to be taken, since it was likely that the capital 'would through aerial warfare become part of the battle front'. Smuts suggested anti-aircraft artillery 'in front of, and covering London' to break up the German bomber formations. Defence aeroplanes might then 'destroy individual machines'.

Smuts was highly critical of the existing Home Defence Forces commanded by his old Boer War adversary, Lord French. There was 'too great a dispersal of Command' between the Observation Corps, 'mostly infantry soldiers, often elderly and not specially qualified', the 'various incomplete units or single machines of the Royal Flying Corps', and the artillery defences.

Henderson had previously proposed that all such forces should be placed under one full-time commander. This officer should be an airman, he believed, because 'the aeroplane is by far the most important means of defence'. Pemberton-Billing had urged the same as early as 1916. Smuts now incorporated this reform as his first recommendation. An air defence chief, responsible to French, was to be 'specially charged with the duty of working out all plans for the London Air Defences'. Naval air squadrons would continue to operate independently, 'but in close connection with the Home Defence'.[80]

The War Cabinet swiftly approved the changes put forth by Smuts. The London Air Defence Area was established at the end of July 1917. The L.A.D.A., as it was called, not only included London, but all of south-east England. Brigadier-General Edward B. Ashmore arrived from France to take over the new command. 'The fact that I was exchanging the comparative safety of the Front for the probability of being hanged in the streets of London did not worry me,' he recalled later with characteristic confidence.[81]

Ashmore was uniquely qualified for his new assignment. Jovial and handsome, he was a dashing figure with his monocle and trim moustache. Friends affectionately called him 'Splash', but subordinates had 'other names for him'. A regular artillery officer, Ashmore was also 'an aviator of no mean ability'. He had become a pilot in 1912 under circumstances that were revealing of his high spirits and brash ways.

Then a major at the War Office, Ashmore took flying lessons at four in the morning so as to be at work by nine. While others awaited their turn on the only available aeroplane, he would push his way to the head of the line. Once in the air, Ashmore further annoyed the other students by staying up beyond his allotted time. Early in the war, he led a wing of the Royal Flying Corps in France under Trenchard. Later, he transferred to a division in the line to command its artillery as a brigadier.

Ashmore reported to French at the Horse Guards, and spent the next few days gathering his staff. Colonel Cyril Hankey, an old friend and formerly a brigade commander of the Medway artillery defences, became his chief of staff. Lieutenant-Colonel T. C. R. Higgins, who had directed the Home Defence Squadrons since February 1917, stayed on as Ashmore's senior air officer. Simon was retained as the London anti-aircraft artillery commander.

Higgins had asked for five additional squadrons after the second Gotha attack on London. But, as later recommended by Smuts, only three were immediately approved. These squadrons, 44, 61, and 112, were quickly activated. No. 44 was stationed north-east of the capital at Hainault Farm. A muddy drab aerodrome, the site was indeed a farm which had been taken over nearly two years before in the fight against the Zeppelins. The airmen were quartered in a large rambling house not far from the field. Since London was less than an hour's ride away, they did not exactly take to country living. 'The pilots spent most of their nights in town,' one of them remembers.

The squadron's old machines were soon replaced with Sopwith Camels. This fighter accounted for some thousand enemy aircraft during the war. A stubby biplane armed with two fixed machine-guns, it could fly at well over a hundred miles an hour and climb at the rate of a thousand feet a minute on take-off. The other two squadrons were assigned Sopwith Pups. While it could not climb as swiftly as the Camel, the Pup was more popular with pilots because of its 'perfect flying manners'.

No. 61 Squadron was stationed at Rochford, then a small village near Southend. Its pilots shared a 'magnificent aerodrome almost a mile square' with the airmen of a few training units. The third new squadron, 112, was positioned south-east of London, far out in Kent. From Throwley aerodrome near Ashford, this squadron guarded the approaches to the Thames estuary.

The L.A.D.A. also included six squadrons organized in 1916. These were equipped with older night-flying machines for use against the Zeppelins. Although the capital had not been attacked by airships for nearly a year, these units were maintained on Smuts's recommendation that 'it would be unwise to abandon earlier defence arrangements'.

Anticipating Smuts's report, Lieutenant-Colonel Simon had proposed the installation of a ring of gun sites about twenty-five miles around London. French strongly endorsed the plan, arguing that 'isolated attacks by aeroplanes on these unbroken formations are, it is clear, a useless sacrifice'.[82] The field-marshal wanted enough guns to cover London on three sides at first, and eventually from the west. He estimated that 190 pieces would be needed to encircle the city. The War Cabinet, already harassed by staggering losses at sea to German submarines, replied that the allocation of 3-inch guns to merchant ships could not be diverted.

The 'eastern gun barrier' was begun in August with only thirty-four guns drawn from London and other areas. Behind this barrier, Ashmore assigned fighters to fly in formation along courses the Gothas would have to cross to reach the capital. A 'green line' divided the two defence zones. Outside this line, the guns were to have priority. But once the raiders crossed it, the guns were to hold their fire to allow the fighters to attack. London and its immediate approaches, where the sound of the guns were calculated to have an uplifting effect on the inhabitants, continued to be defended by anti-aircraft fire.

Notification of approaching raiders was speeded up. In describing how the pilots were scrambled, Captain Cecil Lewis, then a flight leader at Hainault Farm, depicts a scene more reminiscent of 1940 than 1917: 'Each squadron had a telephone operator constantly on duty. When raid warnings came through, he pressed a Morse key close to hand sounding three large Klaxon horns set up on the roof of the men's quarters and the officers' mess. The men swarmed into their kit and warmed up their engines. If the raid warning was followed by the action signal, machines were off the ground within a minute.'[83]

But pilots, once airborne, were not so easily directed to the enemy bombers. Still lacking radio contact with their fighters, the British improvised with imagination, if not success. The so-called Ingram system consisted of a code of dots and dashes communicated by large white panels. Considerable time was required to lay out the cumbersome signals, and the pilots themselves had some difficulty reading them. This impractical arrangement was now replaced by white arrows permanently mounted at widely scattered points. The pointers were large enough to be seen from as high as 17,000 feet on a clear day. The arrows were to be pointed in the general direction of the raiders for as long as they remained over England.

All of these defence innovations were being rushed to completion during the first part of August 1917. Although the work was favoured by a 'distinct pause in the attacks', an uneasiness mounted. Rumours were heard that the Germans were not raiding because they were too busy training new squadrons for a massive blow against London. As the month progressed, the British waited anxiously for the Gothas to strike anew.

CHAPTER ELEVEN

Sunday in Southend

The midsummer lull being put to such good use by the defenders of London was not of Kleine's making. A raid ordered on 29 July had failed to reach England because of the weather. As unfavourable conditions continued into August, the busiest and most harassed man in the squadron was the new meteorologist, Lieutenant Walter Georgii. The days were clear and sunny, but strong west winds were blowing a foam-crested sea against the Belgian coast. While the Gotha crews swam and relaxed by the shallow ponds near the airfields, Georgii hopefully kept busy. Several times daily he sent up pilot balloons and made other observations for his reports to an increasingly impatient Kleine.

Georgii had arrived at Gontrode in late June. Since his name sounded rather strange for a German, he soon became known as 'Ii' (ee-ee) to the other officers of the headquarters staff. The crews, who looked upon his prognosis of the elements with some awe, referred to him as the 'weather frog'. Twenty-eight years old, there was more to the lanky lieutenant than his outgoing manner and the painstaking attention he gave to his duties. A student of physics and mathematics, he had earned his doctorate before the war. For two years he had been a scientific assistant at the Prussian Meteorological Institute in Berlin. Volunteering for the Army in 1915, he became a balloon observer on the Verdun front.

One day late in January 1916, the young scientist was summoned to the headquarters of the German Fifth Army, then located in a palatial villa in the French town of Stenay. Ushered into a large room, he found himself, to his surprise, in the presence of the German Crown Prince and his Chief of Staff, General Schmidt von Knobelsdorf.

Sworn to secrecy, Georgii was told about the planned offensive against Verdun. Knobelsdorf needed a firm forecast of cold weather at least sixty hours before the attack. The ground had to be frozen

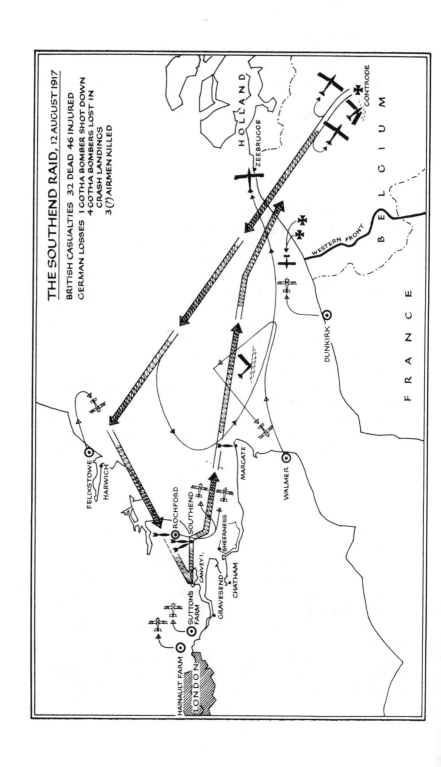

THE SOUTHEND RAID, 12 AUGUST 1917

BRITISH CASUALTIES 32 DEAD 46 INJURED
GERMAN LOSSES 1 GOTHA BOMBER SHOT DOWN
4 GOTHA BOMBERS LOST IN
CRASH LANDINGS
3 (?) AIRMEN KILLED

HOLLAND

BELGIUM

CONTRODE

ZEEBRUGCE

WESTERN FRONT

DUNKIRK

FRANCE

FELIXSTOWE

HARWICH

ROCHFORD

SOUTHEND

MARGATE

WALMER

CANVEY I.

SHEERNESS

GRAVESEND

CHATHAM

SUTTON'S
FARM

HAINAULT FARM

LONDON

hard for the rapid advance of the assault troops. Georgii, his head whirling at what could happen should he be wrong, promised to do 'my best'. The Crown Prince expressed his confidence, and shook the young man's hand.

February was a rainy month. Greatly aided by weather data from Iceland and Norway, Georgii was finally able to predict a freeze of two to three days beginning on the 19th. Despite a stern reminder from Knobelsdorf that 'once these orders for the offensive go out to-night to the entire army, they cannot be countermanded', he stuck to his forecast. The rain changed to snow, and on the 20th the weather turned cold. Georgii was up early the next morning, watch in hand, to time the start of the artillery barrage at the exact hour of 5 A.M.[84]

Soon afterwards, the Flying Corps claimed his services and gave him a commission. Assigned as a weather officer to a squadron in Palestine, he was later sent home with typhoid fever and malaria. While recuperating, Georgii served as an adjutant in the head-quarters of the German Home Air Defence. Then came the sudden orders assigning him to the England Squadron at Ghent.

For Georgii, the greatest forecast 'in all my life' remained the one he had made that night in Stenay before the battle of Verdun. It was a steeling experience that was to stand him well in his dealings with the driving Kleine. 'It was often not easy,' he recalls, 'to convince the Kommandeur that a certain day might be unfavourable for a raid.'[84]

After Haig launched his Flanders offensive at the end of July 1917, Kleine was directed by OHL to bomb British ports. He was only too anxious to comply. His great ambition was to receive the Pour le Mérite which the Kaiser had so grandly bestowed on Brandenburg. A series of smashing raids at this critical moment could well bring the coveted honour.

Kleine's first chance came on 12 August, when Georgii's forecast seemed to permit a flight. The surprised crews were not notified until early afternoon. Since it was a Sunday, many of the airmen had already left to spend the day in Ghent. Kleine could put up only thirteen bombers, but he had them in the air in less than an hour with Oberleutnant Richard Walter, the Führer of Staffel 15, flying in the lead. The objective, decided well in advance, was the British naval base at Chatham. Southend and Margate–Westgate were assigned as secondary targets.

95

The weather seemed ideal at first. Billowing clouds crowded a deep blue sky. Young Delang, setting out on his second attack, was reminded of snowy peaks and yawning gorges 'in whose depths shimmered the green-blue sea'. But the enchantment of the sunlit heights soon passed for the small band of Germans.

The Gothas had never set out for a raid on England in so few numbers before. Soon after take-off, two of the bombers turned back signalling engine trouble. The thinning formation had hardly left the Belgian coast when it was sighted by a British patrol from Dunkirk. In attempting pursuit, the naval pilots were forced to fly straight on to England and land for lack of fuel. As they did so, a warning was flashed to London.

A slashing south-west wind slowed the raiders' advance across the sea. The shielding clouds drifted away, and the blinding sun into which they were flying was without warmth. Fearing the worst, the chilled, tense crews checked their guns and ammunition for the air battle that surely would have to be fought over Britain.

Another Gotha fell behind the formation as it neared the island. Swinging southward on its own, the bomber caused much commotion when alarms were sounded at Ramsgate, Deal, and other places along the Kent coast. Four bombs dropped on Margate, demolished an unoccupied house and injured a woman. The raider then hastened out to sea at a height of 12,000 feet.

Several aircraft from the naval station at Walmer went up, but gradually all abandoned the chase except one piloted by Flight Sub-Lieutenant Harold Kerby. Though flying a Sopwith Pup, a land machine, Kerby persisted nearly all the way across the North Sea before losing his quarry. The ailing bomber barely made it to Belgium. When its engines failed altogether, it came down on the beach at Zeebrugge.

The remaining Gotha crews reported a fierce battle with seven British fighters off the English coast. Delang's view was blocked by the broad upper wing of his bomber. From the moment Ruhl began firing from the back cockpit, the pilot's eyes were glued on his rear-view mirror. A diving fighter blurred the glass and disappeared beneath the tail. Frantically, Delang banked to the right and then to the left. Heavy with a full load of bombs, the Gotha rolled sluggishly.

'The Englishman pulls up steeply by our side,' recounts Delang. 'Lt. Döge and Sgt. Ruhl send streams of bullets flying after him, but the manœuvrable single-seater is already attacking from the rear. Bank! The machine-guns are hammering noisily and the white strands of the enemy's phosphorous bullets zip between the wings of our Gotha like paper streamers.'[85]

As the fighter repeated his angry passes, Delang kept banking and turning. Losing altitude at each turn, the bomber fell farther and farther behind the others. Then, a sharp burst hit one of the wings' ailerons. The Gotha tilted on its starboard side, making further evasive manœuvres impossible. 'Sure of his game,' the Britisher closed in for the kill. He swooped down recklessly, and his shots missed. As he rose vertically on the opposite side, the German gunners found their mark. Its wings shredded, the fighter gave off a white vapour before bursting into flames. A line of black smoke traced its plunge down to the sea.

The fight Delang so vividly describes is not found in British accounts. Confirmation on his side, he states, came later from a German submarine that observed the combat off shore. The presence of British aircraft was not improbable for the bombers approached the coast near Felixstowe where naval machines were based. This victory, and two others the Gotha crews claimed in the course of the raid, were officially recognized in German reports, but the British listed no losses.

Walter, the formation leader, had intended a landfall near the Thames estuary. The delaying wind, he found, had driven him some forty miles to the north. Still determined to bomb Chatham, Walter turned the formation and led it south over Essex. The raiders stayed close to the sea, flying over a flat coastal landscape into which 'the rivers were etched like gigantic veins'. Expecting more fighters at any moment, the Germans kept an anxious watch inland. But they could see very little in the glare of the sun descending in the late afternoon sky. Delang, Döge, and Ruhl were particularly anxious. They were still trailing miles behind the formation.

The British had 133 aeroplanes in the air that day. The ten Gothas took nearly an hour to regain the Thames against a stiff wind. They easily could have been destroyed, had the British not miscalculated Walter's course and target. Ashmore at his Horse Guards head-quarters was notified in good time of the raiders' whereabouts. But instead of seeking immediate battle, he unhurriedly directed the fighters to protect the approaches to London. Then he waited, confident that his 'squadrons would be in position at the required height and in sufficient numbers to overwhelm the enemy formation if it came on'.[86]

At Rochford, near the Thames estuary, 61 Squadron was alerted but ordered to stay on the ground. Ashmore judged that the bombers would by-pass this aerodrome as they came towards the capital from the north-east. White pointers were not yet installed as far out as the coast. The L.A.D.A. commander feared that the pilots from 61 would miss the formation altogether without direction from the ground. He decided to keep them in reserve until the Gothas were on their way out.

The fighter pilots were chatting idly by their Sopwith Pups when, much to their surprise, they saw the German bombers bearing down on them from the north. The squadron commander did not bother to telephone Ashmore in London for instructions. He excitedly dashed out, waving his squadron up to attack. The raiders were equally astonished to see the fighters scrambling for a take-off far below. As if in salute, they dropped three bombs. These fell near some hangars on the aerodrome and wounded two mechanics.

To Walter in the leading Gotha it seemed as if the sky was becoming alive with British fighters. Chatham was still some fifteen miles away. He had to make a quick decision, but the choice was an obvious one. Near Canvey Island on the Thames' north shore, the formation leader turned once more and headed due east. Southend was about five miles ahead between him and the sea. With its hotels, gardened terraces, and promenades overlooking the estuary, the holiday resort was hardly a critical target. And on this particularly warm Sunday, the town was crowded.

Delang, still lagging behind, saw the formation change its course. Doggedly, he kept his damaged bomber on the same track. 'Rochford', he relates, 'is on our right, the open sea glistens on the left, and before us stretches the vast expanse of the Thames estuary. Lt. Döge points downwards. Southend looms below, a town with symmetrical streets and extensive port facilities [sic] along the banks of the Thames. Clumsily, the crippled Gotha turns south-easterly and slowly, ever so slowly, almost centimetre by centimetre, Southend pushes itself under the big aeroplane.

'Down with the bombs! We unload carefully so that the damaged machine will not rise too abruptly. Then the racks are empty, and we take a direct course across the estuary towards Sheerness. Let's join up with the squadron!'[87]

The attack struck Southend at about 6 P.M. and lasted for a quarter of an hour. The crews reported hitting the railway station 'repeatedly'. The jarring explosions tumbled the excursionists converging on the station to board trains for London like bowling pins. In nearby Victoria Street, rescuers found 'a heap of torn and mangled humanity'. A single blast had killed seven people and injured more than a score. In Leigh-on-Sea, outside Southend, seventeen houses were said to have been destroyed. Some bombs were also dropped on Shoeburyness, but most of these fell in the sea.

The guns at Sheerness brought the Gothas under fire as they flew out over the estuary. But the Sopwith Pups from Rochford did not catch up with the Germans until they were some forty miles out beyond the coast. The combats which followed were 'brief and indecisive'. The Royal Flying Corps pilots were apparently not too keen on venturing much farther out over the North Sea.

Kerby, the naval lieutenant who had chased the lone Margate raider nearly all the way to Belgium, had no such qualms. On his way back to England, he sighted the Germans flying in his direction with four British fighters speeding after them. The Gothas were a few thousand feet above his altitude. Kerby rose to 18,000 feet and made a diving attack with no apparent effect. While climbing for another pass, 'he saw a single hostile machine below the enemy formation, but flying with it. He attacked from the front and drove the enemy down to the water. . . .'[88]

Kerby's fire apparently killed or wounded the pilot. The Gotha flipped over as it nosed into the sea. Dipping low, the British pilot saw one crew member clinging to the bomber's tail. He tossed a lifebelt to the German, and then set out to find a rescue ship. A little later, Kerby fired flares to attract four destroyers bound for Dunkirk. These signals were not understood, and the ships went on their way. The gallant pilot received the D.S.C., but it was the frigid North Sea which claimed the final victory, as it did with so many Gotha crews.

The shot-down aircraft was not Delang's. The crippled bomber, once unburdened of its load, had managed to rejoin the formation. Still very much worried, Delang kept in the midst of the other Gothas for protection against any further attacks. The strong breeze which had slowed the Germans on their way out, now sped them home, a cross wind that drove them dangerously close to Dutch territory as they neared the mainland. But the crews were at least spared from having to battle with the Dunkirk naval pilots, who were met by German fighters.

Dusk was settling over the Belgian countryside as the bombers droned over the villages between Bruges and Ghent. With the dangers of flak, fighters, and the sea behind them, the tension of the crews was now measured on the Gothas' fuel gauges. Delang could almost count the litres left in his tanks 'on my buttons'. Finally, the longed for sight of the big Zeppelin hangar at Gontrode loomed ahead.

Delang was gliding down for a landing when another Gotha with motionless propellers slipped in beneath him. He quickly revved up and turned to circle the field once more. Midway in the pattern, his own engines sputtered and fell silent. Barely a hundred feet in the air, the bomber soared silently over a power line and then headed straight for a potato field. Ruhl clambered out of the rear position, and jumped clear as the ground rose up.

The Gotha turned over, 'bursting at all its joints' as its twin landing gear dug deeply into the soft soil. Delang felt a sharp blow on his padded helmet. Unhurt, Döge tugged at his pilot's fur boots to bring him back to his senses. The two shaken airmen took one look at their smashed 'devil's kite', and realized that it would never fly again. Then they ran back to find Ruhl groaning with a broken arm.

Three other Gothas crashed on landing. Add the one Kerby had shot down over the sea, and the total was five out of eleven bombers reaching England that day. The Germans were courting disaster on their daylight flights across the North Sea. Kleine had all the facts, but it was not his nature to concede defeat.

The aftermath of the Sunday raid was no less unpleasant in Southend. Thirty-two civilians, most of them women and children, had been killed. Forty-three others had been injured. Half an hour before the attack the police had been alerted that German bombers were approaching the town. Fire stations, hospitals, and railway officials were notified in turn. But no attempt was made to clear the streets of the milling holiday crowds. The practice of warning the public with sirens, established during the earlier Zeppelin attacks, had been discontinued. Southend had not been raided for two years.

The question of raid warnings outside London was again raised in Parliament. Pemberton-Billing asked whether the Government had 'any power to insist on a system of warning against air raids in any given town of England'. Bonar Law, the Leader of the House, said that he would have to discuss the matter with the Home Secretary. Later, Bonar Law replied that alerts 'must generally be left to the local authorities who know the circumstances and the wishes of the inhabitants. . . .'[89]

The citizens of Southend were quick to make those wishes known in their protest against the 'imbecility of the local authorities'. After a public meeting the angry townspeople marched on the residence of the Mayor. The outcry brought back the sirens which, it was announced, would be sounded for one minute in case of future attacks.

Pemberton-Billing, as usual having the last word, rose again in the House a few days later to indulge in 'a little intelligent anticipation'. This time, the unruly M.P. asked if a warning system 'operative till midnight' might not be introduced, 'in view of the probability of aeroplane raids by night in the near future?'

The Home Secretary, Sir George Cave, answered that the police would circulate with their 'Take Cover' placards during the night hours. The 'maroons' would not be fired, however, 'as they would unnecessarily disturb persons already under cover'.[90]

That much, at least, had been decided should night bomber raids occur. For the moment, the British felt reassured. The 'chief sufferer' had been Southend only because the Germans had turned tail in the face of 'heavy odds'. The real objective of the raid, everyone believed, 'was clearly London'.[91]

CHAPTER TWELVE

Defeat of the Day Raiders

Shortly before noon on 18 August 1917, a work gang was patching a country road outside the Dutch village of Goedereede. From far off in the distance came the faint hum of aircraft. The men stared skyward, curious but unafraid, for their country was not at war. Though German and British warplanes frequently crossed the frontier, they were not likely to appear this far north. Even by air, occupied Belgium was fifty miles away.

Two large aircraft approached from the south-west. White underneath, they were too high for their markings to be recognized. Suddenly, the air was rent by several loud explosions. Slapping shock waves scattered the labourers and showered them with dirt and stones. A crater over ten feet wide was dug only twenty yards from the work site. The breathless Dutchmen were surprised to find that only two among them had been slightly hurt.

The mysterious bombers were Gothas from Ghent. The machines were flying a wild course that would take them right across Holland and end with their destruction. The episode was but a small one in what turned out to be a calamitous day for Kleine and his crews. The memories of the Hollandflug, as they called it, were to last a lifetime.

The flight started as a raid against England. Sunny skies over Belgium extended well into Germany. But the coming weather was being made by a low pressure area over Scotland. Georgii prepared his daily weather report very early that morning, and advised against an attack. Kleine, who could see nothing but bright sunshine, decided otherwise. Feeling morally responsible for the lives of the crews, Georgii firmly repeated his warning of dangerous winds. Not a little annoyed, Kleine dismissed him and alerted his Staffeln to get ready.

Officers in charge of crews came in for the briefing. The whole staff was there: Kleine's adjutant, whom everyone called 'Spatz',

Oberleutnant Gerlich; 'Rabatz', his pilot, tall, blond Lieutenant von der Nahmer, a favourite in the squadron for his lively sense of humour. He was followed by 'Matz', the commander's dark-eyed observer, Lieutenant Buelowius. The young officer's older brother, Alfred, a future general in Hitler's Luftwaffe, was also present as one of the crew commanders.

Georgii was directed to report on the latest weather. His forecast already questioned, he now felt his integrity challenged. He ended by telling the staff and the crew leaders that he frankly did not think it wise to attempt a raid that day. The commander's response was to order an immediate start.

Kleine's plan called for crossing the sea before deciding on a definite objective. He would then know how much fuel remained and what targets were within range. Kleine selected the North Foreland, the outermost tip of Kent, as the place where he would make a decision.

'We're going,' shouted Oberleutnant Fritz Lorenz on rejoining his crew. His pilot, Lieutenant Kurt Küppers, was busy giving his aeroplane its pre-flight checks. He looked up at the beaming observer and yelled back in approval. The suspense was over for the men who became as 'nervous as race horses at the post' during a long wait. The crew hurriedly donned their heavy flying clothes and climbed aboard the loaded bomber.

Painted in large square letters on the Gotha's rounded nose was the inscription, 'Lo-Ri 2'. The first two letters stood for Lorenz. 'Ri' was for Lieutenant Richter, his first pilot, killed the month before while making a trial flight with the original Lo-Ri. Needing a new pilot, Lorenz had persuaded Küppers to transfer to the England Squadron. The two had first met while flying on the Russian front, and they were good friends.

Küppers was no hastily trained wartime flier. As a technically minded youth his interest in machines had progressed from automobiles to aeroplanes. He was only nineteen, and still a civilian, when he qualified as a pilot in 1913. He was serving his one-year tour of military service with the German Flying Corps when the war broke out.

First assigned to flying reconnaissance and spotting for the big guns shelling Dunkirk. Küppers later trained as a fighter pilot on the famous Fokker monoplane. He had three official victories to his credit, all British machines shot down over Flanders, when he came to Gontrode from the Jagdgeschwader Richthofen. It was more his fondness for Lorenz than interest in the bombers which had led him to put in for a transfer. Assured by Kleine that he could return to Richthofen whenever he wished, Küppers agreed to stay on as Lorenz's pilot.

When he took off that 'beautiful morning', Küppers thought he was setting out on his second raid. Lo-Ri 2 was one of twenty-eight bombers. This force—thirteen Gothas from Gontrode and fifteen from St. Denis-Westrem—was the largest ever to start against England. Anticipating strong British fighter attacks, Kleine had ordered up every available aeroplane.

The formation was still over Belgium when it began to be buffeted by a strong south-west wind. Despite the best efforts of the pilots the Gothas inched steadily toward neutral Dutch territory. Near the coast the frontier dips south. The Germans slipped over Holland at this point while still at a low altitude. Dutch border troops at the towns of Aardenburg, Sluis, and Oostburg manned their anti-aircraft guns. They waited a few minutes for some sign of distress from the bombers. When no such signal was given, the guns opened fire. Unable to turn away against the wind, the Germans tried desperately to reach the sea as quickly as they could. Additional batteries near the coast added their fire to the barrage. Possibly because the Dutch intended their shots only as a warning, the Germans escaped without losses.

Hoping for a change of wind, Kleine started to climb. But even at 13,000 feet the Gothas were unable to make much headway. After nearly two hours aloft the crews found that they were still within sight of Zeebrugge. Some swore that they were even drifting back toward the coast. To Lorenz in the open nose of Lo-Ri 2, the unusually strong wind aroused anxieties of a peculiarly personal nature.

While flying over the Russian lines the year before, the chunky lieutenant had been struck in the face by a rifle bullet. Plastic surgeons working with a photograph had devised a plaster mould to equip the disfigured airman with a new nose made of gelatine.

'Each morning he had to cast it anew,' recollects his pilot. 'He was given a paint box and a brush. Standing in front of a mirror, he would adapt the nose to his face. After he had done this with great care and patience, one could not tell that it was a prosthesis. There were drawbacks however. As the day grew older, the flesh-coloured gelatine would darken from grey to black. Also, the nose sometimes came loose. Often, especially at a late hour, Lorenz would grab his tottering nose and hurl it angrily into the nearest corner! He repeatedly lost his nose on combat flights. Unable to withstand the strong wind in the open machine, it would disappear in the North Sea or "land" somewhere in England.'[92]

Lorenz was very likely inconvenienced again that day. The Gothas crept closer to England over a thick cloud cover. After three hours of flight the shore near Harwich finally came into view. Kleine could hardly believe his eyes. A quick calculation showed that he had drifted nearly forty miles from his plotted course. There was no mistaking the port, bombed twice before, with its thin pencil-like mole jutting out into the windswept sea. Now even this familiar target had to be given up. Barely enough fuel remained to fly back to Ghent. The frustrated commander fired a flare to tell his crews that the attack was being abandoned.

Only on changing course did the Germans realize the full force of the wind which had held them back. Their aeroplanes shot forward with a speed that astounded even the oldest crews. 'And now the tragedy began,' Küppers testifies. 'It was not long before we saw two machines go down into the sea. The men aboard were well known to us. The waves swiftly closed in over them! It was heartbreaking having to look on without being able to help. The squadron scattered more and more.'[92]

Like ships caught in a typhoon, the Gothas drifted helplessly toward Holland. Many of them were driven across the estuary of the Schelde and over Walcheren, where they were fired upon from Westkapelle and Domburg. On Schouwen, farther up the coast, alarmed observers reported an overflight by twelve large biplanes. Near Renesse three bombs fell, one exploding in an open field by Moermond Castle. There were fortunately no casualties, and the damage was slight.

Twenty German bombers were seen passing over Cadzand, south of the Schelde. Dutch gunners claimed to have hit one of the intruders, driving it down on the Belgian side of the frontier. Kleine had gathered his dispersed bombers into some sort of formation by this time, and was heading back to Belgium. The crews ran the risk of mid-air collisions, as they lost sight of one another in the clouds blowing in from the sea. To escape the wind and enveloping mist, Kleine led them down below one thousand feet. Even as they flew barely off the ground, the bombers danced up and down violently.

The fruitless five-hour flight ended with the return of the storm-tossed Gothas to Ghent. Their landings described as 'controlled crashes', many cracked up 'with heavy casualties among the crews'. Among those who made it back unscathed were Lorenz and Küppers aboard Lo-Ri 2. Four or five other bombers ran out of fuel before reaching the bases. These came down wherever they could with disastrous losses.

Most spectacular of all was the flight of the two high-flying aircraft whose bombs had stunned the roadmenders near Goedereede. Propelled by a gale-like tail wind, they kept going on a north-easterly course towards the German north coast. About noon the wayward bombers were spotted over the Hook of Holland. Soon after, they were seen near Amsterdam. Continuing across the Zuider Zee, the distraught airmen nearly made it home. When forced down, they were already within sight of Germany.

One Gotha, its fuel exhausted, landed in a meadow near Blyham. The Germans set the undamaged machine afire and ran off into some woods. Dutch border troops fired at the other bomber with rifles. A lucky shot attributed to a Sergeant Lok shattered one of its propellers. The bomber came down at Beerta barely three miles from the border. Both crews were promptly captured and interned.

The proud Dutch raised a fund on behalf of the sergeant. He was presented with a gold watch for giving 'clear proof of our will, where possible, to defend our neutrality by force'. The Dutch press made much of the 'great, unpleasant, and belligerent aerial activity on Saturday last, when fleets of aeroplanes crossed and recrossed our territory, dropping bombs in several places'. Unlike straying Allied airmen who 'might have pleaded that they were over occupied Belgium', the Germans were said to have no such pretext, 'for assuredly they would not drop bombs on the territory they themselves occupy'.[93]

A strong protest was sent to Berlin. The German Government replied that the airmen had lost their way in the clouds, and that they thought they were over the sea when they dropped their bombs. The Dutch rejected this explanation for the two Gothas brought down near the German frontier. Confronted with the evidence, Berlin conveyed its 'deep regrets' and offered 'full indemnity for the material damage'.

'All future flights were started in full agreement between Hauptmann Kleine and myself,' Georgii wrote of the aftermath of the ill-fated flight.[94] The weather still governed the skies. Airmen who went up to battle in frail machines did so at perils often far greater than those presented by the shots and shells of the enemy. When another attack on England was ordered four days later, the squadron had only fifteen Gothas to send out.

Aschoff's 'serpent machine' was one of them. It left Gontrode shortly before 10 A.M. on 22 August, with Kollberg at the controls. The bomber joined the others as the formation took shape on the way to the coast. The land war, now seen in miniature, went on below. Several British warships were shelling German positions near Nieuport as the raiders streamed out to sea.

Once over the water, one bomber after another dropped away. Aschoff counted the disabled machines as they went, and pondered soberly that the attacking formations were becoming smaller and smaller. He knew that shoddy materials and low-grade fuel were the cause. But it also seemed more than a coincidence to him that it was always the same crews which flew all the way to England.

Even greater uneasiness gripped the Germans when the lead machine with Kleine on board turned away. The crews were puzzled when the red flare indicating engine trouble misfired. They saw little more than a wisp of smoke. Walter, the leader of Staffel 15, hastened to fill the vacant spot at the head of the formation. He had little time to worry about Kleine's plight. The British coast was looming ahead, and only ten of the original fifteen Gothas remained.

Within minutes, the sky before them was smeared with the black smoke of exploding shells. The fire was coming from picket ships stationed off shore. Even more disturbing, aircraft were flying in small clusters just beyond the coast. The fighters, fifteen in all, were at varying altitudes below, above, and at the same height as the incoming bombers. They were British naval machines which had come up from air stations at Manston, Eastchurch, Walmer, and Dover on the Kent coast.

On reaching England, the ambitious Kleine had planned to split his formation. One group was to fly in over the estuary for an attack on either Southend or Sheerness, and possibly Chatham. The other was to turn south and bomb Dover. With a much reduced formation and fighters barring his way, Walter realized that this was no longer possible. But he kept on course for Margate, crossing the coast at 12,000 feet.

The Germans were shaken by a devastating barrage over the Isle of Thanet. Walter turned almost immediately for the sea, hoping to reach Dover farther down the coast. As a signal, the frantic leader began to fire a series of three star shells. This confused the crews and some released their bombs instead. The sudden turn was also too late to spare two Gothas from the fighters and intense gunfire.

'One nose-dived, burst into flames and fell spinning round and round like a top,' reported a British official. 'It was a real spiral descent. One of the wings became detached and floated out towards the sea.' The burning wreckage fell in a wheat field near Margate. Trapped in the twisted fuselage, the crew was incinerated.

'The second machine started to drop before the first one had reached the ground,' continued the same observer. 'It was a wonderful sight. In the glorious sunlight one could see the aeroplane turning over and over—alternate patches of grey and flashes of white as the aeroplane caught the sun's rays. In this way it was taken out to sea where it disappeared.'[95] One airman survived the tumbling plunge and was rescued, but his two companions drowned.

A naval pilot, Flight Commander G. E. Hervey, received the Distinguished Service Cross for destroying the Gotha. An air veteran of eighteen months' service in France, Hervey reported firing '100 rounds from straight behind his tail at 100 yards range'. As the machine 'started down into a slow spin, I followed and fired about twenty-five more into him to make sure'. Hervey's gun then jammed, but he saw 'the enemy crash into the sea'.[96]

Some explosives had already fallen on Margate. Ramsgate was 'plastered with bombs'. Because of the fierce barrage, the attack was hurried and indiscriminate. A military hospital and some homes were hit, causing thirty casualties. Half the victims were soldiers, but there were also some women and children among them.

'It is hard to believe,' stated the Deputy Mayor, 'that such things could be done in these days of civilisation and Christianity.' He hoped that 'God would forgive the authors, for our people never could'.[97] Hatred for the 'Huns' long lingered in the little town. In 1920, its residents rioted when a German ship sailed into the harbour with a cargo of coal. Barriers had to be erected to keep hostile crowds from ransacking the ship.

The raiders recrossed the coast at Deal. Most of the Gothas had unloaded by this time, despite Walter's star shell signals. Only nine bombs fell on Dover. These struck an inn, a school, and seven houses. Two soldiers were killed and five others were wounded. One civilian was fatally injured.

The Germans lost a third Gotha near Dover. The apparent victor was Lieutenant J. Drake, but another pilot, Lieutenant Arthur F. Brandon, was awarded the D.S.C. for this engagement. Brandon, whose machine was hit several times, landed to change aeroplanes. Hervey also had to land to have his jammed gun cleared. Both airmen, and many other naval pilots, then chased the remaining seven Gothas out to sea.

Hervey 'caught up with them at 14,000 feet, and engaged them in turn from above and below'. Singling out one bomber, he blasted it with 200 rounds until its guns were silenced. 'I think both German gunners must have been hit, as I was able to get within 60 feet of him without being fired at,' he noted in his report.[96] Though helpless, the Gotha escaped because Hervey had exhausted his ammunition.

The British seemed to have the situation well in hand. Early one morning a few days after the attack, the Royal Naval Air Service sent a burial detail to the farm near Margate where one of the raiders had fallen. The Germans were carried to their graves on a gun-carriage. A military chaplain read the Church of England burial service. Three volleys were fired and the Last Post was sounded. The three coffins had no name plates. These too would have been provided, had it been possible to identify the charred bodies.

What remained of the Gotha was cut up and packed into 1,500 parcels. With Admiralty approval, the packets were sold as souvenirs 'at a minimum price of half a crown on behalf of local deserving institutions and other charities'. The British, it seems, were still a nation of shopkeepers. But this did not make it easier, the Germans were learning, to invade them from the air. Had they gone inland that day, they would have been met by 120 aircraft of the Royal Flying Corps, guarding London above 10,000 feet in squadron formation. Nearly seventy of these aircraft were first-rate fighters.

'The only real security upon which sound military principles will rely is that you should be master of your own air,' Winston Churchill, then First Lord of the Admiralty, had told the House of Commons in March 1914. He had gone on to assure that 'any hostile aircraft, airship or aeroplane, capable of reaching our coast during the coming year would be promptly attacked, and in superior force, by a swarm of formidable hornets'.[98]

Much as Churchill realized the danger even before the war, his fighting promise was premature. His words were later mockingly recalled when German bombs fell on London, but Churchill was then no longer at the Admiralty. In the late summer of 1917, England was now finally defended as he had believed it should be. The Gothas never returned by day. German bombers would await another war to venture forth over the island without cover of darkness; another war that would also return Churchill to the Admiralty and the burdens of leading a Britain at bay.

CHAPTER THIRTEEN

'The Magna Carta of British Air Power'

Smuts was busy finishing his second air report when the tide of battle turned against the day raiders. Completed on 17 August 1917, the hastily written document was to stand as the most important single consequence of the Gotha raids. Defying centuries-old tradition and the opinion then prevailing at the highest official levels, the tenacious Afrikaner recommended that 'an Air Ministry be instituted as soon as possible'. Its avowed purpose was 'to control and administer all matters in connexion with aerial warfare of all kinds whatsoever'. A necessary corollary was the 'amalgamation of the Royal Naval Air Service and Royal Flying Corps' into a co-equal third service.

Unlike artillery, Smuts reasoned, the air service 'can be used as an independent means of war operations. Nobody that witnessed the attack on London on 11th July [sic] could have any doubt on that point.' He foresaw that 'the day may not be far off when aerial operations with their devastation of enemy lands and destruction of industrial and populous centres on a vast scale may become the principal operations of war, to which the older forms of military and naval operations may become secondary and subordinate.'

Smuts thought of 'air predominance' as being essential to Britain's security in years to come. 'Having secured it in this war,' his report went on, 'we should make every effort and sacrifice to maintain it for the future. Air supremacy may in the long run become as important a factor in the defence of the Empire as sea supremacy.'[99]

Smuts has been called a prophet with an 'apocalyptic vision of air-power', the only general who did not have the 'trenches dug deeply into his mind'. But the idea that spawned the Royal Air Force was not originally his own. Decisive in timing, his contribution was to endorse that 'birthright', officially and without reservation.

Claims for a separate air arm had been 'pressed with no small warmth' for some time. Soon after the Zeppelins began to raid

London in 1915, the press demanded a 'Ministry of Aeronautics'. Churchill, already recognized as 'an ardent believer in air power', was proposed 'as a suitable Air Minister'. An attack on the Midlands, which had never been raided before, sparked a more serious uproar early the following year.

The Times blamed the country's 'fundamental weakness in repelling the raiders' on the 'chaotic state of divided duties' under which 'the soldiers and sailors were working'.[100] Fanned by the newspapers, the 'air agitation' swept into Parliament. Arthur James Balfour, Churchill's silver-haired successor at the Admiralty, was jeered in the House of Commons. 'The whole of this flying business is new in practice,' he rebutted. 'How could any Government have foreseen?'[101]

Swift political manœuvring managed to dampen the debate on the immediate need for an Air Ministry. Nonetheless shaken, the Government hastily improvised what it called a Joint Air War Committee. Contrary to what many believed, this body had nothing to do with air defence. It was created to mediate the squabbling of the two Services for aeroplanes and supplies. This dissension was in itself as vexing a problem as the air-raids.

Lord Derby, who was not then Secretary of State for War, agreed to serve as chairman. He resigned in less than two months' time, realizing that his task was an impossible one. The Committee had no power except to recommend, and then only with the unanimous vote of its members. These included the directors of the two feuding air services. In his letter of resignation Derby advised Asquith, then the Prime Minister, that it was 'quite impossible to bring the two wings closer together' unless they were 'amalgamated into one service'. Convinced that 'ultimately they must be', the unhappy chairman viewed such unification as being 'practically impossible' in wartime.[102]

Asquith promptly called on Lord Curzon of Kedleston to repair the political damage. Renowned for his 'treasures of mind and fortune', Curzon was a glittering figure whose only seeming defect was one of body. He wore an uncomfortable steel corset because he was afflicted with a curvature of the spine. Once Viceroy of India, the haughty peer saw the air as a new realm in which, as Secretary of State for Air, he might recapture some of his past majesty.

'I paint myself a dream of a single service under a single hand, under a single roof, with a single organisation,' he told the House of Lords. 'Such a unification I cannot believe to be beyond the administrative genius of our race.'[103] *The Times* advised Curzon to confine himself to a committee on merchant shipping. The air post, it commented, was 'not a job for a politician, however eminent'.[104]

Balfour and Lord Kitchener, the War Minister who would soon be lost at sea while on his way to Russia, quickly checkmated Curzon's ambitions. The legendary 'K. of K.' was opposed to any Air Board with independent powers. Speaking for the Admiralty, Balfour informed the Prime Minister that 'a fighting department should, as far as possible, have the whole responsibility of the instruments it uses. . . . The Navy should be autonomous. . . .'[105]

Curzon's 'large changes' were soon watered down. Though given Cabinet rank as President of the Air Board, and not bound to a unanimous vote of its members, he could do little more than make suggestions to the two Services on aviation matters. If the War Office or the Admiralty failed to act on them, Curzon had no recourse but to appeal to the War Committee of the Cabinet. This large, cumbersome group included Kitchener and Balfour. The effect was to shift any dispute to a higher level of irresolution.

Churchill, whose only forum was now the House of Commons, attacked the Air Board as 'a mere attempt to parry the demand for an Air Ministry'. He chastised the Government 'for following no principle except that of postponement to the last possible moment, and then taking the line of least resistance'.[106] Churchill also predicted a 'first-class row' which finally crystallized in August 1916.

By-passing Curzon completely, the Admiralty secured nearly three million pounds from the Treasury for the purchase of aircraft and engines. The aspiring Air Minister was incensed. He bitterly complained of the Navy's 'intransigence' in a thirty-page, carefully drafted protest to Asquith. While calling for unification as the 'only solution', Curzon granted that this would have to be postponed as 'the war is still proceeding, and in the face of the dislocation that might be caused'. But, as an immediate step, he asked that the Air Board be given 'the whole responsibility for the supply, design, inspection, and finance' of aircraft. He further proposed that the Admiralty should dignify its air service by appointing an additional Sea Lord to command it.[107]

Balfour retorted that the Admiralty would feel 'the greatest misgiving', if the number and design of its aircraft were decided 'by an independent and (I suppose I must now add) a hostile department. . . . I do not propose to discuss the constitution of the Admiralty,' he went on acidly. 'It was created some generations before the Air Board, and its framers had not the wit to foresee that it would some day be required to carry out its duties in subordination to another department. . . .'[108]

Aggravated by Asquith's 'habitual mental wobbliness', the dispute deteriorated into a hopeless deadlock. Curzon threatened to resign if the Air Board were not given control over the supply of aircraft. He was described as being 'prepared to die fighting—and the Government are afraid to let him die'. But it was Asquith, not Curzon, who died politically early in December 1916. Scornful of the Prime Minister's indecision, Curzon was among the 'conspirators' who brought about the Government's downfall. He then abandoned the Air Board to become Lord President of the Council under the new régime.

Led by Lloyd George, the new Cabinet moved swiftly. Within a few weeks a bill was passed in Parliament to provide the Air Board with 'the sanction of statutory existence'. Lord Cowdray, 'a self-confident man whom an earthquake would leave undisturbed', succeeded Curzon. A financier and construction engineer of international repute, Cowdray was widely recognized for his ability to direct large undertakings. He was charged with 'organising and maintaining the supply of aircraft'.

Up to this time the actual production of aeroplanes had been a divided concern of the Admiralty and the War Office. The Army had its own Royal Aircraft Factory, the original R.A.F. Production was now centralized under the Ministry of Munitions. The Navy was particularly upset by the change, and there were some 'flesh-creeping reports' on the consequences of 'civilian control of manufacture'. Yet, by late spring 1917, even the highly critical *Daily Mail* was proclaiming that 'aeroplanes are fluttering out of the factories like butterflies in June'.[109]

The Cowdray Board was far from being an Air Ministry, but it did allow for some degree of unification. 'We who are concerned with the air all live in one house,' said Major John L. Baird, the Board's Parliamentary Secretary. He was referring to the Hotel

114

Cecil, an 'architecturally deplorable, dreadful building' in the Strand, which was requisitioned for the Board. Cowdray had his office on the first floor. Henderson of the Royal Flying Corps, and Commodore Godfrey Paine, newly appointed as Fifth Sea Lord of the Admiralty, were on the floor above. Sir William Weir of the Ministry of Munitions, who managed the 'colossal' increase of aircraft production, was on the third floor. All were members of the Air Board.

The campaign for a separate air force had fed on the anxiety over the Zeppelins, but they were no longer a serious threat by the end of 1916. With the setting up of the Cowdray Board, the air agitation all but petered out. *The Times*, reversing its earlier policy, reflected this new calm. 'For the moment,' it stated editorially, 'the supply of machines and engines is the thing that really matters. . . . The ideal plan is not necessarily the wisest to adopt in the midst of a great war.'[110]

Some of the 'fanatics', such as Pemberton-Billing, remained unsatisfied. Churchill, who was not so easily laughed off, was another dissenter. Speaking out again in Parliament in April 1917, he scoffed at a recent 'portentous oration' Curzon had made in support of the Air Board, 'as if it were the constitution of a new international republic'. He went on to criticize the House for dropping 'the whole question of inquiry into the Air Service'. Churchill warned that 'never since the Battle of the Marne has the situation been more serious than at present'.[111]

The Gothas over London, if not Churchill's oratory, renewed the urgency of the air debate. By late June, the press was openly hinting at an impending Cabinet crisis. Within ten days of the raid of 7 July, Lloyd George not only turned to Smuts, but also offered the Ministry of Munitions to Churchill. With the Cabinet having to recall fighters from the front, there was less talk of 'aeroplanes fluttering out of the factories'. *The Times* was now blaring that 'the crying need for 1917 is for aeroplanes, as it was for shells in 1915. The Government must be compelled to realize that the aeroplane will be the ultimate and deciding factor of the war.'[68]

Smuts went a long way in satisfying this point of view by calling for an Air Ministry. That he should have done so must remain no small wonder. Nearly all the military and civilian officials he consulted were opposed to unifying the air services. These included all of the senior officers of the Royal Flying Corps, Henderson excepted. His strong endorsement of unification was a decisive factor in Smuts's historical verdict.

Since Henderson is all but forgotten today, it is all the more ironic that Lord Trenchard should be hailed as the man most responsible for bringing the Royal Air Force into being. Lord Beaverbrook, who has provided some pungent profiles of the leading personalities of the period, writes that Trenchard 'can hardly be considered as the founder of the Royal Air Force. . . . He was a father who tried to strangle the infant at birth though he got credit for the grown man.'[112]

As commander of the Royal Flying Corps in France, Trenchard enjoyed Haig's fullest confidence. 'The War Cabinet has evidently decided on creating a new Department to deal with Air operations . . .' the field-marshal noted in his diary for 28 August 1917. 'Trenchard is much disturbed as to the result . . . just at a time when the Flying Corps was beginning to feel that it had become an important part of the Army.'[113]

Those who knew Trenchard before he was lifted 'over the threshold of history', and seated at Douhet's right hand as a prophet of air-power, credit him with 'common sense, but limited ability'. He was said to have 'uncanny intuition', and a rare knack for arriving at 'a just conclusion by an apparently erroneous process of thought'. Anything but articulate, he 'often confused people he was trying to enlighten or persuade'.[114]

As a young lieutenant in India, he was called the 'Camel' because of 'the loud grunting noises he emitted when anyone addressed him and he had nothing to say'.[115] The allusion was made perfect by the slight forward tilt of his small head perched atop a lean, very tall frame. Though unclear in expression, Trenchard was not without a voice, whose resonance later won him the lasting nickname of 'Boom'.

Urged on by a fellow officer to 'come and see men like ants crawling', Trenchard had turned to flying in the summer of 1912. He did so with the despondency of a man approaching middle age, and whose career, after nearly twenty years in the Army, was at a dead end. His prospects as an applicant for pilot training were hardly any more promising. Standing a full six feet three inches, Trenchard was far too tall to fly the small machines of the day. He was also nearly blind in one eye, but this disability he managed to conceal. He was accepted and earned his wings in thirteen days with a total flying time of sixty-four minutes. He did so only months away from his fortieth birthday, the age limit for pilots seeking to join the Royal Flying Corps. By all accounts, he was never a very good pilot.

Only a major in the autumn of 1914, Trenchard's mercurial rise was due to his strength of character and qualities as a leader. His is largely the credit for the dash and fighting spirit of the Royal Flying Corps in the skies over Flanders in the First World War. But had he had his way as an 'Army man', there would have been no Royal Air Force in 1918.

'I thought,' he wrote years later, 'that if anything were done at the time to weaken the Western Front, the war would be lost and there would be no air service, united or divided.... Henderson had twice the insight and understanding that I had. He was prepared to run risks rather than lose a chance which he saw might never come again. He did so with no thought of self-interest, and it is doubtful whether the R.A.F. or Britain realises its debt to him, which is as least as great as its debt to Smuts.'[116]

On 24 August 1917, two days after the last daylight raid, Smuts reported to the War Cabinet. Bonar Law presided in the absence of Lloyd George who was suffering from 'overwork and depression'. Churchill and Curzon were the only Cabinet members favouring prompt action on an Air Ministry. Bonar Law had fought over much the same ground in the House of Commons the year before. The renewal of that controversy held little appeal to him. Predictably, the decision was to form another committee.

Called the Air Organization Committee, it was to examine the problems of uniting the two Services and draft the necessary legislation. The task again fell to Smuts who promptly asked for Henderson's full-time assistance. Chief of the Royal Flying Corps since 1912, he gave up his post 'to undertake special work'. The shift marked the beginning of a stormy transition. Conceived in battle over London, the Royal Air Force was to have a long and painful pregnancy with abortion threatening at every turn.

The Admiralty had a new First Lord, Sir Eric Geddes, who closely guarded his interests. The telephone installed in his home was said to be on 'the pay-box system'. He was agreeable to an Air Ministry, provided that only the Royal Flying Corps was taken over. The Army's own case was not presented in full until mid-September, when Haig forwarded his views on the proposed reorganization.

Though resigned to the Cabinet's decision, Haig provided little encouragement. He rejected Smuts's 'future possibilities' as going 'far beyond anything that can be justified in my experience'. Nor did he take kindly to the notion that 'the older forms of military operations' might become 'secondary and subordinate'. The whole idea, in his estimate, required 'very considerable modification' after 'consultation with officers who have wide practical knowledge'. No visionary, Haig single-mindedly limited his consideration 'to our requirements in this war, the winning of which demands the concentration of all our energies'.[117]

Smuts, on the other hand, was speaking of the day that 'may not be far off'. He did not turn to the past where there was none to consult. The test of his wisdom did not lie in the winning of Haig's war in France, but over Britain in 1940, when the 'older forms' of warfare stood by and awaited the outcome of a classic clash of air-power.

As the testimony against a separate air force mounted steadily in the late summer of 1917, even Smuts began to doubt his own counsel. But destiny is often better served by battle than by debate. Beaten by day, the Germans returned by night to prod the British the rest of the way in their reluctant 'revolution of arms'.

And by Night . . .

It is improbable that any terrorization of the civil population which could be achieved by air attack could compel the government of a great nation to surrender. Familiarity with bombardment, a good system of dugouts or shelters, a strong control by police and military authorities, would be sufficient to preserve the national fighting power unimpaired. In our own case we have seen the combative spirit of the people roused, and not quelled, by the German air raids.

Winston Churchill (October 1917)

CHAPTER FOURTEEN

Trials and Experiments

The drone of engines from somewhere above a thin haze made radiant by the light of a full moon caused no alarm at the Chatham Naval Barracks. Notice had been given earlier in the day that there would be an air defence exercise during the night. It was already late in the evening of 3 September 1917. In a large drill hall several hundred recruits were sleeping in hammocks slung so closely together that they nearly touched. The hall had only recently been converted into a dormitory to cope with overcrowding at the big naval base.

'We had no warning of any kind,' grieved one sailor. 'Before we knew what was happening, the roof was lifted off the shop, blown into the air, and fell in a thousand pieces among the men. It was flying glass, which was thick and heavy, that did the damage. We were dashed out of our hammocks to the floor, all mixed under broken glass. The men on either side of me were killed.'[118]

Two large clocks were hurled into an adjacent parade ground, their hands stopped at 11.12 P.M. Seconds before, four 110-pound 'crashing Christophers' had tumbled on the base. Two exploded harmlessly but the others struck the stuffy drill hall squarely. Another Gotha raided the town itself. One house was destroyed and several were damaged.

At Sheerness, some ten miles away, the Germans 'narrowly missed important targets'. Margate had been shaken half an hour earlier. There were only seven casualties at these places. But at the naval barracks, 131 naval ratings died and ninety others were injured. The survivors were taken to a gymnasium the next morning to identify their messmates. The task was not easy for many of the dead had to be gathered up in sacks.

The night before this attack two low-flying aeroplanes had bombed Dover. There were eleven victims, and some damage was done to houses, a stable, and a timber yard. The machines apparently belonged to another German squadron whose target was Calais on the French side of the Channel.

The Dover incident had moved Ashmore to call a night practice alert that evening. He and Lord Derby, the War Minister, were already at the Horse Guards headquarters when the rehearsal turned out to be a real raid. Derby very considerately left to give Ashmore a free hand. The defence commander had more than enough to do trying to track the night raiders. Ironically, an attempt had been made to alert Chatham by telephone. But the bombs fell before the message got through owing to some delay at the exchange in that town.

The British experienced other difficulties during the first Gotha night attack. The moon's hazy brilliance diffused the probing rays of the searchlights. The guns on the Isle of Sheppey fired only sporadically and without effect. There was no opposing fire at Chatham. The raid was even more perplexing to the defence pilots. The situation at Hainault Farm was typical of the confusion caused by Kleine's sudden change of tactics.

'Nobody expected it,' recalls a flight commander assigned to 44 Squadron. 'Most of the pilots were in town. We were thoroughly unprepared. At that time scout [i.e. fighter] aeroplanes were considered tricky enough to land in the day-time, nobody thought of flying them at night. Moreover, most of the pilots had no experience of night flying. None of the machines were fitted with instrument lights, so to go up in the dark meant flying the machine by feel, ignorant of speed, engine revs, and of the vital question of oil pressure. If this gave out, a thing which happened quite frequently, a rotary engine would seize up in a few minutes, and the pilot might be forced down anywhere.'[119]

Ashmore decided that it was impossible for the Camel pilots to go up. But the squadron commander at Hainault Farm, Captain Gilbert W. Murlis-Green, was not one to sit idle during a raid, day or night. He had first met the Gothas over Macedonia where they bombed such targets as Salonika even before their first attack on England. In March 1917, Murlis-Green had encountered six of the bombers in formation, and brought two down before his ammunition ran out. The very next day he blasted a German two-seater out of the air. That two-day stint had earned him the D.S.O. One of his previous victories was said to have been against Count

Schwerin of Mecklenburg, a cousin of the Kaiser. Murlis-Green seemed to have a natural bent for thrashing Germans. While a student at Bad Godesberg a few years before the war, he had won a German schools' boxing championship.

The twenty-two-year-old captain called London during the Chatham raid, and insisted that he be allowed to take off. Two other pilots, Captain C. J. Q. Brand and Lieutenant C. C. Banks, volunteered to go up with him. The trio patrolled for about forty minutes without seeing any Germans, but the flight alone was considered no small feat at the time. 'The exhilaration of our new adventure,' Brand noted in his report, 'created the most intense excitement and eagerness among the other pilots.' Ashmore was so pleased that he cited the night flight as being 'perhaps the most important event in the history of air defence'.[120]

Instrument-lighting equipment was installed in the Camels the very next morning. 'Two-gallon petrol tins with the tops cut off, half filled with cotton waste and soaked with paraffin,' were set out to illuminate the aerodrome. And the pilots were told to practise night landings immediately. One of them judged that 'in twenty-four hours the Home Defence squadrons ceased to be looked upon as anything but night fighters'.[121]

The transition had been equally swift for the Gotha airmen. Night attacks had been decided on in late August because of the formidable British day defences. The Germans, equally untried in night flying, had to find their way over a dark sea and a blacked-out England. Their only navigational aid was a compass. Despite the risks, Kleine was quite willing to gamble with the lives of a few crews. From among volunteers he had selected five of the most experienced, including his own, for the trial flight to Chatham.

The moon was low on the way out. The Kent coast was effectively darkened after the bombing of Dover the night before, but the chalk cliffs could be seen well enough. Four Gothas reached England, one having to turn back with mechanical trouble. Significantly, the British estimated that at least ten bombers had flown in. Kleine was satisfied that night raids were feasible. The crews were jubilant over the absence of British fighters. It was also apparent that the anti-aircraft gunners could not find them in the darkness.

Anxious to exploit these newly found advantages, Kleine ordered another attack the very next night. The target was London, some forty miles from the coast. Eleven crews, all volunteers, roared off at five-minute intervals starting at 9.30 P.M. They headed for the coast in a long, loose chain. The bomber ahead could be seen only by the small flames glowing from the exhaust pipes of its engines. The pilots followed one another for a while, but the tiny flashes gradually faded away and each crew was on its own.

Signal flares were fired from behind the German lines to guide the bombers over Belgium. The airmen could also recognize much of the dim landscape below. Canals stood out and the roads appeared as light lines against the open fields and dark woods. Leaving the signal lights behind, the crews flew on over the darkness of the sea. Their greatest concern was the drift of the wind, which was all but impossible to detect at night. The moon rising in the east was of some comfort. Before long, its light flickered reassuringly on the waters.

Shortly before 10.30 P.M. the bombers were heard passing over Margate. Straying far off course, some crews missed this checkpoint. Dover, twenty miles to the south, was attacked by at least one raider. One or two more bombed Margate with negligible results. The other Gothas followed the Thames to London. Single searchlights along the way betrayed the bombers for a brief moment against the night sky. The lights were too few to illuminate the invaders for very long. Thus handicapped, the guns at Chatham and Gravesend fired in futile anger. Only off Sheerness was a bomber seen going down into the sea. The British found no traces of it, but one Gotha failed to return.

Once beyond the capital's outer gun defences, the Germans easily found their target. 'In the western sky appears a bright glow—London; the city is not blacked out,' describes Walter, the flight leader who had taken over the formation on the last daylight attack. 'Tens of thousands of lights suddenly emerge out of the darkness, and looking straight down, every street is clearly discernible.'[122]

The first bombers were over the city at 11 P.M. The streets were practically deserted. Shouting policemen shepherded what few people were about into the nearest buildings. Others toured the streets on bicycles with 'Take Cover' placards, noisily ringing their bells as they went. Then the guns opened up with a barrage.

Flying high above London, Walter saw the gunfire as too 'sparse and badly aimed' to interfere with the dropping of the bombs. His pilot was able to break away from the 'many searchlights by repeatedly turning and banking'. Walter knew that his bombs had found a mark by the 'glaring flashes' of their explosions. One of the first to fall that night struck an empty factory which had been used, until very recently, as quarters for interned German civilians.

A row of Victorian shops was wrecked in Castle Street, and a nearby cigarette factory was damaged. A salvo of four 110-pound bombs was apparently aimed at Charing Cross Station. One of the bombs exploded just outside the main entrance to Charing Cross hospital in Agar Street. The blast blew in the front door and hundreds of windows. Another plunged to the rear of the Little Theatre in John Street. The Canadian Y.M.C.A. had converted the concert hall into a soldiers' canteen. The dining room, already laid out for breakfast, was left a shambles. The third bomb exploded in the gardens near the Hotel Cecil, the home of the Air Board.

A fourth crashed into the road opposite Cleopatra's Needle on the Victoria Embankment. The shaft itself was scarred, and one of the large bronze sphinxes at its base was pierced by fragments. A crowded tram was passing by at that moment. The conductor and two passengers were fatally wounded, and eight others were taken to hospital. A deep hole in the roadway ruptured a gas main. The Underground line beneath had to be closed until the following day because of escaping gas.

The city was quiet for half an hour before another Gotha arrived to bomb the northern suburbs. The last attack came just after 1 A.M. The streets were filled with people during the early morning hours. Wearing coats over their night clothes, they strolled aimlessly along the glass-littered pavements. Many murmured angrily at being turned out of bed. London had had raid warnings for three nights in a row, and this time the Germans had reached the capital.

British officials were amazed at the seemingly light casualties (19 dead, 71 injured). They estimated that no less than twenty-six aeroplanes had bombed the city. Some reports mentioned 'a number of separate formations' attacking 'in succession'. Eight to ten bombers were believed to have been in the first 'wave' alone. Actually, only five Gothas had struck at the capital.

Kleine, judging from the haphazard blackout of the city, sensed the confusion generated by the protracted bombing. 'Either the

Londoners thought that the raid was over after the first attack,' he informed OHL, 'or else some of the streets had to be lit temporarily because of fire or some sort of panic.' He could make no definite appraisal of the night defences from the varying reports of his crews. 'I myself saw only two guns firing in London.'[123]

It was even more apparent to the British that night attacks had rendered their elaborate day defences virtually useless. This was underscored by Smuts who was asked, once again, 'to favour the War Cabinet with his views'. The Government was distressed by the renewed outbursts of indignation in Parliament and the press.

The *Manchester Guardian* called for 'overwhelming supremacy in the air to redeem our shores from outrage'. The aerial invasion was described as the worst event 'since the Normans conquered England'. Noting that Ashmore was 'evidently in the wrong place', one newspaper invited him 'to make way for people who can and will do his work'.[124]

The air defence commander was swamped with all kinds of advice. One suggestion called for turning night into day by floodlighting much of the south of England with 1,800 lights. Actively entertained for a time, the plan was later rejected because 'it would have been cheaper to move London'. Another idea was to sprinkle the raiders with sulphuric acid. This was hardly practical as long as they were over the country. Experiments in which carborundum powder was blown into the engine of an aircraft were actually made. The tests were given up when the powder failed to have any damaging effect.

Ashmore's own answer to the 'new danger' was the balloon barrage. Such obstacles were already in use in Germany. Venice was also protected against Austrian bombers by single balloons raised from rafts in the city's canals. The British innovation was to form an 'apron' of dangling 1,000-foot streamers held aloft by three to five balloons joined together by heavy steel cables. Anchored at three points, the 'apron' could be raised to any height between 7,500 and 10,000 feet.

The first 'apron' was ready for trial in mid-September. Ashmore himself was present to watch it go up over Richmond Park on the outskirts of London. The test was about to begin when a strong gust of wind suddenly scattered the balloons. The 'apron' was swept into the air, causing the streamers to cut through thick boughs 'like twigs'. Two men failed to let go of their lines in time. Dangling helplessly, they were carried skywards as Ashmore and others looked on horrified. One man, his strength exhausted, plunged to his death in the park from above 1,000 feet. The other scrambled into the rigging of the balloons, only to fall from an 'immense height' over Croydon. The runaway balloons were later shot down by gunfire.

Despite this tragedy the 'nets' won quick approval. Their main purpose was to force the bombers up to predictable altitudes so that the gunners and the pilots might more readily find them. There was also the odd chance that an unsuspecting raider would fly into the streamers. Immediate plans called for twenty 'aprons' to be erected on the eastern and northern approaches of London. Owing to the difficulties in finding a suitable type of balloon and wire, less than half that number were in position when the raids ended in May 1918.

Ashmore, mindful of the success of aeroplanes against the Zeppelins, felt that the fighters would be more effective than the guns against the night raiders, provided they could be found. Aircraft patrol lines were reorganized to give the pilots a broad search zone free of anti-aircraft fire. Guns were taken out and searchlights were moved in. The pilots were told to stay within the patrol zone at night. Any aeroplane heard outside its limits was assumed to be hostile. The re-sited guns, plus some mobile batteries withdrawn from other parts of England, were used to extend the outer anti-aircraft defences.

Lieutenant-Colonel Simon, the London artillery commander, and Captain A. R. F. Kingscote, devised an elaborate system of barrage fire to combat the unseen raiders. The London metropolitan area was divided into numbered squares. German aircraft were plotted by their sound, and screens or 'curtains' of shells were aimed in their path as they passed from square to square. Some rather colourful code names were assigned to the 'curtains'. 'Woodpecker' extended across the Thames between Dartford and Gravesend. The 'Ace of Spades' curved to the south and east of Woolwich. 'Pot Luck', 'Pip Squeak', and 'Cosy Corner' shielded London from the north. 'Dandy Dick', 'No Trumps', and 'Cold Feet' ran between Croydon and the Thames to the south. By October 1917, the inner defences of London consisted of some ninety such screens.

The British also developed sound locators which were an

improvement on a French device. Two pairs of 'gramophone trumpets' were mounted at the ends of two long poles. One pole rotated horizontally, while the other was adjusted vertically. A listener was assigned to each set of trumpets which were connected with tubing with a stethoscope attached. The set-up was much like a massive hearing aid, and indeed blind persons were used for this work. The trumpets were moved about until the listener heard the sound of a distant aircraft with equal intensity in both ears. The direction from which it was coming, and at what angle with reference to the horizon, were then read from a compass card. This information was quickly relayed to the searchlight and gun crews.

One listening device was installed on the south-east coast. A concave surface was carved into the face of a cliff to collect sound waves. This made it possible to hear the drone of an aeroplane from as far away as twenty miles. Such were the beginnings of an early warning system against German bombers. In the next war Britain would have something better.

With these defence improvements Ashmore was in a better position to deal with his critics. But he was hardly prepared for the affront he suffered one day while inspecting 44 Squadron at Hainault Farm. Ashmore and his aide were standing on the aerodrome talking to Murlis-Green when a Camel came in for a landing. The light-headed pilot had taken off 'for a flip' after downing several drinks at the squadron mess. Unaware who the three figures were, he impulsively dived down on them 'like a hawk'.

Ashmore, recalls an onlooker, 'was at first amused, screwing his monocle tighter into his eye; but he soon became alarmed, and finally sat, panic-stricken, in the mud while the undercarriage of the Camel shrieked by about a foot above his head and the slipstream from the prop blew his beautiful brass hat off'. The general 'replaced his hat and, making some quite unprintable remarks about the pilot, resumed his dignity. The three walked on.

'But Sandy was not satisfied . . . so he gave them the other barrel . . . and dived again. The result was precisely the same, except that the General managed to hold his hat on! By this time the seat of his trousers was sopping. . . . Sandy, zooming up to about five hundred feet, half rolled on his back . . . and fell out of his half-loop into a third and more gorgeous pounce. His objectives were still sitting angrily in the mud. This time he shaved them even closer than before, so that the General thought his hour had come and lay flat on his back, cursing!'[125]

Reputedly, 'the unfortunate Sandy' was 'deprived of his Sam Browne and put in irons for three days'. Ashmore left no record of this little fracas at Hainault Farm. If he had, he undoubtedly would have indicated that it was safer, and certainly much more comfortable, to deal with German bombers over London, than it was to visit one of his own squadrons out in the country.

Captain Kleine, the first officer ever to lead sustained strategic air strikes with bombers, was no devil-may-care airman. Stern-faced and reserved, he could well have been an ambitious young executive as he sat behind a large polished desk at Villa Drory, his headquarters near Gontrode. An ornate French telephone, his link with OHL, stood within easy reach. Closer by were three buzzers with which he could summon his staff aides. A large map of the south of England covering much of the wall served as a constant reminder of the enemy across the Channel.

Another handy item was a large, wooden-handled reading glass. Smoke-blurred views of London and the clutter of British ports had been closely scrutinized under its magnifying power earlier that summer. Kleine was concerned now that the glass would be of little further use except as a weight for his papers. That there should be no more photographs of British targets taken by day was unacceptable to him.

'The two successful night flights made by a small and experienced part of the Geschwader must in no way signal a complete and definite change to night operations,' he wrote to General Hoeppner. 'They were necessary to keep England harassed while the Geschwader is being speedily and completely equipped with new machines, the Gotha G.V.'[126]

Kleine had hopes of eventually conducting a rapid series of massive day and night attacks on London. Later that autumn, he prepared a plan for raids with 120 to 150 bombers. Oberleutnant Weese, one of his flight leaders, undoubtedly contributed to the scheme. In a study entitled 'Air Attacks on England', written in February 1917, Weese had proposed 'rolling day and night attacks' (rollender Tag und Nachtangriff) on the British capital.

129

The weather permitting, these sequential assaults were to consist of a morning raid followed by one in the afternoon made by separate Geschwadern of forty-five bombers each. Still another Geschwader of thirty aircraft was to attack in the evening. Weese predicted that the British would become so distraught under such steady bombing that their 'will to fight would be broken'.

Weese cautioned against any raids at all until all 120 bombers were 'ready to go'. His analysis concluded with a remarkably accurate estimate: 'The possibility of attacking London by day can be calculated to last two months, three at the most, by which time the effectiveness of the defences will force a change to attacks by night.'[127] The daylight raids had lasted exactly three months less three days.

Kleine's expectations of attacking again by day were never realized. The Gotha G.V. was an improved, more streamlined bomber. The crews welcomed it because, unlike the G.IV, its fuel tanks were located in the fuselage instead of under the engines. This greatly reduced the chances of fire in a crash landing. But the newer model was only slightly faster and its ceiling was no higher. After August 1917, even the G.V. could not be used by day.

The daylight concept lingered until the following spring when the Gotha G.VIII was expected. With more powerful Maybach engines, and carrying only a two-man crew, this aircraft was designed to reach a height of approximately 20,000 feet. It too was a vain hope. The German aircraft industry lacked the resources to build the bomber in quantity that late in the war. None was ever flown against England.

Kleine was anxious to resume daylight attacks because they allowed the bombing of military targets with greater accuracy. Their abandonment radically changed the raiders' methods. It was hardly possible to single out and hit the railway stations of London, or the docks of Harwich, at night. Flying individually, the Gotha crews henceforth had no other objective but the British capital itself. If the city could not be reached, any other place marked on their maps of the south of England could be bombed at their discretion. None too specific, their orders simply read: 'To raid targets of military importance in Great Britain.'[92]

Kleine met with another setback when his plans for large-scale raids were overtaken by events at the front. OHL denied his pleas for additional squadrons. At the same time he was ordered to assist Captain Alfred Keller, the commander of Kagohl 1, in mounting raids on the Channel ports. Dunkirk, a funnel through which the British were pouring troops, ammunition, and supplies for Haig's Flanders offensive, had become as important a target as London.

The England Squadron thus lost its exclusive and unique function of long-range strategic bombing. 'With this, a split which was contradictory to the aim of the entire undertaking occurred,' concluded Major Freiherr von Bülow, a German staff officer who carefully analysed the first Battle of Britain after the war. 'This division of the mission into two parts was an operational error. While justified by the emergency situation of the Army, it precluded any decisive results against England in the future.'[128]

OHL was satisfied to have the raids continue for purely psychological reasons. For purposes of 'frightfulness', much was expected of the Giant bombers which were now ready to attack England after long trials on the Eastern Front.

CHAPTER FIFTEEN

Giants to the West

The German Giant bombers of World War I have been described as 'the ugliest aeroplanes ever built', the product of 'an ambitious idea, an idea that was grandiose in the Wagnerian manner'. The Giants were no more fantastic than the much publicized Zeppelins, yet their raids on England remain a little known episode. Soon after the flights began, a London newspaper published an 'unconfirmed' report from Stockholm. The Germans, it was rumoured, were flying four-engined aircraft carrying five men, and capable of staying aloft for ten hours. 'If not true at the moment,' commented C. G. Grey, 'this seems useful as to the future. . . .'[129]

Despite this disbelief, Igor I. Sikorsky's 'Le Grand', the world's first four-engined aeroplane, had thrilled a Russian crowd by taking off for the first time in May 1913, and 'flying smoothly at about sixty miles an hour'. Less than a year later the larger 'Ilia Mourometz' had risen with sixteen people on board. Inspired by these Russian successes, the Germans began constructing multi-engined machines in the autumn of 1914.

One of the first to be delivered was the R.I., built at the Siemens-Schuckert factories in Berlin. Originally ordered as a G-type aircraft, the R.I. was later designated as a Riesen or R-type. The bomber had three 150 h.p. Benz engines and a wing span of nearly ninety-two feet. The craft, a mammoth at the time, made its initial flight in May 1915. On its way to the Eastern Front in September, the R.I. was grounded at Warsaw and drenched in a heavy rainstorm. The next day the bomber was unable to leave the ground. One member of the crew discovered the difficulty when he jabbed his bayonet into the Giant's upper wing; gallons of rainwater poured out.

A special tent was requisitioned for the bomber, but endless mishaps and technical problems prevented it from carrying out any raids. Dismantled, the R.I. was later shipped back to Germany where it was used as a trainer until 1918. Pieces of the aircraft were preserved and displayed in a Berlin museum until they were destroyed by Allied bombs in World War II.

The first Giants were assigned to Feldfliegerabteilung 31, a field aviation squadron which had its base at Slonim on the Eastern Front. Oberleutnant George Krupp commanded the unit. Though of little military significance, the initial Giant raids were important for training and experimental purposes. Detailed crew reports enabled German engineers at home to improve upon the earlier bombers.

OHL, losing all faith in the Zeppelin, ordered the production of the large aeroplanes to be stepped up. They were the only aircraft which approached the airship in range and carrying capacity. Because of their size and complexity the Giants were eventually organized to operate separately from the Kagohls. Two Giant Aeroplane Squadrons, Riesenflugzeugabteilungen 500 and 501, were activated in 1916.

Squadron 501, the unit later transferred to Belgium to bolster the raids on England, first attacked the Russians that August. From its base at Porubanok near Vilna, the squadron bombed railway stations, troop camps, and other targets in support of the German Tenth Army. Varying in strength from one to three Giants, the squadron also had single-engined aeroplanes which flew as escorts.

When OHL recalled Squadron 501 from the Russian front, its commander was Captain Richard von Bentivegni. Thirty years old at the time, he was a regular officer but not a pilot. He had served in Africa before the war and occupied various staff posts. Bentivegni ran the squadron, which had indulged in too many late parties before he took it over, on a strict régime. But, for all his Prussian efficiency, he was at heart a pleasure-loving man with the jovial manner of his Italian forbears. He survived the war to marry three times.

Leaving their Giants behind as training machines, Bentivegni and his crews returned to Germany in the late summer of 1917. At two airfields near Berlin, Staaken and Döberitz, they were equipped with improved R-type aeroplanes. Bentivegni was assigned the R.39, a Staaken R.VI. This model was the largest German aircraft produced in any quantity during the war. The parent firm was the Zeppelin-Werke at Staaken.

The designation of Giant for the R.39 was no misnomer. Compared to World War II aircraft, its wing span (138ft. 5½in.) exceeded that of the Handley Page Halifax by over thirty-four feet; it came within three feet of equalling that of the B-29 Superfortress. The German bomber was powered by four 245-h.p. Maybach engines mounted in pairs facing front and rearward. The engines were housed in streamlined nacelles supported between the upper and lower wings by struts. Each nacelle had a small cockpit which was occupied by a mechanic who could service or repair the engines in flight.

The number of crew members varied from seven to nine men, depending on whether any full-time machine-gunners were added for any given flight. The basic complement consisted of the aircraft commander, two pilots, a wireless operator, the two flight mechanics, and a fuel attendant. In addition to the commander, at least one of the pilots was a commissioned officer. Some of the sergeant pilots disliked flying the Giants which acquired a reputation for being 'even more dangerous than the Gothas' during landings. They complained that their officer counterpart made them land the aircraft, thereby making them responsible for crashes.

A sturdy undercarriage did lessen the chances of serious damage in a rough let-down. Sixteen wheels over three feet in diameter were mounted on two massive axles. A smaller two-wheel gear was attached under the bomber's nose. This auxiliary gear touched the ground only on landing. A standing Staaken R.VI rested on its tail skid with its nose high in the air.

R.39 was essentially a monstrous biplane, but its fuselage was surprisingly modern. The forward section was constructed of plywood and completely enclosed. The two pilots, Lieutenant Freiherr von Lenz and Lieutenant Buth, sat up front with the throttle controls between them. Facing them was an array of dials and gauges which included altimeters, tachometers, temperature indicators, an air speed indicator, a variometer to measure the rate of climb, and even an artificial horizon. The pilots communicated with the mechanics in the engine nacelles with electrical switches. These lit up a series of bulbs which the occupants, Unteroffiziere Matern and Walter, read according to a prearranged code.

Bentivegni, the aircraft commander, was also the navigator and bombardier. While navigating he sat at a map table directly behind the pilots. A gyro-compass supplemented by ground navigational aids such as beacons and flares guided the bomber's course. Bentivegni could obtain a position fix over England by sending out a radio signal. Taking a bearing on his signal, two ground stations determined the Giant's position and transmitted this information back to the aircraft. Klickermann, the wireless operator, was the fourth crew member in the control cabin.

During wireless silence the bomber's Bosch generator produced current for the lighting system and the crew's electrically heated flying suits. The spacious Giant also carried oxygen and parachutes for the crew. They were similar, if not identical, to the ones provided for the captive 'kite' balloon observers at the front. Loosely packed in a heavy canvas sack, the parachutes were deployed by a static line. The equipment was never used in flights over England.

Bentivegni's R.39 could strike at a target nearly 300 miles away. Ten fuel tanks installed in the upper centre fuselage had a total capacity of 660 imperial gallons. The fuel attendant was occupied full-time transferring fuel so that the trim of the aircraft would not be disturbed in flight. Depending on the fuel loading, the bomber could carry nearly two tons of explosives. Internal racks beneath the fuel tanks could accommodate eighteen 220-pound bombs. Larger bombs were carried semi-externally. The projectiles were sighted and released electrically from the nose of the bomber which was reached by a gangway.

Though it flew alone, R.39 was no easy prey for fighters. Fully armed, the bomber was defended by as many as six machine-guns. One gun was installed in the nose while two others could be fired from the top of the fuselage. A single machine-gun, mounted on a small platform so that it could be lowered for firing, covered the underside of the bomber.

Some of the Staaken Giants had two machine-guns installed in the upper wing directly above the engines. The firing of these guns called for some daring. To reach them, the mechanics had to climb a ladder leading up from their engine nacelle cockpits. The ladder was exposed to the wind and only a few feet away from the whirling propellers. All six guns were rarely carried, and three became the standard armament. The official German Equipment Tables for the Giant bombers specified that these should be Lewis machine-guns, a British weapon. The Lewis was ideal as a free gun because of its extreme lightness.

Other Staaken R.VI aircraft which flew against England were R.25, the first of the type to be built, R.27, and R.33. These were powered by four 260-h.p. Mercedes engines. The cruising speed of the Giants, which varied slightly, was in excess of 80 m.p.h. An improved version of the bomber with a speed of 100 m.p.h. and a ceiling of nearly 20,000 feet never saw combat service.

R.12, a veteran of the Eastern Front later used to bomb England, was a Staaken R.IV. Of the same gigantic proportions as the R.VIs, R.12 had six engines generating a total of 1,200 h.p. Two engines mounted in the bomber's nose powered a large tractor propeller. The other four engines were installed in pairs in the outboard nacelles to drive two four-bladed pusher propellers. The mechanics occupied open positions at the front of the nacelles. The bomber's armament included upper wing guns. Attempts to equip the predecessor of this type with a 2-cm. cannon were given up when tests indicated that 'the recoil endangered the fuselage structure'.

R.13, another England raider, was a Staaken R.V. The forward and rear crew positions were open, as in the case of R.12, but its three large four-bladed propellers were all of the tractor type. The mechanics of this five-engined bomber were located in the rear section of the highly tapered engine nacelles. A streamlined pod in the centre of the upper wing, known as the 'swallow's nest', served as a machine-gun outpost.

Another unique feature of R.13 was its pneumatic tube message system. At each of its six stations a crank could be turned in alternate directions to create either air pressure or suction. A signal light alerted the receiving station that a message had been placed in the tube. The bomber's crew, which included three mechanics and three gunners, totalled eleven men.

R.13 was assigned to Squadron 501 in December 1917. Bentivegni eventually received six Staaken aircraft for operations against England. The Giants flew to St. Denis-Westrem, and later occupied other airfields in the Ghent area. Early in 1918, the squadron moved to its permanent base at Scheldewindeke, near Gontrode, where larger hangars and a concrete apron had been constructed for the big bombers.

Bentivegni received his orders from Hoeppner to whom he reported daily by direct line. After informing Kogenluft of the weather and the number of Giants ready for flight, Bentivegni was told what targets he was to bomb. Late in September 1917, Squadron 501 was ready to launch its first attack in the west. As Bentivegni expected, the target assigned was London.

CHAPTER SIXTEEN

The First Blitz

For over a week at the end of September 1917, a handful of German airmen held sway over millions of Londoners. In retrospect, their almost nightly visits were but an intimidation compounded of moonglow, concealing clouds, and the sinister throbbing of aeroplanes multiplied thrice over by the inflamed imagination of a much alarmed population. Yet no other attacks 'remained more vividly in the memory of those who lived through the air raids on England' during the First World War.[130]

Charles H. Grasty, a London correspondent for *The New York Times*, was told by an American air officer in mid-September that 'a fleet of 500 Gothas would come to London within a few months'. The British capital, he reported gloomily, 'contemplates the great event in Russia and the crisis in France with less concentration than they deserve. She has troubles of her own. The average citizen goes to bed wondering at what hour he will be hauled out by German air raiders'.[131]

'Strangely quiet and deserted were the streets,' recalled one Briton many years later. 'Petrol restrictions had reduced the motor traffic almost to zero. Street lights were no more than glowing pinpoints along the shadowy chasms between the houses . . . pedestrians hurried by quickly in the shadow of walls, glancing apprehensively at the sky. Would they come tonight? London seemed breathless, in the tense expectancy of disaster. . . .'[132]

The attacks began on a Monday, 24 September. The alert of bombers off the coast came at about seven in the evening. The raiders were early since the moon was in its first quarter and would soon fade away. Searchlights nervously probed the skies over London, and star shells lit up the darkness like fireworks. The empty streets echoed with the sound of the crunching barrage. Only later were bombs heard exploding in various districts of the city.

One struck the pavement just outside the entrance of the Bedford

Hotel in Southampton Row. The foyer was jammed with guests and people who had come in for cover. Splintered woodwork and slivers of glass cut down thirty persons, injuring thirteen fatally. These casualties were the worst of the raid, but there were many near misses that night. One bomb fell dangerously close to the Ritz, leaving a large crater in Green Park. Westminster Abbey escaped damage when another failed to detonate in Dean's Yard. One missile exploded in the Thames opposite St. Thomas's Hospital on the Albert Embankment. Burlington House was blasted. No one was injured since the premises were closed at the time.

Less than two hours after the 'All Clear', a fleet of ten Zeppelins appeared off the Yorkshire coast. Hampered by low clouds and strong westerly winds, few of the airships found targets. Three women injured at Hull were the only casualties. The ghostly ships, their bellies painted black to make them less visible, then withdrew over the North Sea. The real threat was clearly the bombers reaching London, but the Zeppelins added to the apprehension.

On Tuesday, the capital braced itself for another bombing. Shops and offices began closing in the afternoon so that employees might get home before nightfall. Theatres and cinemas ran notices in the evening papers: 'Moonlight Nights—Open as Usual—Ample Bomb Proof Shelter.' Many Londoners held out for more exciting entertainment. As evening came, they gathered in the parks and at other vantage points to see 'the Hun Air Show'.

They were not disappointed. Bombs fell in Bermondsey and Camberwell on the south side of the Thames where several houses were wrecked. Two projectiles splashed into the river near London Bridge, sending columns of water high into the air. But the bombing was far less severe than on the previous night. The people sheltering in the Underground stations were reportedly unconcerned and in high spirits. Some read newspapers and books, while others told jokes and laughed. Some were said to have had 'such a good time in the tubes that the police had a hard time dislodging them after the raid'.[133]

Thousands returned on the two succeeding evenings, even though no raiders flew over the city. The nightly excursion was almost as pointless on the Friday, despite the Germans' best efforts to fulfil the worst expectations of the London populace.

The air crews rode out to the waiting bombers at dusk. A large pale moon slowly emerged from behind some distant trees on the edge of the airfield at Gontrode. Rising higher, the radiant disc became blurred as thin clouds crept in from the west. The airmen became slightly uneasy as they waited for the last bombs to be shackled.

The 'weather frog' had assured them that the clouds would not be solid, and their height would remain below one thousand feet. Georgii, continuing his observations to the last minute, appeared just before take-off with some parting advice. Less certain now about his earlier forecast, he cautioned the crews to turn back rather than to fly on blindly over a solid cloud cover.

The Startdienst, the ground party charged with readying the field for the bombers' departure, had taken up its positions. Two search-lights mounted on small lorries had been driven out. The lights glowed briefly as their crews checked them, and then stood by for further orders. A rescue team and a medical officer waited alongside the Startwagon. The vehicle was loaded with axes, saws, and other equipment needed to extricate airmen from a crashed bomber.

Guided through the darkness by its mechanics, the first Gotha was rolled out to the starting point. The two searchlights suddenly pierced the gloom, their horizontal rays joining far down the strip to form a large 'V'. The bomber swayed forward at the signal of the Startoffizier, and began to gather speed down the lighted path. As it neared the green lights at the end of the field, the heavy biplane rose slowly into the darkness.

The lights faded out quickly so as to not attract patrolling enemy aircraft. Another Gotha was brought up, the lights were flashed on again, and it too disappeared into the night. The bomber was fol-lowed in turn by another, and another, until all were finally on their way. As the lights went out for the last time, the spell cast by the hustle and excitement of launching a raid was broken. An empty stillness gripped the men left behind—the riggers, the bomb loaders, the mechanics. Now the long wait began.

The Gothas were off that evening, 28 September, after being grounded for forty-eight hours by rain and murky weather. The sky had not cleared until late afternoon. Some of the airmen were in Ghent, and messengers had to be sent out to round them up. The Döge-Delang crew was among them. Having little time to prepare, the young pilot realized just before take-off that he was not wearing

his 'England trousers'. Delang had superstitiously worn the same
pair on every raid thus far. His observer laughed at this, and
reassured him that the ones he had on would 'fly just as well'.

Kleine was anxious to make up for the two lost nights. Although
some machines went out to bomb Dunkirk with those of Kagohl 1,
twenty-five Gothas were ordered to London for the third strike of
the week. With two Giants from Bentivegni's squadron, the raid
was one of the heaviest ever attempted.

The crews had no difficulty navigating to the Belgian coast. Once
over the North Sea, they encountered towering clouds building up
ahead. Fearful of losing their way, fifteen Gothas returned. Another
did so because of a faulty engine. Despite Georgii's warning, the
more adventurous crews continued as if beckoned by the beauty of
the moonlit scene aloft.

'We flew on over a milk-white sea of clouds,' remembers Lorenz,
the observer with the gelatine nose. 'A full moon was shining above
with a brightness that was almost unreal. In addition to our compass,
a beautifully clear, star-filled sky showed us the way. We had
learned from experience with the Geschwader that Arcturus, a
fixed star of the first magnitude, was an exact finger post to the
target of London for those machines starting out in the early
evening. . . .'

Lorenz was now in charge of Staffel 14, whose leader had been
killed earlier that month. The stocky Oberleutnant was intent on
keeping faith with his motto, 'Iron and Madness' (*Eisern und Irre*).
The words were painted in large letters on the upper wing of his
new Gotha, Lo-Ri 3. Badly damaged in a British attack on Gontrode, Lo-Ri 2 had been scrapped.

The 'gallant Küppers' was still his pilot. The two airmen were as
unconcerned about British fighters as they were about the weather.
After a few night flights they had removed the rear machine-guns
and left their gunner behind, making up the weight in bombs. An
OHL staff officer visiting the squadron occupied the rear position
on this trip. Wanting to see for himself, he had telephoned his headquarters for permission to fly on the raid.

Over England, the three Germans found the sky strangely free of
anti-aircraft fire. 'Probing in vain, the searchlights painted large
yellow saucers in the clouds below us,' continues Lorenz. 'Where a
devil's cauldron of bursting shrapnel had never let a machine pass

without inflicting at least some hits, there prevailed this time in this silvery solitude a peace which was like something out of a fairy tale. On the white blanket beneath, the moon cast a silhouette of our machine.'

Even the broad Thames could not be made out. Relying solely on his watch, compass, and the stars, Lorenz claims to have found London 'by the play of its numerous searchlights whose faint glow shimmered within the clouds all around. . . . A few twists of the levers, a slight shudder of the machine, and the long, torpedo-shaped missiles silently find their way down through the clouds. . . .'

Lo-Ri 3 was the only Gotha credited with having bombed London that night. According to the British, no bombs fell on the capital. London or not, Lorenz and Küppers had their worse moment on the way back when they let down through the overcast to find their bearings for Ghent.

'We dived deeply into the white foam, and, a few seconds later, found ourselves in an impenetrable darkness—an indescribably oppressive sensation, suffocating and stifling. Even from a distance of only a few centimetres, the eye could barely read the instruments through the wet fog. Down and down we went.'

The Gotha went into a spin as Küppers lost all sense of direction in the enveloping mist. Lorenz tried to stand upright in the nose position, holding his arms out horizontally to guide his pilot. At the same time he was 'searching desperately for some point below on which to fix the eye'. The wings creaked under the strain of the dive. Suddenly, a 'connecting strut snapped with a ringing sound and trailed behind the upper wing like a sinister streamer'. Küppers, struggling with the controls, had his own thoughts: 'Are we going to dive into the sea and drown, or crash on land and burn?'

The Gotha broke through the haze barely a few hundred feet above the water, and Küppers levelled off. Lorenz did not know in which direction was the coast. His compass was spinning crazily. Crawling back to the pilot's cockpit, he sought to steady Küpper's compass for a heading. The crew kept flying hopefully, until 'all of a sudden a blinker light was flashing comfortably close across the waves—long-short, short-long-short, short—Ostend'. Lo-Ri 3 finally landed at Gontrode after a flight of nearly five hours. 'No one at the Geschwader', concludes Lorenz, 'counted any longer on our safe return. . . .'[134]

Delang and Döge were not so fortunate. They had gone on also, bombing what they believed to be Sheerness through breaks in the clouds. On the return flight Delang found that the Gotha's elevator control failed to respond. Sergeant Jödicke, replacing Ruhl injured in the earlier crash landing, went forward to the pilot's cockpit to help balance the bomber. Still unaware of the trouble nearly an hour later, Döge calculated that they should be nearing the Belgian coast. The observer pointed downward to signal a descent.

Controlling as best he could, Delang managed to dip the machine slowly into the haze. A 'stinging rain' began to beat down on the airmen in their open cockpits. Delang could not see anything through his goggles. Buffeted by the wind, the Gotha suddenly plunged down out of control. As it neared the ground, a 'black line' loomed ahead. A wincing jolt was followed by the splintering of wood and the tearing of fabric.

The bomber had crashed into the tops of some trees along a country road, and crumpled in an open field beyond. The crew awoke in a German military hospital behind the front the next morning. Döge admitted ruefully that his pilot did not fly as well without his 'England trousers'.

Confused by the clouds and low on fuel, five other crews crashed on the way home. A British reconnaissance aircraft photographed three wrecked Gothas in a meadow near Gontrode the next day. Another Gotha came down near Sas-Van-Gent, just across the border in Holland. The observer, Lieutenant Martin Emmler, was badly injured. His companions abandoned him and tried to escape. They were captured and interned, and the lieutenant died shortly afterwards. Three Gothas, the probable victims of British guns along the coast, were lost without a trace.

The two Giants returned safely, but without bombing London. Hoeppner, who had long awaited their first raid on England, was pleased nonetheless. He wired Bentivegni to congratulate him and 'the participant crews on the first successful attack with which the R-aircraft have begun their important assignment in the West'. Kogenluft was confident that the Giants would 'grow from flight to flight into an ever stronger offensive weapon'.[135]

The British counted some forty bomb hits north of Harwich, and in the coastal areas of Kent and Essex. There was no significant damage, and no casualties. After accomplishing next to nothing, nine Gothas rested at the bottom of the sea or were scattered about the Flemish countryside.

Undaunted, Kleine ordered another attack the very next night with a much reduced force of seven Gothas. Visibility was still greatly obscured by clouds. The British estimated 'that at least eighteen aeroplanes' flew in over Kent and Essex. Lord French's raid communiqué announced 'a determined and simultaneous attack on London by three groups of raiders. Each of these groups, which approached from different directions, was broken up by anti-aircraft fire. . . .'[136]

The barrage fire was believed to have driven at least a dozen aeroplanes away 'without dropping any bombs'. The multi-engined Giants, then not known to be flying over England, misled the listening posts. A Giant twenty miles away sounded like a Gotha overhead. On hearing one of the mammoth bombers, the British mistook it for a whole group of smaller aircraft.

Only two Gothas and one Giant went as far as London. The capital nonetheless 'suffered heavily' in a half-hour bombardment which began at 9.10 P.M. Two large bombs apparently released from R.39 rocked Waterloo Station, mauling the tracks and many railway carriages. Oddly enough, no one was hurt. London Bridge Station, not very far away, was the scene of a poignant episode when a train pulled in at the height of the raid. A special train, it was loaded with wounded arriving from the front. Many were immobilized, some were in pain, and all were weary from their long journey. As the shells burst overhead, the troops were transferred with 'calm and celerity' to waiting ambulances.

A few scores of Londoners sought shelter at the Eaglet, a public house in the Seven Sisters Road. A bomb crashed through 'a wooden cellar-flap' and exploded in the cellar. With a roar 'the floor of the saloon was blown upwards, and many of the refugees were hurled into the street'. Rescuers found four of them dead and thirty-two others injured, 'many seriously'.[137] Private houses were battered in Notting Hill, Kingsland, and Kensington. Along the coast, at least one Giant attacked Sheerness, scoring some hits on the railway. Bombs were also strewn in the vicinity of Ramsgate and Margate.

After four raids in less than a week, the number of Londoners flocking into the Underground rose to 300,000. Without waiting for a warning, entire families took to the streets with pillows and blankets, food baskets, dogs, cats, and caged birds. Once safely below ground these people settled down as comfortably as they could, hoping all the while that they would find their homes as they had left them.

The 'tubes' soon reeked with the stench of crowded humanity. Sanitation facilities were simply not available for such swarms. There were curses and frequent scuffles as the refugees trod each other underfoot. Many 'did not prove amenable to the best efforts of the railway officials to distribute them to best advantage'.[138] Some trains ran as usual, but at many stations passengers were unable to get on or off because of the blocked stairways and platforms.

In addition to the ninety-odd Underground stations, the tunnels under the Thames were popular places of refuge. To accommodate the overflow, police stations and other Government buildings were opened to the public. Sturdy structures at least afforded protection against fragments. By such emergency measures nearly one million Londoners could be sheltered. Stay-at-homes, even on the occasion of an air raid, were offered sandbags 'in large or small quantities'. One enterprising firm warned buyers living in 'ordinary houses' that overloading 'could cause a roof to collapse, and so anticipate the intentions of the Huns'.[139]

Thousands more went outside London altogether to sleep in open fields, or whatever accommodation could be had in the outlying towns. The nightly invasions much disturbed these localities, but shopkeepers were happy at the thriving business they brought. In the morning, the influx of people trying to make their way back disrupted suburban commuter travel into the city.

Sunday, 30 September was a beautiful autumn day, but the invigorating weather only aroused anxiety. The sky was cloudless and the moon would appear at its fullest that night. Places of amusement were avoided, and the streets were noticeably deserted. Evening church services, normally conducted at 6.30 or 7 P.M., were advanced to five in the afternoon. By early evening, many Londoners were on the verge of panic.

'I was prey to the acutest anxiety,' recalled Lieutenant-Colonel A. Rawlinson, who headed a sub-command of the London anti-aircraft defences; 'the exhausted state of my magazines was *horrible to contemplate*'. In barrage fire each gun could fire a round every four seconds. The night before, 12,700 shells, or more than 1,800 for each German aircraft actually engaged, had been fired. A large hulk of a man, Rawlinson was given to improvisation in an emergency. He ran about all day Sunday for the 'necessary motor-lorries' to haul ammunition from the Woolwich Arsenal to his widely scattered gun-stations. 'This vital manœuvre was not yet complete when, at 6.42 P.M., we received the warning that the enemy were again on their way to London.'[140]

Although the raid lasted twice as long as the one of the previous night, the destruction was 'comparatively slight'. Some houses were hit near the docks in the East End, and the Midland Railway cleaning sheds at West Ham were damaged. Operating on the theory that 'The louder the guns, the fewer the Huns', the British really outdid themselves that evening. They set the sky on fire with over 14,000 shells without scoring a single hit!

Calling the action 'a terribly anxious and trying ordeal', Rawlinson writes that many of his guns had 'fired over 500 rounds apiece. . . . In many instances the guns were red-hot, and "fire" had to be temporarily ceased to allow them to cool, in spite of the constant streams of water which were poured over them. Everything breakable in the gun-stations quickly succumbed to the constant concussion; the men, in many instances, were temporarily "blinded" by the flashes of the guns, and "deafened" by the incessant concussions, until they became entirely bewildered and practically useless. Burnt hands from the hot guns also were the rule . . . and the guns' crews were thoroughly exhausted by their well-sustained exertions.'[141]

By Sunday, some of Kleine's airmen were also showing signs of nervous exhaustion. Staffel 18 at Gontrode was put on a stand-by status. At the last minute its crews had been told they would not have to fly. Kleine had been satisfied to attack with eleven Gothas. Gerlich, his adjutant, also took off in a single-seater which he often flew as a night interceptor.

One Gotha soon returned with a misfiring engine, but the others reached England. Shortly after ten o'clock the first of the empty bombers were heard approaching their bases. One after another appeared in the moonlit sky, identifying themselves with blinking lights and coloured flares. Landing lights were switched on, and the aircraft came in without incident. When the count reached eleven, the ground crews let out a loud cheer.

Gerlich reported proudly that he had dropped his four small

bombs on Dover. They had done slight damage to the Dover Engineering Works, and injured one man. Six Gotha crews claimed to have flown all the way to London in perfectly clear weather. They said they had seen several fires in the city.

Ashmore's grand barrage of over 14,000 shells must have deterred the others. Many random bombs fell in Kent, and more people were killed in Margate than in London. Kleine nonetheless described the attack to OHL as one of the most successful since the start of the night raids. The following night, 1 October, he continued his bombing marathon by dispatching eighteen Gothas to England.

Londoners with an incorrigible gambling instinct had been making bets the previous week on whether there would be a raid on any given night. By Monday, they were wagering on the hour that the alert would be given. Those betting on 7 P.M. that evening won the pool. Shortly afterwards, the Volunteer Corps sped through the streets with automobiles on which lighted 'Take Cover' signs had been mounted. At the telephone offices, operators went into action to notify subscribers. The exodus out of the East End, which was always in the raiders' path, was heavier than ever.

Attacking at intervals between 7.45 and 10 P.M., the Germans were apparently still trying to hit the railway termini. In the vicinity of Victoria Station bombs fell on Belgravia, an area of fine houses and foreign embassies. Some houses near the station at Euston were ravaged. A 112-pound projectile splashed in the Serpentine in Hyde Park, and reportedly killed all the fish. Highbury, then a suburb of gracious villas and walled gardens, and Edmonton were bombed in the last assault. *The New York Times* gave the prolonged attack a banner headline—'Biggest Raid on London Made by Four Squadrons'.

A heavy mist rising from the Thames spared London from the full brunt of the bombing. Only the first raiders to arrive were able to see the city clearly. Two Gothas missed the capital altogether, flying far to the north past Luton and into Buckinghamshire. Two more flew across east London, from Tottenham to Woolwich, without releasing their bombs. Some raiders unloaded on Ramsgate, Margate, Sheerness, and Harwich. No appreciable damage or casualties resulted at these places.

The Prime Minister had called an emergency meeting of the War Cabinet that morning to consider the deteriorating anti-aircraft defences. Shells were in short supply. Many guns, good for only 1,500 rounds, had been fired into uselessness. Lord French insisted that he should be given more guns to replace the ones worn out, and to extend the outer defences completely around the capital. A special committee was created on the spot to deal with the problem. Smuts, to whom Lloyd George invariably turned in time of crisis, was appointed chairman. Churchill and Ashmore were included as members.

Before the group could give a report, London had had another air raid. The news that the barrage fire had been reduced for lack of ammunition jolted the Cabinet. It promptly instructed the War Office to step up the supply to 30,000 shells per month, and to build up a reserve stock of 100,000 rounds. French was at his gloomiest. He predicted that, if the raids continued as they had, London's artillery defences would 'cease to exist' within a few months' time. Churchill interjected that he had arranged to have the guns relined at the rate of twenty a month. This was regarded as hardly enough. The Cabinet earmarked the entire production of 3-inch guns for October, already allocated to merchant ships, for the city's defences.

The havoc inflicted by the barrage was another item of serious concern. Churchill was particularly aroused, calling the guns 'instruments of self-bombardment'. Public sentiment found expression in a letter one irate citizen addressed to Smuts:

'As to your defence of London by this infernal Barrage I do trust you will stop it, as it is a remedy worse than the disease. We have lived under showers of this odious shrapnel (purely home-made) and it is costly in life and property. A woman close to me was killed in bed thereby.'[142]

So had seven other people in the past week. Another sixty-seven had been injured. British fire during one raid alone had damaged nearly 300 houses, 'about half of them seriously'. Nineteen French 75-mm. guns, which fired only shrapnel, were moved from London to Birmingham and other places not as likely to be raided. Unlike explosive shells, the cases of shrapnel projectiles came down intact.

For all their 'well-sustained exertions', the gunners of London had yet to bring a bomber down since the start of the Gotha raids. British pilots, taking off at considerable risks in the darkness, made 151 sorties during that one-week period. Most of them were assigned to night squadrons organized in defence against the Zeppelins.

Their B.E. and F.E. aeroplanes were of little use against the German bombers. Few airmen of the day squadrons had sufficiently mastered the unstable Sopwith Camel to fly at night. Only two indecisive combats were reported.

The attack of 1 October, the sixth in eight nights, brought 'the raids of the Harvest Moon' to a close. Sixty-nine people were killed and 260 were wounded, mostly in London. These totals included the barrage casualties. Although losses were far from excessive, the first blitz was a bewildering experience of profound psychological effect.

'Londoners have been put to the test recently,' a young woman wrote to friends overseas, 'and I confess we might have shown ourselves to better advantage. Our nerves have been somewhat shaken. For a week German airmen . . . succeeded in seriously disorganizing the lives of the whole population. . . . As soon as the signal "Take Cover" is heard, one by one the taxis stop and refuse to take passengers, the buses turn out their lights and line up in some wide thoroughfare, the Underground trains cease running, and the stations are darkened. And one is stranded.'[143]

As Minister of Munitions, Churchill was concerned with stoppages of another kind. After the first few raids he had asked for a report on the output of the arsenal at Woolwich. It showed that only one-third of the night shift in the filling factory was at work on 25 September. Production that evening was less than 20% of normal. The following day, it was still below 75%. Then, as a result of a brief attack that night, the output was down to nearly 60% of capacity. The survey was only a sample, but Churchill concluded that the disruption at Woolwich was 'typical of what was taking place over a wide area'.[144]

The authorities were particularly alarmed at the abandon with which the people had taken to the streets, especially in London's East End, in search of shelter. Much of the blame was placed on the news coverage given the attacks because 'panic paid the press'. Even the Prime Minister was personally involved. Two newspapers published a brief item hinting that Lloyd George had left 'his official duties' in London for the safety of his home in the country. He angrily brought suit and received both damages and 'unreserved apologies'.

Cowdray of the Air Board owned the newspapers concerned. His relations with the Prime Minister were never quite the same after the incident. Cowdray was already being criticized for his support of the proposed Air Ministry on the ground of personal ambition. 'When London is half levelled,' he lashed back, 'someone will have to be lynched, presumably the Cabinet, since no one else has any clear responsibility. Hence I do not personally desire the job, but someone must face the music and step into the breach.'[145]

As for the London press, Lloyd George summoned the editors and told them to tone down their accounts of the bombings. He particularly objected to photographs showing the damage. Owners of bombed out buildings were later required by law to put up board fences to conceal the destruction from sightseers and passers-by.

The raids also touched off a furore for more shelters. A committee headed by the Home Secretary considered several possibilities, including large dug-outs in the parks of London. Rejecting this proposal because of the labour and materials it would have required, the committee advised the conversion of suitable buildings into public shelters instead. A Defence of the Realm Regulation was enacted to empower the authorities to requisition privately owned premises for this purpose. As the shelter placards went up, the mood in London was one of siege.

On 4 October, the Kaiser awarded the Pour le Mérite to Kleine. The decoration had long been his desire, and it was well deserved. Flying by night in adverse weather and with only a few dozen bombers, he had flustered the British with a spectre of German aerial might. Londoners could have slept much more soundly on moonlit nights, had they known the full extent of the raiders' difficulties.

All told, ninety-two Gothas had been sent out that week. Only fifty-five crossed the British coast, and less than twenty found their way to London. The Giants made five sorties, and only one raided the capital. Kleine lost thirteen aircraft, the equivalent of two Staffeln or one-third of his squadron. An undetermined number of Gothas was also destroyed at the Ghent bases, when the British countered the raids with a blitz of their own.

Beginning on 25 September, the German bases were attacked nearly every day and night for over a week. The Dunkirk naval squadrons dumped eight tons of bombs on St. Denis-Westrem alone. The Royal Flying Corps concentrated on Gontrode, dropping hundreds of darts in addition to explosives. On 29 September, two

British squadrons struck the aerodrome. The old airship hangar was set afire.

Both bases were raided the following evening while the Gothas were off to England. Waiting ground crews were sent scurrying into ditches dug as shelters. Bombs whistled down helter-skelter in the darkness, their detonations piercing the gloom like giant fireflies. Damaging hits at Gontrode were few, but over St. Denis-Westrem the sky turned a fiery red. A blazing hangar could be seen for thirty miles.

The harassed Germans were not entirely unprepared. Belgian farm carts, loaded in advance with rubble, were rolled out from behind the sheds. Using as little light as possible, the men quickly filled the bomb craters on the landing strips. The returning Gothas landed without mishap a few hours later.

The steady bombing forced Kleine to disperse the flights concentrated at Gontrode. Staffeln 13 and 14 were moved to Mariakerke, while 17 and 18 were relocated at Oostakker. These airfields were also in the immediate vicinity of Ghent. Kleine and his staff later moved from Villa Drory near Gontrode to a large house owned by Countess Hemptin in Ghent itself. The old Geschwader headquarters had become too cramped, and it was 'not well suited for the winter season'.

CHAPTER SEVENTEEN

'We Will Give it All Back to Them'

The Germans had started a game which even the phlegmatic British could play. After the September blitz they were not to be content with bombing the Gotha bases alone. 'The raids of the last ten days,' read one report, 'have virtually convinced the entire British press and public that the policy of passive defence must be dropped, and that a strong air offensive against Germany must be waged immediately.'[146]

Once again, an urgent message was sent to Haig at the front. This time, the call was not for fighters, but bombers. 'Cabinet desire immediate action against those German objectives which can be reached from neighbourhood of Nancy,' wired Robertson on 1 October 1917. 'Send Trenchard over at once to discuss scale on which you can undertake these operations. . . . Cabinet wish for at least one squadron to be employed and with least possible delay.'[147]

Hasty improvisation was the order of the day. Smuts's latest committee, which now included Churchill, was instructed 'to report as quickly as possible' on the organization of a bomber force, the aircraft to be used, and the detailed planning for a raiding campaign against the German homeland.

The Cabinet met again the next morning. Smuts said that he was hard at work on the bombing questions, but that Trenchard had not as yet arrived. French had just finished bemoaning the exhausted state of the London gun defences. He was very obviously in need of some fresh air. Taking him along, the restless Prime Minister dashed out for a quick morale-building tour of the districts bombed the evening before.

At one stop a crowd of 'poor people' gathered around Lloyd George. There were cries for raids on German cities. 'We will give it all back to them, and we will give it to them soon,' the Prime Minister shouted back. 'We shall bomb Germany with compound interest!'[146] Lloyd George was no air strategist. But, as an astute

151

politician, he realized that it was high time to take 'the bull not only by the horns but by the tail as well'.

London newspapers had come out that morning with large maps of Germany on their front pages. Enemy population centres within range of British squadrons in France were pinpointed. A few days later the mayors of the metropolitan boroughs gathered at the City Hall in Westminster to urge air attacks 'on the largest possible scale . . . against German cities and towns without distinction'.[148]

The British had yet to consider seriously the alternative of bombing solely for military effects. They were more intent, as C. G. Grey put it, 'on getting our own back'. The outspoken editor of *The Aeroplane* was a notably calm exception to all the 'speechifying and writing and talking and shouting about reprisals'. As far as he was concerned, 'the very word reprisal is enough to make one sick'.[149]

Grey had put forth a militarily sound bombing policy early that summer. But the thinking which now impelled the War Cabinet to take up the cudgel of long-range air attacks did not exactly follow his reasoning. Grey's open letter to the Air Board had read:

> Behind Germany's army lie the sources from which it is fed. The iron mines, the steel works, the armament factories . . . lie within reach of the weapons of war which are made under your direction. . . .
>
> Instead of bowing to popular clamour for reprisals—mere retaliatory raids in revenge after every enemy attack—let us take the invasion of Germany from the air as a serious problem of the war. . . .
>
> The two-dimensional soldier has now seen enough air fighting to remove most of his prejudices against third dimension war. . . .[150]

Though somewhat reluctantly at first, Britain's soldiers would learn well enough what this new kind of warfare was all about. As important as the bludgeon they were called upon to shape was the spirit behind it. The British temper in war was undergoing a profound change.

An anger bent on vengeance had been building up ever since the first Gotha raid on London. A mass meeting sponsored by the *Daily Express* had been held at the London Opera House in mid-June to protest against 'the brutality and horror of high explosive bombs being dropped upon small children who were blown about like bundles of bloody rags. . . .' The Lord Mayor of London presided. He moved a resolution urging Lloyd George and his Cabinet 'to initiate immediately a policy of ceaseless air attacks on German towns and cities'.[151]

Churchmen, on their side, tried to restrain the mounting rancour. The Bishop of London admonished his flock not to 'break with God's righteousness and love' by asking for 'an eye for an eye, and a tooth for a tooth'. At the instigation of the Archbishop, the Bishops of the Province of Canterbury also passed a resolution. 'The principles of morality,' it reminded, 'forbid a policy of reprisal which has, as a deliberate object, the killing and wounding of non-combatants.' The public response was such that the Archbishop complained of being 'curiously and even persistently misunderstood'.[152]

The Government remained above the debate until later that month. Derby, the War Minister, then told the House of Lords 'that we are not going to try to imitate the German in his brutality'.[153] At least not until it is possible for us to do so, he should have explained.

Lloyd George had proposed the bombing of Mannheim after the 13 June raid. Haig discussed the matter with Trenchard. 'The enemy would almost certainly reply "in kind",' responded the commander of the B.E.F. on 16 June. He added that 'unless we are determined and prepared to go one better than the Germans, whatever they may do . . . it will be infinitely better not to attempt reprisals at all. At present we are not prepared. . . .'[154]

Unaware that the Prime Minister had tried to appease them, the people reacted with violence to the second raid on London. Rioting broke out in the streets. On 9 July, a boisterous crowd gathered on Tower Hill. A telegram, 'paid for by the pennies of the people', was sent to Buckingham Palace. It petitioned the King 'to instruct your Ministers at once to make vigorous and continual air attacks on German towns and cities'. If this were not done, the King was further implored 'to dissolve Parliament, and appoint Ministers who will do their duty'.[66]

The telegram was forwarded to the Prime Minister. He had, this time, already directed Haig to bomb Mannheim, provided it did not interfere with the forthcoming offensive in Flanders. Haig was exasperated enough at having to send fighters to England. Such a reprisal attack, he replied, would require that 'our plans will have to be reconsidered entirely and the operations may have to be abandoned'.[155] The Rhine city was spared for a second time when the Cabinet relented.

Anti-German feelings found another outlet after the July raid with the formation of the 'League of Londoners'. 'We have been fighting the war too much under the Queensberry rules,' protested Lord Tenterden at its first rally, 'and the time has come when we should attack the Germans with "knuckle-dusters".' The Mayor of Poplar called the British 'a nation of lions governed by asses'. He warned that the country was headed for revolution, 'unless the Government is exceedingly careful'.[156]

Passions cooled as the summer passed without any further raids on the capital. But in Southend the people did not take very kindly to the Sunday raid of 12 August. The Town Council asked the Government for 'an assurance that the engineering of the [reprisal] scheme will leave little doubt that German civilians shall suffer to as great an extent as civilians in England'. Commented Grey: 'We have now got rid of our hypocrisy, and have evidently come back to the good old Mosaic Law.'[157]

The decision to bomb Germany, as finally announced by Lloyd George in a London street, evoked some wistful regrets. Without blaming Londoners 'for asking what they do', *The New York Times* held out the hope that a 'competition in savagery may be avoided. . . . The bombing of undefended German cities promises no better result than the depriving of the Allies of a moral superiority they now possess. And that is not worth while.'[146]

Speaking at a Chamber of Commerce luncheon, Smuts sought to justify that decision: 'We did not begin this business of bombing industrial and populous centres; the enemy began the practice. . . . We are now most reluctantly forced to apply to him the bombing policy he has applied to us. . . .' Smuts decried 'these developments of the art of war as utterly bad and immoral'. But he hoped that this 'will be borne in mind when it is ultimately found that my words are not bluff, but serious and far-reaching in their import'. Smuts blamed the stupidity of the Germans even more than their 'calculated brutality'. Because 'the Germans have never understood the psychology of their enemies', he predicted that they would 'continue to blunder to the end of the chapter'.[158] That chapter was not written in 1918.

Trenchard inadvertently caused a great commotion when he arrived in England by air on the morning of 2 October 1917. Three two-seaters, carrying him and a few staff officers, became separated in a dense mist over the Channel. The groping machines were mistaken for enemy bombers, and air-raid alerts were sounded all along the coast and in London. One of the three aeroplanes came up the Thames to be met 'with a violent barrage from all the aircraft guns along its course'.

Trenchard's own pilot prudently made an emergency landing at Lympne aerodrome near Folkestone. The general went the rest of the way by car. The streets of London were still half-deserted when he arrived. Trenchard was 'amazed and less than amused' to find that a few unidentified aeroplanes could virtually paralyse the capital during the noon rush-hour. The 'All Clear' was not sounded until about 2 P.M.

The Cabinet quickly convened to hear what Trenchard had to say. Lloyd George was most anxious to know just how soon British bombs could be sent crashing through German garrets. Explaining that Ochey, an aerodrome near Nancy, had already been set aside, Trenchard replied: 'Six days after arriving there.'[159] The Prime Minister, looking tired and drawn, lectured him at length on the importance of the attacks 'to the morale of the people at home'.

Trenchard was being a good soldier. Actually, he was 'irate at the folly of the press', and the outcries of the public for reprisals. The Royal Flying Corps in France had only four bombing squadrons of some eighty aircraft. What machines could be spared would have to be moved to the right of the French line because of their limited range. Later that same day, Trenchard confided to a journalist friend 'that the long-range bombing squadrons are not ready yet, and will not be till winter'.[160]

Trenchard was still grumbling ten days after his return to his headquarters near St. Omer. Convinced that bombing Germany would neither spare London nor 'win the war', he was 'not going to alter his offensive battlefield tactics until the present operations are suspended'.[161] Haig, whom Smuts called an 'unimaginative man', was far from being the sole author of the Army view that the

aeroplane had no valid military use other than in the tactical sense.
Very much alike in 'outlook and character', Haig and Trenchard
were in 'complete harmony' on this point.[162]

The Royal Naval Air Service, on the other hand, had been keen
on attacking targets in Germany from the very first days of the war.
The daring raids on the Zeppelin bases at Düsseldorf and Friedrichshafen were instances of what could be done even in 1914. The
dream of bombing Essen and Berlin persisted even after Churchill
left the Admiralty.

In May 1916, the Navy organized at Luxeuil in eastern France a
special wing for systematic raids on German war industries. Three
months later the unit had twenty-two machines, much less than
planned, but it was hoped to equip it eventually with 100 aircraft.
Trenchard opposed the naval venture as a 'luxury of war'. The
Army, he estimated, was short of twelve squadrons for the Somme
offensive. The Navy was compelled to give up some of its aircraft
when Henderson, the Director-General of Military Aeronautics,
interceded on Trenchard's behalf.

The Luxeuil wing nonetheless began making sizeable raids against
industrial targets in the Saar in October. The attacks were made in
co-operation with French squadrons. That same month, the Admiralty proposed to 'keep an effective force of at least 200 bombers in
France, to include Dunkirk'.[163] Much perturbed, Trenchard
appealed to his Commander-in-Chief. Haig, in turn, sent 'a real
snorter' of a letter to the Cabinet.

'I disagree entirely,' he wrote. 'The fighters are of first importance, for it is evident that we shall have to face a new struggle
for the command of the air in the spring of 1917; and if we lose that,
then neither reconnaissance machines nor bombers will help
us. . . .'[163]

Haig's hostility and the unfavourable winter weather ended the
Admiralty's experiment of strategic bombing. The Luxeuil machines
were moved to Dunkirk from where they operated tactically on the
Flanders front. The idea of bombing Germany was revived from
another quarter early in 1917. Its proponent, this time, was the
Ministry of Munitions' representative on the Air Board, Sir William
Weir.

'You prove that your factories can deliver the machines,' Trenchard responded sceptically in May. 'Then leave the bombing to

me.'[164] The Royal Flying Corps had yet to receive the squadrons ordered nearly twelve months before. The delay seemed reason enough to discount any long-range operations that year.

Trenchard was not so certain after German raiders appeared over England in battle formation. The latest plan from London called for forty bomber squadrons. On odd days in July and August, whenever the weather interrupted air operations, he went out surveying likely bases in eastern France for the 'mythical bombers'. Trenchard had promised as much to Lloyd George after the first Gotha raid on London.

Haig went to great pains to point out the futility of the entire project. 'The German air routes' were 'short and lie over the sea' while 'the distance we have to go . . . is much greater and our routes lie over hostile territory. . . . In this regard it is well to remember that the science of defence against aircraft may develop considerably . . .' he informed Robertson on 15 September.[165]

Considering that the Flanders offensive, then raging, was to cost some 250,000 British casualties, Haig's reluctance to face up to the difficulties of bombing Germany was most remarkable. He had a much better case when it came to 'suitable machines', of which he was 'improvided'. The Royal Flying Corps had nothing comparable in the autumn of 1917. The D.H.4, a single-engined aircraft, was a good daylight tactical bomber. Another machine used for bombing, the F.E.2b, had been designed as a reconnaissance-fighter. Its performance limited it to night missions.

The situation did not escape C. G. Grey's scathing attention:

What has really happened is simply that the Germans have developed a special branch of warfare which we have neglected in a manner which can only be described as idiotic.

Until quite recently, it was never worth the while of any designer to design a machine specially for bombing because the authorities did not want it. . . .

And yet we are surprised when the German goes to the trouble of building as good a bombing machine as he knows how, and proceeds to use it for the purpose for which it was built.[149]

It was not that the British were incapable of building big

aeroplanes. As early as December 1914, Sir Frederick Handley Page had gone to work producing Britain's first heavy bomber. He did so at the request of Churchill at the Admiralty, who 'had the foresight to see that large planes were necessary to carry war into other countries'. The original order was for four machines. Owing to development troubles, the Royal Naval Air Service did not receive its first Handley Page until November 1916.

Another was sent over straight from the factory at the turn of the year. Losing its way in a storm, the aeroplane landed in 'Hunland' near Laon. The Germans captured it intact along with its crew. Though it was of dubious propaganda value to say that they were being bombed with their own creation, the British later claimed that the Gotha was 'only a copy of one of ours'. One of the minor myths of the war, the story still persists.

Powered by two 275-h.p. Rolls-Royce engines, the Handley Page o/400 was the largest British bomber actually used in the war. In appearance, it was indeed similar to the Gotha. In performance, it surpassed its German counterpart with an endurance of eight hours and a bombload of nearly 1,800 pounds. For all its capabilities, the Handley Page was largely neglected as a strategic bomber. By September 1917, there were only eighteen of them in France. These were assigned to the naval squadrons in Dunkirk.

The Navy used them for long-range patrols over the North Sea, and some bombing of the U-boat facilities at Ostend and Zeebrugge. The bombers also participated in the concentrated raids on the Gotha bases at Ghent. The Royal Flying Corps did not order 'any Handley Pages until the Cabinet directed reprisal raids. Trenchard had dismissed the big machines as 'a useless type'. Hence, his complaint that 'the long-range bombing squadrons' would not be 'ready till the winter'.

Lloyd George had no intention of waiting that long after the September raids on London. At the Cabinet meeting of 2 October, Smuts announced that one R.F.C. squadron of D.H.4s, No. 55, was being transferred to Ochey. Robertson added that twenty additional D.H.4s, already crated for shipment to Russia, would be diverted to France. The Chief of the Imperial General Staff promised twenty more from the same source within six weeks.

The Admiralty dispatched eight Handley Pages based in England for U-boat patrols off the Yorkshire coast. Within ten days these aircraft were assembled, along with the F.E.2b aircraft of 100 Squadron, to form 41 Wing. The commander, Lieutenant-Colonel Cyril L. Newall, 'knew his business'. The special task of the wing was to bomb 'targets of military importance in German territory'.

On 17 October, exactly six days after the aircraft arrived at Ochey, two flights of D.H.4s took off to bomb the Burbach iron factory, near Saarbrücken, as Trenchard had promised. The daylight raid was the Royal Flying Corps' 'first long-range attack on a German target'. A week later, the Navy's Handley Pages joined the Army aircraft for a strike on the same target, the first British strategic night raid of the war.

Berlin was still a long, long way off. If any additional incentive was needed, a Manchester civic group provided it during 'reprisal week'. A reward of £1,000 was offered 'to the British aviator who dropped the first bomb on Berlin'. Reminded that officers were prohibited from 'accepting tips', the group's chairman suggested making 'the sum payable to charity'.[166] Even so, British airmen had started too late to collect that bounty in the First World War.

CHAPTER EIGHTEEN

'All that Flies and Creeps'

German hopes of ravaging London were revived in the autumn of 1917, with the development of a ten-pound incendiary bomb. Unlike high explosives, hundreds of these small projectiles could be delivered by comparatively few aircraft. The Germans calculated that panic and confusion would reign in the British capital, as scores of fires broke out. Should there be a strong wind, the fires were expected to join and sweep unchecked through the older districts of the city.

In November 1914, Grand Admiral von Tirpitz had argued for such measures with classic Teutonic logic: 'I am not in favour of "frightfulness". . . . Single bombs from flying machines are wrong; they are odious when they hit and kill an old woman, and one gets used to them. If one could set fire to London in thirty places, then what in a small way is odious would retire before something fine and powerful. All that flies and creeps should be concentrated on that city.'[167]

Tirpitz's noble sentiments found practical expression in a 'bombing plan' drawn up for the Zeppelin raiders that year. Gas works, oil and petroleum tanks were singled out for attack along with such obvious targets as the British Admiralty and the Telegraph Office. In a later revision, Admiral Behncke, the Deputy Chief of the Naval Staff, 'urged particular attention to the "dangerous zone" in the heart of the City of London between Aldersgate Street and Moorgate Street—the "soft goods quarter" crowded with inflammable textile warehouses.' Recollections of a 'disastrous conflagration' in that area in 1897 inspired the fire raid planners.[168]

Everything 'between Aldersgate Street and Moorgate Street', and much more, was finally consumed in the great fire raid of 29 December 1940. The Zeppelins had no such luck in 1915, although more than 70% of the bombs they dropped on London in four separate raids that year were incendiaries. Serious fires resulted from only one attack, that of 8 September. Warehouses in the narrow lanes north of St. Paul's were set ablaze at a loss of over half a million pounds.

Materially, the raid was the most destructive of the war. But apart from this isolated success, German plans for waging war with fire were clearly ahead of the current technology. Now, some two years later, it remained for the Gothas to attempt the same tactics with what was believed to be a much improved fire bomb.

The England Squadron waited for the new moon. Although it was nearly full on 29 October 1917, stormy weather was also advancing across England. Postponing the fire raid, Kleine sent a token force of three Gothas to bomb the coast. As clouds obscured the moon on their way over, two aircraft elected to attack Calais. The other reached the Essex coast, dropping eight bombs on villages near Southend. Damage was slight and no one was injured. But even a single raider could cause quite a stir.

Observer posts reported that 'three or four detachments of enemy aeroplanes, numbering perhaps ten in all, came overhead by way of the mouth of the Crouch, the Blackwater, and the Thames estuary'.[169] An alert was sounded in London. The next morning, French confidently claimed another victory. A raid had been attempted, he announced, but the bombers had been unable to penetrate the city's outer defences.

Jittery Londoners were badly in need of reassurance. The capital had been attacked quite by surprise on a very dark moonless night less than two weeks before. Despite a raid warning, the searchlights did not probe the skies nor did the guns fire a barrage. Shortly before midnight loud explosions were heard in the city. A brief communiqué issued during the early morning hours revealed that 'hostile airships' were over the country, and that a few bombs had been dropped 'in the London area'. There was an immediate protest in the newspapers and in Parliament. An airship attack on London had been assumed to be virtually impossible. And how was it that not a single shot had been fired?

The 'silent raid', as it became known, was one of the most fantastic of the war. Eleven Zeppelins had struck out from North Germany for an attack on the Midlands. Gale winds above 16,000 feet had driven them south over England. One airship, much to the distress of its crew, drifted clear across London, the first to do so in over a year. More intent on rising higher than causing injury, the Germans revealed their presence by dropping ballast and bombs.

One 660-pounder exploded in Piccadilly Circus. Shop fronts were caved in and pedestrians were strewn about the street. Another fell in Camberwell across the river. Two houses were 'swept away' and two hundred others were damaged. A third 660-pounder crashed on a row of houses at Hither Green. Eight children perished in one family. All told, the bombs killed thirty-one persons and injured forty-eight in London.

Seeing nothing, the gunners had held their fire rather than guide the Germans on their 'sinister and murderous course'. Only twenty-two rounds were fired, mostly along the coast. Four Zeppelins, however, never returned to Germany. Driven ever southward by the winds at high altitudes, they met with disaster over France. The raid was London's last by airships. Until March 1918, when Zeppelins again set out to attack the Midlands, the air campaign against England relied entirely on the Gothas and the Giants.

Kleine launched his first incendiary raid on the evening of 31 October with twenty-two Gothas. They were loaded with over six tons of bombs, nearly half of them incendiaries. A departure schedule was worked out to stagger the take-off over a period of almost three hours. The attack plan called for a stream of bombers to reach the south-east coast at Deal. From there, they were to fly across Kent and approach London from the south, thereby avoiding the heavy defences to the east. Because of rising winds over the Channel and low clouds over Kent, this route proved to be a mistake.

Over half of the attacking force released their bombs on random targets. Incendiaries and some high explosives were aimed at Dover, Chatham, and Gravesend. Several bombs fell on military camps near Canterbury. Herne Bay, Ramsgate, and Margate were also attacked. The British reported no damage of any consequence in Kent, 'except in Ramsgate where a gasometer was burnt out and much shop and house property was demolished'. The absence of casualties at these places was largely due to the few explosive bombs used.

While Kent was under attack, more Gothas were taking off from Gontrode. Aircraft from nearby Oostakker were already in the air. Piloting one of the departing bombers was Kollberg. Aschoff, his observer, held a flare pistol as he listened intently to the engines. Should they falter, he was ready to alert the ground crew on the field below to turn on the lights. The Gotha circled the aerodrome once, another precaution against engine failure shortly after take-off.

Aschoff crawled forward to his 'pulpit'. Standing over a lighted compass, he raised his arm and the bomber banked into a turn. The needle danced in the dim light. When the right heading was reached, Aschoff dropped his arm and Kollberg knew that he was on course. Gontrode and the blacked out city of Ghent were left behind. Small clusters of red, white, and green lights showed the way to the sea. Guns firing tracer ammunition marked the Dutch border. To the south, the front was quiet. Now and again, a flare rose from some unseen trench, and burned itself out over no man's land.

At Ostend, German gunners were shooting at precisely timed intervals as a signal for the Gothas. Kollberg checked the engines once more before flying out to sea. The drone of the bombers had awakened the defences along the French coast. Bright beams flittered about for any German raiders which might be heading for Dunkirk.

As the lights receded, Aschoff realized that he was being blown off course. He became alarmed after nearly an hour had passed. Deal should have been reached by this time, but he could see nothing of the English coast. How far could the Gotha have drifted? The dark shadow of the shore did not appear until some thirty minutes later. Aschoff judged from its broken contour that he was off the estuary of the Thames, somewhere between Southend and Harwich. He signalled Kollberg to fly on a south-west heading for London.

The fiery bursts of shells speckled the sky over Sheerness across the river. And directly below were lighted aerodromes from which fighters could be seen taking off. A cloud bank rolled in from the west to obscure the disturbing sight. Though the searchlights persisted, their beams were now blotted out by the haze. Unable to see the ground, Aschoff navigated by the stars and counted the minutes to determine when he should be over London.

He finally spotted the city, immense and unmistakable in the gloom, beyond a sharp break in the clouds. Flak puffs floated past the bomber in weird frightening shapes. The electrified Germans became prey to hallucinations. Clutching at their guns, they were ready to fire as they mistook the smoke for British fighters. On the north-east outskirts of the capital they caught sight of a balloon apron, ghostly and menacing with its dangling steel cables. Kollberg gingerly flew around the barrier, and kept on course for the city.

Half a hundred lights weaved and turned, and more red splotches broke out in small clumps against the sky. Over north London the Gotha turned for Woolwich with its 600-acre arsenal. Aschoff waited for the Thames to slide beneath his wings. Once across, he jerked one lever after another to release his bombs. Leaning far over the side, he waited for what seemed a very long while before seeing small flashes far below.

The crew had little time to see much else. A light beam side-swiped their machine, and then returned to hold it in a blinding cone. Kollberg immediately banked and went into a dive. As the glaring beam held on, several more converged to trap the Gotha with their searing light. The guns began to concentrate their fire on the bright speck in the sky.

Kollberg could do nothing but fly as fast as his engines would allow. Aschoff and the rear gunner crouched low in their positions to avoid being blinded. Their guns at the ready, they squinted in all directions for attacking British fighters. Kollberg held the bomber on a speedy course until it finally escaped the lights. Leaving London behind, he flew south-east over Kent.

At least eight other Gothas braved the barrage to bomb the out-lying districts of the city. Woolwich suffered no damage, but bombs fell all around that borough. At Erith, a few miles to the east, much harm was done to house property. Hits were also clustered on the docks of the Isle of Dogs and in Greenwich. One crew reported 'a fierce and distinctively visible fire on the eastern rim of London'. The destruction was actually limited because most of the incendi-aries had failed to ignite. The attack killed ten persons and injured twenty-two. British shrapnel caused seven of the casualties, in-cluding one death.

Two U.S. senators clad only in pyjamas watched the raid from their suite on the top floor of a London hotel. 'We welcomed it,' one of them said of the bombing, 'in the sense that it nerved us for our coming visit to the trenches in France and Belgium.' The senators promptly left London the following afternoon, reportedly to inspect shipyards in the north of England.[170]

The 'All Clear' in the capital was rather unusual. After experi-menting with whistles and car horns, London officials had decided to adopt the Paris system of bugle calls. Several hundred Boy Scouts, responding to an appeal for buglers, first appeared in the streets early that morning. Blowing cheerfully, they undoubtedly roused anyone who had managed to sleep up to this point.

The Home Office promptly disowned any responsibility 'for Boy Scout buglers who may be injured while on air raid duty'. A business firm then offered to pay for a Lloyd's policy covering '350 of the lads'. The parents of any 'little patriot killed by bombs or shrapnel' were to receive an indemnity of fifty pounds. In case of injury, half that sum was payable 'for medical expenses'.[171]

The House of Lords had given the airmen of the Home Defence squadrons a vote of thanks, if not compensation, only a few days before. 'I sometimes think,' spoke Lord Curzon in support of the resolution, 'that when Gothas are shrieking over London, and when the civil population are cowering in their cellars, we might give a thought to those brave men who are riding in the darkness above and risking their lives to save us from destruction.'[172]

Since the Germans had attacked in relays of one or two bombers flying in at long intervals, the British had had time to put up fifty aircraft. Over one-third of them were fighters of the latest types, but few pilots saw anything of the raiders. Two of the defenders crashed, and all the Gothas left England unscathed.

Once over Belgium, Aschoff was anxious to reach Gontrode. The eastern sky was lightening to a drab grey. He was worried about being spotted by British aircraft out on patrol. As the sun started to rise, Aschoff caught his first glimpse of the aerodrome's large Zeppelin hangar still far in the distance. Nearer Ghent, a thick fog hugged the ground. Kollberg could see nothing of the field except for the vertical beams of the searchlights which served as a beacon.

Waiting for a break, the Gotha circled low above the fog. The tops of tall trees, looking like little islands in a flooded landscape, gradually emerged. Kollberg finally had to risk going in, for his tanks were nearly empty. Grimly, he plunged into the shroudlike haze and held his breath until he saw the firm earth beneath. Aschoff made a final entry in his log and noted the time—5.22 A.M. Plain good fortune was still flying with his crew. Five other Gothas crashed as they came in to land that misty morning.

Kleine had other reasons to be unhappy about the flight. Although more than twenty Gothas had bombed England for the first time since the start of the night attacks, the reports of the crews were too inconclusive to proclaim the fire raid a success. His frustration was complete when the moon faded away without a spell of good weather.

Still feeling glum, the Kommandeur rode out to one of his aerodromes early in November. The cordial reception given him at the Kasino, the scene of many enthusiastic toasts and carefree parties in the past, failed to cheer him. Never very friendly with his officers, Kleine found such social interludes increasingly depressing. They only reminded him of the absence of many of his best crews.

Küppers, for one, was no longer with the squadron, Developing a 'deep-seated dislike' for night flying, he had asked to go back to his old fighter unit. Soon after he left, Lorenz crashed in a Rumpler biplane. Taught to fly by Küppers, the exuberant observer nearly killed himself with the fast and tricky aircraft. He went home minus a leg, as well as his nose, and became a state lottery collector after the war. Richthofen made Küppers commander of Jagdstaffel 48 early in 1918. By the Armistice, he had six official kills to his credit. Now over seventy, he lives in quiet retirement in West Germany.

Not many of the airmen raiding England in 1917 would live to see such an age. They were steadily being replaced by young fliers fresh from the training squadrons in Germany. Flight leaders complained to Kleine about their inadequate training. Too many observers were unable to find London after reaching the coast. Too many pilots were wrecking Gothas in night landings.

All through November, when the weather made flights across the Channel impossible, the crews were kept busy with a crammed training programme. Pilots went up for practice landings, and gunners were sent to the firing range. Observers were lectured on celestial navigation, and they studied maps of the south of England until they were able to trace its coast and rivers from memory. Inexperienced observers were first flown as gunners with veteran crews. There were some objections to this exchange in the rear cockpit, even on a temporary basis. But it served to introduce an observer to combat flying before risking a bomber to his command.

Closer attention was given to the weather. Moonlight alone was not enough; it had to be accompanied by cloudless skies. Beginning in December, single-engined Rumpler C.IVs equipped with two-way radio telegraphs were sent out to observe conditions off the

English coast. Whenever the weather was unfavourable for a raid, the squadron was promptly alerted and the Gothas remained grounded.

In London and the coastal towns, a sullen uneasiness returned with the moon toward the end of November. Although no alerts were sounded, the Underground stations were crowded on several moonlit nights. The anger of the people in the threatened areas was turned on Coventry during this tense period, when thousands of workers in the local aircraft engine industry went on strike.

Coventry was denounced as 'the centre of the contempt of the British Empire'. The Lord Mayor pleaded in vain with the workers to serve as 'loyal soldiers in the munitions shops'. A Royal Naval Air Service chaplain was flown from the front in France to preach patriotism in the strikebound city. Aircraft even dropped leaflets on Coventry on 2 December, calling 'for an increase in aircraft production'.

Taking the 'aircraft shirkers' to task, C. G. Grey invoked the wrath of the raiders on their city. 'When the Germans are good and ready to invade England by air in the spring, they may well find London fully protected against air raids,' he wrote. 'It will then be a small matter for their new and improved aeroplanes to cover an extra hundred miles or so to some other munitions centre. Obviously, Coventry is the next nearest. . . . Then Coventry will get precious little sympathy. . . .

'Meantime, and pending this just retribution, Coventry has deprived the British Army of much-needed aircraft. . . . Later on, doubtless, the Hun raiders' bombs will pay Coventry as a whole for the results of last week's disgraceful work. . . .'[173] The curse on Coventry, a lasting one, was fulfilled on the night of 14 November 1940.

Late on 5 December 1917, Georgii could finally confirm that the weather across the Channel was nearly perfect for a raid. The air was cold and the sky was clear. There was little time to lose. The moon, now only a thin crescent in its last quarter, would soon be gone. London received its first warning at 1.30 A.M., as a Giant and one or two Gothas crossed into Kent. The raiders went only as far as Sheerness where they dropped 3,000 pounds of bombs. More than two-thirds of this load were incendiaries. A few fires were started but they were quickly put out. High explosives released by the Giant demolished five houses. The town suffered seventeen casualties, including five dead.

Because of a five-week lull, and the fact that an attack had never started at such an hour, the alert caught some of the defence pilots unawares. 'I was on duty that night,' recalled Captain Cecil Lewis, then a flight leader with 61 Squadron at Rochford. 'There was nothing to do but play poker, put on the gramophone, and drink— but not too much, in case you had to take to the air.

'The Mess was strangely quiet on such nights. The voices of the pilots calling their hands, Kreisler's *Caprice Viennois*, the chink of bets dropping into the saucer on the table. . . . Then—suddenly the raucous Klaxons right overhead. Their nerve-shattering blast jolted our hearts into our throats. Instantly everything was confusion. . . .

'Pilots dashed about, frantic, picking up odd bits of kits, and tumbled through the door of the Mess, pell-mell. There was the sound of many feet as the men doubled up to the sheds. In a minute the engines were running.'[174]

Lewis was desperate for an aeroplane. He had been up a few hours earlier, stunting over the aerodrome. While landing in a cross wind, he had sheared off his wheels and turned over. Now he had no machine to fly. Realizing that his 'place was in the air', Lewis decided to go up in an S.E.5 he had ferried in that afternoon. The 'new bus' had no lights and its oil pressure was low. Lewis took off with a 'torch' strapped to his shoulder and plugged into his flying suit.

'I rose over the dim river and climbed up to patrol height. . . . I wheeled up and down my beat for half an hour, trying to judge where the Huns might be from the anti-aircraft bursts; but, as usual, saw nothing. Then I caught my hand in the flex of the torch and pulled off the wire. The cockpit was plunged into darkness. I tried to get the wire back on the terminal, but couldn't manage it. The bus was new; it wouldn't fly hands off. . . . This was altogether too tricky. Home, John. . . .'[175]

Having flown the first patrol, Lewis was allowed to sleep when the second warning was received some two hours later. This time, Bentivegni's R.39, and three or four Gothas, came in over the north coast of Kent. Incendiaries were showered on Whitstable, Herne Bay, Margate, and Ramsgate. After dropping its fire bombs, the Giant dumped more than half a ton of high explosives in the vicinity of Dover. Mistaken for a Gotha flying at very low height, the gigantic bomber was fired at with machine-guns as it passed out to sea.

The main attack was still to come. Beginning at 4. A.M., Gothas were tracked over both Kent and Essex as they flew on converging courses for London. The alerted city readied itself for simultaneous attacks from three different directions by 'five groups'. In truth, the assault was attempted by nine Gothas, and only six reached the city. These dropped over 5,000 pounds of bombs, mostly incendiaries, in a 'well distributed pattern'. Since the fire bombs were released in driblets to cover a wide area, the actual bombing lasted well over an hour.

The 'cock-crow raid', so-called because of its unusually early hour, has been described as 'the most formidable effort to implement the Fire Plan in the history of the War'. Thanks to the foresight of the London Fire Brigade, headed by Lieutenant-Commander S. Sladen, the city was spared from any serious conflagration. Men and fire-fighting equipment from the outlying districts had been moved into the potentially dangerous sections of the city the evening before. There were only four big fires, and these were checked before they could spread.

'All kinds of things happened to incendiary bombs,' reported *The Times*. 'One went through the roof of a house and plunged into a cistern where it was extinguished. Another fell in a dust-bin. One which dropped on the pavement of a street broke two plate-glass windows and set fire to the stock displayed behind the glass. The flames were extinguished before they had extended to the shop. . . . Many of the bombs fell in open spaces and did no damage.'[176]

The total damage was estimated at more than £100,000. Such losses were covered by a Government insurance scheme inaugurated in 1915. Rates on private houses were a few shillings for each hundred pound evaluation, with higher rates for industrial property. In March 1917, the rates were reduced by half. Free coverage was later provided for losses up to £500. Even so, the raid insurance plan netted a profit of over eleven million pounds by the end of the war. The incendiaries also had little 'killing' effect. There were only eighteen casualties in London, and half these were inflicted by shell fragments.

This time, the guns had not fired in vain. Farmers living near Canterbury were awakened by the glow of a roaring fire in the early morning hours. A Gotha had come down in the darkness in an open field. The Germans set the machine ablaze, and then surrendered to the parish clergyman. He had been called to investigate in his capacity as a special constable. The pilot, a handsome youth with close-cropped hair, explained that he had been forced to land after one of his engines had been damaged over London.

Another Gotha was struck by a shell near Canvey Island. With one propeller shattered, the anxious crew spotted a lighted aerodrome not far away. It was Rochford where Lewis had come in without any lights in his cockpit. Following the usual procedure, the Germans fired a signal before attempting to land. The aerodrome had three colours—red, green, and white—which were alternately changed as 'a sort of password'. Quite by chance, the raiders gave the colour of the day, but the pilot was not familiar with the field. He struck a tree on his approach, and the bomber came crashing down on a nearby golf course.

Mechanics, thinking it was one of their own, ran to the crash site. They were much surprised to see three 'Huns' crawling out of the wreck. The Germans were quickly hustled away before they could do any further damage to their aircraft. Except for bruises, all were quite unhurt. British officers went out to inspect the broken, petrol-soaked bomber. One of them found a flare pistol. As he was showing his prize to another officer, it went off with a glorious flash. A magnesium flare bounced along the ground, and the whole heap exploded in flames. By morning, only the charred engines and a twisted framework remained.

'Thus it happened that I never saw a Gotha,' grieved Lewis. 'We were very upset about this, because, at the time, a great controversy raged as to whether the rear gunner in the Gotha had a tunnel to enable him to fire under his tail. . . . Examination of it would have solved our problem. . . .' Lewis did get to see some of the Germans he had searched for on many a moonlight night.

'Next morning,' he continues, 'we went in to look at our prisoners. They were very quiet and rather sorry for themselves. I believe they feared victimization: raiders were not popular with the general public. However, whatever the public thought, we knew they were very brave men and had a fellow-feeling for them. So we gave them a good breakfast, and took them round the sheds. Then they were ordered an escort to take them into town. I accompanied them.

'We had a reserved first-class compartment, locked, with the blinds down. But somehow the news had got around, and at every station there was an angry crowd. The officer in charge had to keep them off at the point of a revolver, otherwise we should have all been lynched. The Germans were anxious. . . . One cut off the flying badges on his tunic and gave them to me. I suppose he thought they made him a little too conspicuous. At Liverpool Street there was a heavily armed escort, and the wretched men were marched away, through a hostile mob, to the safety of an internment camp.'[177]

The capture of two crews in one night was almost too good to believe. Actually, the barrage fire had been even more successful than the British realized. Two machines limped back, so badly battered that they barely made it to Belgium. Another bomber never returned. It went down, very likely, into the sea after being crippled by gunfire. Still another crashed while landing at its aerodrome. The toll was six of sixteen Gothas reaching England.

Such losses would have been less galling if London had been set aflame. Kleine informed OHL on 9 December that 'only two or three persistent fires' had apparently resulted from the five hundred incendiary bombs dropped on the raid. Noting that the British had reported 'a large number of fires', he conjectured 'that the enemy is deliberately mentioning these fires to trick us into continuing the use of incendiaries instead of heavy calibre demolition bombs. . . .'[178]

The Gothas never again dropped incendiaries on England. Ten years later, Major von Bülow added a final postscript to the fizzle of the fire raids: 'A great deal of time and effort had gone into the design of these incendiary bombs, on whose effect on the densely settled London area such high hopes were based. The bomb was a complete failure. . . . The sound idea of creating panic and disorder with numerous fires came to nothing owing to the inadequacy of the materials employed.'[178]

Despite this discouraging failure, the Germans did not abandon their 'sound idea'. Working with the greatest secrecy, they began searching for a foolproof incendiary bomb early in 1918. By August, they had found such a weapon and their factories were producing them in quantity.

The Elektron bomb, as it was called, was made of almost pure magnesium. It burned with a fierce heat of 2,000 to 3,000 degrees Fahrenheit. Exhaustive tests left no doubt that this new type of bomb would ignite on contact. Nor could it be put out with water; dousing only added to the intensity of the fire. Since it weighed only two pounds, thousands could be dumped in a single attack. Even if half were to burn themselves out in the streets or other paved areas, more blazes would be started than any fire brigade could possibly fight at one time.

Devastating fire raids were planned late that summer. The England Squadron was to assault London, while three other Geschwadern were to fly to Paris on the same night. The bombers were to return the following day, that night, and continue to do so until all were shot down or their crews were too exhausted to take off.

The Allied capitals escaped this ordeal only because of the shifting tide of battle at the front. On 8 August 1918—'the climax of the war' —the British cracked the German salient on the Somme with over 400 tanks. OHL realized that the war was lost as its troops wavered, straggled, and surrendered by the thousands. The fire raids would only boomerang when it became necessary to negotiate for an armistice.

'Our position,' Ludendorff recalled, 'was now so serious that General Headquarters could not hope that air-raids on London and Paris would force the enemy to make peace. Permission was therefore refused for the use of a particularly effective incendiary bomb, expressly designed for attacks on the two capitals. . . .' The Chancellor, Count von Hertling, was opposed to the use of the fire bombs 'on account of the reprisals on our towns that would follow'. But 'the general military situation' was 'the real ground for the decision'.[179]

That decision was made none too soon. At Ghent, the message quashing the attack was received less than an hour before the Gothas were to set out for London. And at one other squadron, whose target was Paris, some of the crews were already in their cockpits and about to start their engines.[180]

The terrible scourge of the fire raid would have to await another world war to be flown. Then it would inflict its greatest havoc not so much on London, but other cities even farther away from the old Western Front. The fate of Hamburg and Dresden was far beyond anything the Germans could have possibly achieved in 1918. But, as a concept for strategic air warfare, little was to be added to the German idea in the intervening years.

1a and b. Gotha G.IV bombers, like the twelve lined up above for take-off from Nieuwmunster near Ostend on the Belgian coast, were first dispatched to Flanders for the daylight raids on London in the spring of 1917. Note the distinctive crew markings on the bombers and, in both photographs, the crashed aircraft in the distance.

2a. A German airman inflates a life jacket worn on the flights to England. His other equipment includes heavy gloves, fur-lined boots reaching above the knees, and a padded crash helmet.

2b. Ground personnel pour liquid oxygen into containers prior to loading into the crew positions of the Gotha bomber. A valve regulated the flow of oxygen into the rubber bladder, to which a breathing tube was attached.

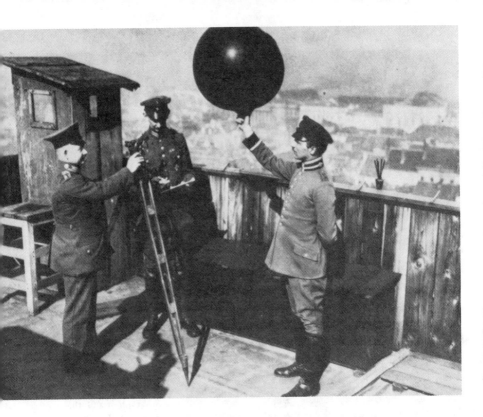

3a. A meteorological team headed by Lt. Walter Georgii, centre, the England Squadron's weather officer, prepares to release a pilot balloon from the rooftop of the University at Ghent to measure winds aloft prior to a raid on England. Dr. Georgii became a foremost German authority on aerology and gliding after the war.

3b. Barrage balloons joined together by heavy cables guarded the approaches to London in the autumn of 1917. General Ashmore conceived the idea of the aerial 'apron' with its dangling steel streamers on the morning after the first Gotha night attack on London.

4a. A rare German photograph of a Gotha bomber over London. Victoria Park and Gardens may be seen to the right. Running diagonally across the lower left corner is the Mile End Road.

4b. A smoke-blurred view of London as seen from a bomber during the late morning raid of 7 July 1917. A blaze at the Central Telegraph Office, immediately to the north of St. Paul's Cathedral, was quickly extinguished, but warehouses in nearby Bartholomew Close were burnt out. Other points of orientation include the Mansion House roof, and, upper right, the circular outline of Finsbury Circus and Finsbury Square.

5a. The funeral procession for fifteen of the children killed in an infants' class in an East End school during the first Gotha raid on London. Public shock and sorrow is evident from the huge crowds and the floral tribute of over five hundred wreaths.

5b. Major-General Hugh Trenchard, seen at extreme right, escorting Queen Mary on a tour of an R.F.C. aerodrome at St. Omer, France, on 5 July 1917, was much concerned over the diversion of British squadrons from the front for home defence. The aircraft are Bristol fighters.

6a. The Sopwith Camels of No. 44 Home Defence Squadron at Hainault Farm Aerodrome, near Romford, Essex.

6b. A Gotha three-man crew occupy their respective positions aboard a G.V. The camouflage design was printed on the fabric. The colouring of the irregular polygon pattern varied from green, brown and purple on the upper surfaces to black and different shades of blue on the sides and under surfaces.

7a. Completely equipped for battle over England, an observer-gunner sucks on an oxygen tube in the forward turret of a Gotha G.V bomber. Behind the observer may be seen the pilot's rear view mirror and windscreen. The bomber's weight, fully loaded, is given as 3,975 kg., or 8,763 lbs.

7b. The Gothas carried a greater bomb load on the night raids against England since they were flown at considerably lower altitudes than the daylight attacks, averaging from 6,500 to 8,200 feet. This G.V is being loaded with nearly half a ton of explosives—five 110-pound bombs and two 220-pounders already in position beneath the fuselage.

8a. While the rear fuselage of the Staaken R.VI was covered with fabric, the forward section was constructed of plywood. A pilot and co-pilot sat up front in the enclosed control cabin. The open nose position, in which a machine-gun could be mounted, was occupied by the aircraft commander on the bomb run.

8b. Each nacelle of the Staaken R.VI bomber housed two engines with a small cockpit for a flight mechanic in the centre. The tractor and pusher propellers measured fourteen feet from tip to tip.

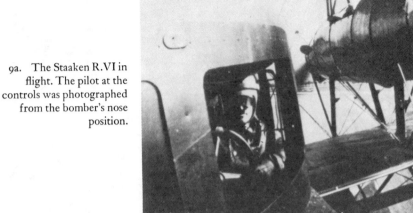

9a.   The Staaken R.VI in flight. The pilot at the controls was photographed from the bomber's nose position.

9b.   The port gunner-mechanic of R.12, a Staaken R.IV, clambers up the ladder to his upper wing gun. He was also equipped with another machine-gun firing forward from the nacelle. The bomber's armament, when fully armed, totalled seven machine-guns.

10a. The incessant noise and vibration of the two 160-h.p. Mercedes engines mounted in the nose of R.12 were particularly trying to the occupants of the flight engineer's compartment located immediately aft. The incongruous radiators atop the nose account in part for the bomber's maximum speed of 77 m.p.h.

10b. A flight mechanic apparently strapped to the struts rides outside the port nacelle of R.12. Four 220-h.p. Benz engines mounted in tandem pairs drove the aircraft's pusher propellers.

11a. The gunner-mechanics of R.13, unlike those of R.12 whose cockpits were located forward, occupied the aft section of the nacelles. The airy positions were directly behind the aircraft's huge four-bladed propellers, whirring noisily some twenty-two feet forward.

11b. R.13's two pilots rode well forward in a large open cockpit. The aircraft commander occupied a similar position immediately aft of the pilots'. The ladder leads up to the gun pod atop the upper wing.

12a and b. Lt. Kurt Küppers, wearing light greatcoat, and Oblt. Fritz Lorenz, third from the left, with other crew members of Lo-Ri 3. The lower photograph shows the crew's earlier Gotha which had to be scrapped after being narrowly missed by a British bomb in an attack on Gontrode aerodrome. In the crater behind the notice 'Lori 2 before the Grave' are the ground crews of Staffel 16.

13a. A solemn-faced German airman disembarks from a lorry after his capture in the early hours of 6 December 1917. Two crews surrendered when their Gothas were forced down in England with battle damage. The prisoner was a rare catch for the British, who seldom had any survivors to interrogate.

13b. Wreckage of a Gotha bomber shot down on 28 January 1918, near Wickford, Essex, by two Camel pilots of 44 Squadron. The German crew was buried in a church graveyard.

14a. The first one-ton bomb to fall on England, dropped on the night of 16 February 1918, struck the North Pavilion of the Royal Hospital, Chelsea. The home of a hospital staff officer was destroyed, and many other buildings in the area were damaged.

14b. Despite the best efforts of the British, the England Geschwader lost more aircraft in crash landings than it did to the guns and fighters over Britain. This Gotha fell on a farmhouse while making a night landing approach. A Belgian farmer and his wife were killed in bed.

15a. R.13, seen with its crew, became operational with Squadron 501 in December 1917.

15b. The 'indestructible' R.12 on its return to Germany after the war. On the night of 16 February 1918 it rammed a balloon apron of the London air defences. Badly shaken, the crew regained control of the six-engine bomber after a thousand-foot drop, and flew on to attack Woolwich and Beckenham. In this photograph the raider's remarkable record, chalked on the fuselage by its crew, lists places attacked on the Russian front as well as in England and France. The total weight of the bombs dropped by R.12 is given as 25,000 kg., or 55,115 lbs.

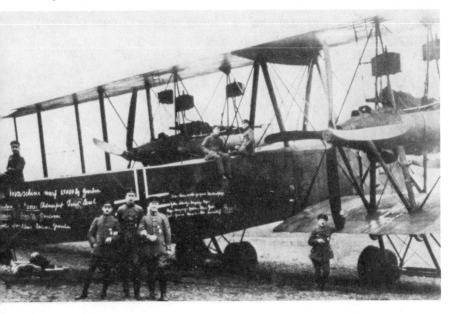

16a. Lord Weir, Secretary of State for Air, bares his head in salute as he reviews Royal Air Force cadets on the seafront at Hastings in 1918. An early advocate of long-range bombing, Weir was the driving force behind the strategic air offensive the British launched against Germany.

16b. Twin-engined Handley Page o/400s of the Royal Air Force at an aerodrome near Dunkirk in April 1918. Flown as a night bomber, the o/400 became the backbone of the Independent Air Force the British specifically organized for the large-scale raids against the German homeland. The hundred-foot upper wing of the o/400 was thirty feet longer than the lower span. The pilot occupied the open cockpit immediately aft of the observer in the nose position. Armed with as many as five Lewis guns, the o/400 dropped single bombs weighing 1,650 lbs. in the last months of the war.

Winter Twilight of the Gotha Bombers

The battered engine of a Gotha bomber was displayed in London's Trafalgar Square after the last fire raid. The trophy was placed alongside a tank to spur a war loan drive. For fund-raising, a whole Gotha, complete with black crosses and mottled camouflage, would have been much better. But the engine alone, however unexciting, at least gave sign that the cover of night was failing the raiders.

Kleine was well aware of that fact after the attack of 6 December. In a special report to Hoeppner, he indicated that his bombers had been held 'in the cones of searchlights for minutes at a time' even along the coast. Beyond Sheerness, 'the illuminated machines were passed from group to group' of four to six lights. The 'flak zone' was observed to stretch 'far to the north and south of the Thames'. Emphasizing that 'many enemy fighters were seen', he estimated that there were twelve 'lighted' aerodromes between Dover and London.[181]

The disturbing survey was Kleine's last. On 12 December 1917, his squadron made a daylight attack on British troop encampments near Ypres. The Gothas set out early in the afternoon. The flight was a short one and they were soon back, circling over Ghent 'under a canopy of very dark clouds'. As the men on the ground made the usual count of the returning bombers, they quickly realized that one was missing. The first crews to touch down brought the stunning news that the lost Gotha had the Kommandeur on board.

Kleine's undoing was described in an official statement issued the next day: 'Reports establish beyond any doubt that the aeroplane was shot down by enemy anti-aircraft artillery between Le Touquet and Croix le Bois, half-way between Warneton and Armentières.'[182] That this was not exactly so is evident from the story of a Canadian pilot published many years later.[183] That pilot was Captain Wendell W. Rogers, then a youth of twenty assigned to 1 Squadron of the Royal Flying Corps in Flanders.

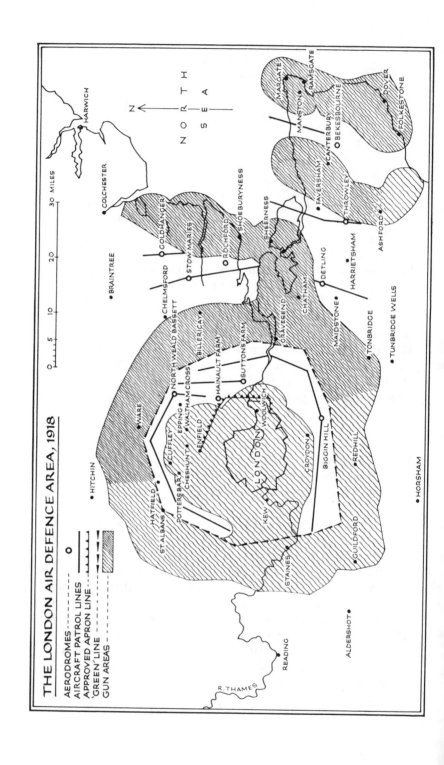

THE LONDON AIR DEFENCE AREA, 1918

AERODROMES --------- ○
AIRCRAFT PATROL LINES ——————
APPROVED APRON LINE - - - - - -
'GREEN' LINE - - - - - -
GUN AREAS - - - - - -

0 5 10 20 30 MILES

NORTH SEA
N

HARWICH

COLCHESTER

BRAINTREE
HITCHIN
GOLDHANGER
STOW MARIES
CHELMSFORD
ROCHFORD
SHOEBURYNESS
SHEERNESS

WARE
NORTH WEALD BASSETT
EPPING
CUFFLEY
HATFIELD
ST ALBANS
POTTERS BAR
CHESHUNT
ENFIELD
WALTHAM CROSS
HAINAULT FARM
BILLERICAY
SUTTONS FARM
GRAVESEND
CHATHAM
DETLING
HARRIETSHAM
MAIDSTONE
FAVERSHAM
THROWLEY
ASHFORD
BEKESBOURNE
CANTERBURY
MANSTON
MARGATE
RAMSGATE
DOVER
FOLKESTONE

LONDON
WOOLWICH
KEW
CROYDON
BIGGIN HILL
REDHILL
GUILDFORD
TONBRIDGE
TUNBRIDGE WELLS
HORSHAM

STAINES
R. THAMES
READING
ALDERSHOT

Rogers took off at one o'clock that afternoon to lead a patrol of five Nieuports over the front. The weather was grey and very cold. He had been told to 'wash out the patrol and come home' if the sky was clear of Germans. The Nieuports found a hole in the clouds over Armentières. Once above the overcast Rogers sighted seventeen 'specks' which he soon recognized as Gothas. Flying at 10,000 feet, the Germans were heading west for the Allied lines.

Although two of his pilots had strayed off in the ascent through the clouds, Rogers pressed on towards the enemy formation. Gaining easily, the fighters pounced on the three rearmost bombers. Rogers levelled off and nosed straight into the rear of one of the stragglers. The gunner in the back cockpit hammered away at him frantically. The tracers from the top gun passed over the Nieuport; those fired through the tunnel beneath went under. The Canadian coolly held his track into this wedge of flying bullets until he was barely thirty feet from the Gotha's towering tail.

Shot through, 'the great aeroplane' veered on one side and went into a steep glide 'towards the trenches in front of Armentières'. Shortly after the riddled craft had crossed the trenches at 4,000 feet, it suddenly burst into flames. Fanned by the wind, the fire leapt from the blazing tanks and raced along the taut fabric of the fuselage. Rogers, following close behind, saw some figures plunging, dark and doll-like against the sky. Two Germans had jumped without parachutes rather than burn. The Gotha exploded moments later into 'a mass of fluttering, smoking wreckage'. Australian troops in the front lines near Warneton saw the bomber crash in no man's land.

Killed with Kleine were von der Nahmer and Buelowius, the popular 'Rabatz' and 'Matz', who had the reputation of being the 'best crew'. Georgii, the squadron meteorologist, confirms that the bodies were scattered. The two lieutenants, he recalls, 'were not interred by the Geschwader as we had no information about them'. Kleine was returned to Ghent for burial. A German shock trooper had found a broken body which he immediately recognized as being that of no ordinary airman. About its neck hung the Maltese cross of the Pour le Mérite.

Hoeppner eulogized Kleine as 'one of whom I expected much. His name, and the air raids he led against England, stand indelibly inscribed in the annals of this war and the honour roll of the

Luftstreitkräfte.'[184] Yet, time and circumstances were virtually to consign this resolute pioneer of bomber warfare to oblivion.

'Congratulate the pilot who shot down the Gotha machine in flames,' wired Trenchard, unknowingly applauding the death of the one German who had done the most to bring about the birth of the Royal Air Force in 1918. Rogers received the Military Cross. Years later, he was only aware of having 'brought down the first Gotha in France'. The Germans, on their side, were not about to publicize a loss from which their England Squadron never quite recovered.

Oberleutnant Walter, whom Kleine had regarded as one of his best flight leaders, became acting commander. Within a week, the crews returned to London. They did so with an increasing sense of futility, but the raid's timing and destructiveness dismayed the British. London had never been attacked by the light of so small a moon. With the onset of winter the Germans had another means of finding the city at night. A light snowfall had fallen on England. Against a white background, the darkly etched course of the Thames was clearly visible from the air.

The raid of 18 December was believed to have been 'carried out by five separate divisions, each consisting of numerous groups of aeroplanes advancing in succession on a broad front on both sides of the river'. There were really only thirteen Gothas; two others had turned back before reaching the coast. As the bombers were 'met by barrages and concentrations of searchlights at upwards of 12,000 feet', the number reaching the capital dwindled down to seven. These dropped high explosive bombs 'at various times between 7.10 and 8.30 P.M.' Five other raiders raked north-east Kent, and one attacked Harwich with little effect.

The Gothas were followed by a single Giant, R.12, which arrived over London shortly after nine o'clock. Commanded by Oberleutnant Hans Joachim von Seydlitz-Gerstenberg, the lumbering aircraft released, among others, a 660-pound bomb which fell in Lyall Street near Eaton Square. The missile was the first of its size to be dropped from an aeroplane over England. Its terrific blast damaged a score of houses without injuring anyone.

The House of Commons was in session when the alert came. On receiving the message, the presiding officer left the Speaker's Chair. Shouts of 'No! No!' from Pemberton-Billing and a few other stalwarts did not stop the scramble to the basement storerooms. The

176

protesting M.P.s were still angry after the 'All Clear'. Pemberton-Billing called it 'humiliating' that the House should have 'retired in the face of the enemy'. In other countries, he added, 'men are shot for leaving their posts!' The view that the sensible thing to do was also patriotic prevailed.[185]

The press, complying with the ban on 'lurid' air raid stories, gave scant attention to the damage. The destruction was actually the worst since the devastating Zeppelin raid of September 1915. Thirteen fires raged in London, one being visible over fifty miles away to the returning German crews. Despite the property losses, there were only twelve dead and sixty-six wounded. The barrage fire injured nineteen others, two fatally.

A cannonade of over 10,000 shells bagged no raiders, but Captain Murlis-Green chalked up a drawn-out air victory. While patrolling at 11,000 feet over Essex, the British pilot saw the exhaust glow of an aircraft engine. As he approached, a searchlight lit up a Gotha in his path. Murlis-Green opened fire with short bursts to avoid being blinded by the flashes of his machine-gun. The bomber escaped in the darkness, but only temporarily. One of its engines had been knocked out.

The Germans doggedly stayed on course for London, releasing their bombs on Bermondsey ten minutes later. The disabled aircraft steadily lost altitude on its retreat over Kent. Soon after it reached the sea near Folkestone, the other engine failed. The bomber landed in the water from a low height and stayed afloat. A trawler was sent out to take the prize in tow, its crew still on board. As it was being taken into port, the Gotha was suddenly ripped by an explosion. German machines carried a charge for their swift destruction in the event of imminent capture. Two of the airmen were fished out of the water and made prisoners, but the third drowned.

The attack had not followed the predictable pattern of the night raids to which Londoners had adjusted. They had not bothered to shelter in the Underground, as they did when the moon was full. Observer posts along the coast had not been on the alert for raiders. With a preliminary warning of only eight minutes, the police had had no time to take to the streets with their 'Take Cover' placards. A disquietude not felt since the September raids surged anew in the capital and the coastal cities.

Indignant trade unions called a mass meeting in Sheerness.

Resolutions were sent to London to protest 'the complete absence of warning at night', and 'the continued refusal of the military authorities to provide suitable bomb-proof shelters'.[186] In London, the agitation centred on the use of sound alerts at night. The firing of maroons, a daylight warning, had been considered after the September raids. The War Cabinet had then refused approval for fear that the cardboard shells would induce panic during hours of darkness.

The authorities now reluctantly decided to use the charges as a warning both day and night. But 'in deference to invalids, the aged, and the feeble', they were not to be fired after 11 P.M., unless the police had insufficient time to alert citizens with placards. The question of adequate shelters was not so easily resolved. The Government begged off by saying that air raid shelters were 'a matter for local authorities'.

Officials made one concession by extending military honours to civilians killed in the raids. Relatives were instructed to apply at the Horse Guards in London for the attendance of troops at funerals, and 'for the loan of a Union Jack to cover the coffin'. Applicants were reminded, however, that 'approval can be given only if troops are available locally, and if military exigencies permit'.[187]

The burial of a bombing victim could be quite an elaborate affair. In the case of a special constable killed on 18 December, the procession included a brass band. Leading it was a solemn, white-haired old man on whose uniform dangled the medals of other wars. Helmeted policemen lined the street. Grim and silent, a large throng gathered to watch the horse-drawn, flower-bedecked hearse go by on its way to the grave. Such pomp contrasted sharply with the assembly line internment accorded British soldiers in Flanders. But the killing of civilians still could not be accepted as incidental to the far greater tragedy of the Western Front, or as a justified act of war.

On Christmas Eve, the Royal Flying Corps made its first avowed reprisal raid on Germany. Ten aircraft droned over the misty Rhine valley to bomb Mannheim in daylight. A bridge over the Neckar was demolished, and fires were seen burning in the city. Four bombs crashed on the main railway station. A Swiss account of the mid-morning attack was read in London with considerable satisfaction and some regrets. The Kaiser's special train, it informed, had left the station only half an hour before the bombs struck.

Murlis-Green's air victory was the first since the start of the moonlight raids. However encouraging, the fact remained that nearly fifty British aeroplanes had been up on patrol that night. In Ashmore's words, 'a large number of pilots were risking their necks for pitifully small results'. Far from satisfied, he reorganized the defences toward the end of 1917.

Aircraft patrol lines were extended with the activation of two new Home Defence squadrons, 141 and 143. Fighters were to fly at 1,000-foot intervals between 11,000 and 8,000 feet, the upper height of the balloon aprons. A loaded Gotha was not expected to attack at a much higher altitude at night. When the British later learned differently, they turned to larger balloons to raise the barrage up to 10,000 feet.

In addition to the Sopwith Camel and the S.E.5, the defence squadrons were now receiving the Bristol Fighter, an aircraft flown by a two-man crew. The pilot and the observer-gunner sat so closely together, back-to-back, that the machine was often mistaken for a single-seater. But unlike other fighters, it had 'a sting in its tail as well as its nose'—one or two Lewis guns fired from the rear cockpit, and a Vickers fired through the propeller. A big but extremely manœuvrable aircraft, the 'Brisfit' could fly at 120 m.p.h. and reach 20,000 feet.

The introduction of the Neame gunsight increased the 'kill' probability of these latest types. The sight had an illuminated ring whose diameter was filled by a Gotha at a distance of 100 yards. Machine-guns were also equipped with a 'flash eliminator' to keep pilots from being blinded when firing in the dark. Sparklet or tracer ammunition was eventually discarded for the same reason.

The greatest stumbling-block to effective air defence remaining was the lack of a ground-to-air radiotelephone. The British were now making serious efforts to perfect airborne radio communications. But, as yet, the defence pilots received only one instruction after leaving the ground. Transmitted by blinking searchlights, that message was 'to come down at the end of a raid', a signal which 'seldom failed to be read'.

Ashmore further concluded that 'the organization on the ground was not keeping pace with progress in the air'. Searchlight crews were regrouped into companies, and those working with aircraft were placed under the control of air squadron commanders. Observer

179

posts, upon which the entire system depended for timely warning and the tracking of the bombers, were held to be too sluggish. Many of these posts had a direct line to a Warning Control centre where messages were sifted and relayed to the Horse Guards. Some relied on private telephones reserved for military use. Clearing the lines with the code word 'Airbandit', operators could report a hostile aircraft to headquarters in London within three minutes. But, more often, 'it took three or four times longer and the information was scrappy and unreliable'.[188]

Observer posts, for the most part, were still manned by soldiers physically unfit for duty overseas. Dulled by long periods of idleness, they lacked the 'quick and cool intelligence' the work required. Beginning in December, the police took over the posts except for those along the coast where a twenty-four-hour watch was maintained. The police observer posts were occupied only after a preliminary warning had been received.

Citing 'the peril to which London is exposed', one member of the House of Commons asked the Prime Minister if there was 'what might be called a thinking department whose duty it is intelligently to foresee the effects of German activities and to advise appropriate and adequate preparations. . . .' Assured that this indeed was being done, the M.P. retorted: 'If a thinking department exists, why does it never commence to think until after the event?'[189]

Aside from such political needling, the Government was beset by genuine apprehension that the enemy was out 'to terrorize us and break our resolution' with massive air attacks in 1918. The upshot was a flurry of studies and reports in January. The War Office estimated that raids of well over a hundred German bombers could be expected by early summer.

Lord French was asked if the L.A.D.A. could meet such an invasion with the forces available. South-east England was defended at the time by 224 fighters. About one-third of these were too old to be of much use against the Gothas and the Giants. London was further protected by 150 anti-aircraft guns. Another 100 pieces were assigned to Harwich, Chatham, Sheerness, Dover, and there were two mobile artillery brigades in Kent and Essex. The entire complex had 325 searchlights.

French demanded an additional forty fighters of the latest types, 100 guns, and 300 searchlights. A separate inquiry led to the approval of five underground hangars. After their construction began, it was decided that only two were to be completed. Nor were all the extra guns and aeroplanes delivered before the Armistice. Despite the fears of the British, the scale had already been turned against the raiders. Victory in the air over London would come much sooner than they dared hope that final dreary winter of the war.

The cold weather at least brought the blessing of Britain's famed fog. An impenetrable blanket, it often provided far better protection than that of the fighters and the barrage. Late in January, three Giants set out from Ghent only to be forced back by a dense mist over England. Three nights later, the Germans tried again.

The early evening of 28 January 1918 was crisp and clear. The moon was full and the sky vibrant with stars. Only a little later did a heavy haze rise along the English coast. Much the same conditions developed in Belgium. Many Gothas, already fuelled and loaded with bombs, were unable to take-off as the low-lying fog engulfed their aerodromes. Thirteen did get off, but six crews gave up the flight when they found that the mist persisted well over the sea. Those which flew on reached the coast shortly before eight o'clock. Almost simultaneously, one raider crossed into Kent and two came in over Essex.

Since much had been done to soothe public alarm over sudden attacks, the alert set off a wide variety of warning devices in London. Coloured lights atop high buildings and towers, and even street lights dimmed and flared ominously in some boroughs. One district resounded with the wail of two steam sirens which could be heard for five miles. And the controversial maroons, 'sounding like guns', were fired over a wide area. That night, the doubts of the authorities about using rockets after dark were tragically confirmed.

An expectant crowd had gathered outside the Bishopgate Goods Depot to be admitted for shelter. At the Olympia Music Hall, directly opposite, a long queue was waiting for the second performance. Then the maroons were fired. The jarring bangs were mistaken for falling bombs. Panic-stricken, the people surged towards the depot entrance. Before a railway policeman could open one of the double gates completely, they bolted through like cattle. One refugee tripped and was trampled underfoot. Shoved from behind, others stumbled and piled up at the entrance. Some were suffocated, and still more were crushed against the pillars and abutments of the station. 'A woman had a baby swept from her arms,' notes one account. 'She next saw it in the mortuary.'[190]

A similar tragedy occurred at a railway station in nearby Mile End. The stampedes ended in twenty-eight casualties, including fourteen dead. Twenty-five years later, and not far away from Bishopgate, the sirens sent some fifteen hundred Londoners pouring into the Underground station at Bethnal Green. As they cascaded down a darkened stairway, a woman carrying a child fell. Nearly two hundred died in that crush.

The first assault was carried out between 9 and 10 P.M. The bombers came in above 12,000 feet along both sides of the Thames, their paths crossing over the city. 'This had the effect of rendering "location by sound" extremely uncertain,' complained Rawlinson, the gun commander. 'Accurate identification became impossible' owing to the 'many contradictory reports from the same locality as to the direction of the flights of planes.'[191] A barrage of nearly 15,000 shells had no effect other than to injure eleven citizens and damage more than three hundred houses.

Nine bombers were believed to have reached the capital, but there were only three. Three others attacked Sheerness, Ramsgate, and Margate. One raider was intercepted over Essex by two Sopwith Camels from Hainault Farm. Repeatedly machine-gunned, the Gotha crashed in flames on a farm near Wickford. In London, the guns became quiet shortly after eleven o'clock. Believing the raid to be over, many people emerged from the Underground. Then, at about midnight, the barrage began to crackle again above the city. A single Giant, R.39, was approaching to renew the attack.

The huge R-bomber gave ample proof on this flight that it was a fearsome weapon in its day. A British pilot tried to overtake it on its way in over Essex. Bentivegni altered his course momentarily and lost his pursuer in the darkness. A short time later, a Bristol Fighter was soundly initiated into the perils of tangling with a German Giant. After a brief air battle, the 'Brisfit' was forced to land with a wounded observer, a bullet in its engine, and a punctured fuel tank. Still on course for the capital, the Staaken sideswiped a balloon apron over Chingford. Two of the steel streamers were torn away and never found, a feat which much astounded the British at the time.

Barely damaged, R.39 finally arrived over central London where it unloaded over 2,000 pounds of explosives. Weaving and turning, the bomber rode out the furious barrage and left the city unscathed. Bentivegni was challenged by still another fighter before reaching the coast. Manœuvring into 'a favourable position for attack', the pilot was unable to fire because of a jammed gun. R.39 passed out to sea over the Thames estuary and safely returned to its base.

During the first hour of that homeward journey Bentivegni could see the 'red glow' of a large fire burning in the heart of London. He attributed the blaze to a 660-pound bomb which had struck 'close to the Admiralty'. Actually falling in Long Acre, the bomb wreaked a havoc long remembered for its horror and what then seemed an appalling toll. The point of impact was a three-storey brick building housing the Odhams Printing Works. The structure, a sturdy one with concrete floors nine inches thick, had been designated as a public air-raid shelter. On this particular night upwards of five hundred people crowded the basement in refuge.

Missing the building itself by inches, the projectile plunged through a pavement grating. Its full explosive force was directed within, as it detonated below street level. The building was dangerously shaken on its foundations, but did not immediately collapse. Fire broke out in the large rolls of newsprint stored in the cellar. Finding one exit blocked, the terrified occupants ran about blindly in the basement. The police arrived quickly to evacuate a considerable number through another entrance. Before all could be rescued, an outer wall fell and the heavy printing presses came crashing down.

The task of extricating the survivors became a nightmare. Water being poured on the fire was rising rapidly. While some of the trapped victims faced death by smoke and flames, others were on the verge of drowning. Doctors stood by to amputate limbs, as a rescue party cut their way through the large rolls of paper with saws. Eighty-five persons were finally removed with severe injuries and grievous burns. Thirty-eight others were taken out dead.

Bentivegni's bomb was the deadliest to fall on London during the entire war. The overall casualties of the raid stood at 233, including sixty-seven deaths. Such losses had not been suffered since the daylight raids, a consequence of harsh fate and the huge bombs the Giants were now ferrying to England.

In early February, a broken figure of a man hobbled before the assembled crews of the England Squadron. Wearing an artificial leg, he tried to hold his broad frame as erect as he could with the help of a cane. The Kommodore, as he was remembered with affection, was back to command the squadron once more.

Brandenburg had pleaded with Hoeppner to be returned to Ghent after Kleine's death. He did not want to sit out the war as the decorated cripple who had led the first Gotha raid on London. Reluctant at first, Kogenluft finally agreed. Lame or not, Brandenburg was probably the only officer capable of breathing new life into the sagging Geschwader. Behind him were long months spent in hospitals, recovering from his near-fatal crash at Kreuznach. Feeling very much alive, he had even courted and married one of his nurses.

Brandenburg had been told of high losses among the crews, but he had hardly expected to return to a ghost squadron. Despite the steady flow of men and machines the six Staffeln were at little more than half-strength. On the last England raid alone, one Gotha had been shot down and four had crashed while trying to land in the fog. Delang's observer, Lieutenant Döge, was among the dead. Transferred to another crew after his previous crash with Delang, Döge was killed when his bomber rammed a row of trees while letting down near Oostakker.

The frequent raids on the French ports and at the front also added to the toll. And perverse luck continued to hound the squadron. The Geschwader prided itself on having three young counts among its officers. On 16 February, 'a sad day', all three titled airmen were killed in air accidents. One was the observer of a Gotha which plunged almost vertically into the ground shortly after take-off. The other two were aboard the same bomber. It exploded while attempting a night emergency landing. The leader of Staffel 14, Oberleutnant Count von Adelmann, died in that resounding crash.

Brandenburg did not have to lose three counts in one day to realize that the squadron was exhausted and deteriorating rapidly. Unlike Kleine, who would have kept up the raids down to the last crew, he proposed to halt all combat flights until late March. At least six weeks were needed to reorganize and re-equip the Geschwader. A listing of the machines, crews, and technicians required was attached to the report.

Kogenluft gave his approval with assurances of speedy replacements, and a new, faster bomber, the Gotha G.VIII. Heartened by the news, Brandenburg set to work planning even larger raids on London, much as he had done the year before. But it was now 1918. Lacking in neither courage nor ability, Brandenburg's real plight was having to serve a lost cause.

CHAPTER TWENTY

The Nights of the Giants

As if in prelude to the great German spring offensive of 1918, OHL ordered a show of strength in the air in late January. Captain Alfred Keller, a Luftwaffe general in World War II, bombed Paris with two squadrons. Over 250 people were killed or injured. The French capital had had no raid casualties since a Zeppelin attack two years before. Shuttled by train from Flanders, another German squadron was attacking Venice and other Italian cities of the Venetian plains.

The alarm over these simultaneous blows on London, Paris, and beyond the Alps was even heard in the United States. Admiral Robert E. Peary, the famed explorer, then heading the National Aerial Coast Patrol Commission, warned that 'our large cities near the coast may be subjected to the same death-dealing and destructive air raids'. He urged the appropriation of one billion dollars for air defence.[192]

Berlin explained that Paris was being bombed in reprisal for French attacks 'on open German towns'. The air campaign against England was called a 'systematic action'. The Germans candidly admitted that the destruction of military targets was secondary. The 'principal object' was to compel the British to maintain 'an enormous barred aerial zone' with forces which otherwise would be used at the front.[193] This diversion was an undeniable success. Until May, only half a dozen Staaken bombers and the Zeppelins were engaged against Britain.

The nights of the Giants began on 29 January, when Squadron 501 raided London without the Gothas for the first time. The sounds and flashes of aerial combat filled the skies over the south of England, as the British put up seventy-three opposing fighters. Mistaken for Gothas, the R-bombers baffled the defence pilots with their tremendous wing spans. A Giant, filling the diameter of the new Neame sight, was almost twice as far away as a Gotha. Thus misled, British airmen consistently fired at too long a range for their shots to have effect.

The heroic but futile effort of Captain A. Dennis of 37 Squadron was typical of many engagements. The pilot was patrolling out of Goldhanger aerodrome when he detected a Giant on course for London at 12,000 feet. He attacked repeatedly in the face of the bomber's blazing guns. Despite his steady firing, the raider cruised on closer to the capital. Over Hertford, the Germans turned south to skirt London's West End. His own aircraft riddled, Dennis kept up the chase well into the zone of barrage fire. Ground observers thrilled at the sight of the two aeroplanes 'visible at the same moment against the moon, the smaller pursuing the larger, quite double its size'.[194]

Probing the gun defences, the Giant made a few half-hearted attempts to turn in toward the centre of London. The blistering barrage was apparently too much for the crew. The bombs fell on Brentford, Kew, Isleworth, and Richmond, killing ten people and injuring ten more.

Another Giant was even less successful, but it too seemed impervious to fighter attacks. Four British aeroplanes set upon it soon after it came in over Essex. The fighters followed it inland, harassing it almost continuously with their fire. Thoroughly shaken, the Germans swerved away from London on the northern outskirts, not far from Tottenham. Minutes later, the Giant unceremoniously dumped its 2,200-pound load of explosives. The bombs all struck within an area of 300 yards in an open field at Wanstead. Still pursued, the raider slowly headed back for the coast. Its besieged crew seemed convinced that they would not escape the sniping fighter attacks. Flying very low, the Giant was apparently seeking a place to land when it finally reached Eastchurch on the Essex shore, and 'disappeared in the darkness over the sea'.

The outer barrage sufficed to prevent another R-bomber from going any farther than Billericay, some twenty miles north-east of London. The German commander claimed to have bombed Southend effectively on the way out. The explosives actually fell on some villages miles away, and even in the sea off the Blackwater. Three houses and a farm building were damaged. A fourth Giant never reached England. Shortly after taking off, it developed engine trouble and returned to its base.

The British, believing that the attack had been made by fifteen bombers, hailed the night's work as a notable victory. Though determined pilots and the popping barrage had kept the raiders away from central London, none of the Giants had been shot down. Had their crews been more experienced, the city could have had a bad raid. As it was, the capital was quite safe throughout the three-hour foray. But to the average citizen, who heard the warnings and the thunderous barrage, the attack was as unnerving as any other.

'What an ordeal we are living through,' an Englishwoman wrote to a friend in America, 'in dread and expectations of air raids, in spite of knowing how wonderfully London is being defended! Do not worry about it; there is no panic here. . . . The one thing we hope for is a cloudy, stormy night when we go to bed, and when we get up we are grateful to be able to say, "Well, we're safe for another day!" '[195]

The British are often credited with dropping the largest bomb in World War I, one of 1,650 pounds, but that dubious honour easily belongs to the Germans. Their biggest, truly a monster by the standards of that war, weighed one metric ton (2,204·6 pounds) and measured thirteen feet in length. R.39 delivered the first such projectile to London on the night of 16 February, as part of a five-plane assault.

Carrying only that one bomb, the Giant droned over the capital at about 10 P.M. Bentivegni evidently aimed it at Victoria Station, but his one-shot load tumbled more than half a mile away into the grounds of the Royal Hospital at Chelsea. The residence of a hospital staff officer in the North Pavilion was blown sky-high. Five members of the family were killed; three children were miraculously found alive in the wreckage. Chelsea Barracks and several other buildings in the area were damaged.

A second Giant, R.12, roared up the Thames a short time later. East of Woolwich, the bomber made a sudden vertical detour when it flew straight into a balloon apron. Violently swatted, the Staaken lurched from side to side before 'sideslipping out of control' in a thousand-foot plunge. 'The first pilot, Lt. Götte, immediately throttled-down all engines, then opened up the throttles on only one side, whereby the aircraft regained equilibrium,' reported Seydlitz-Gerstenberg, the crew commander. One of the mechanics riding in the engine nacelles was thrown against 'the glowing exhaust stacks' and 'severely burned his hands'. The ponderous aircraft slipped under the cables with only 'minor damage to the leading edge of the starboard wing, propeller, and mid-fuselage section'.[196]

R.12 fluttered on to attack Woolwich with two 660-pound bombs. Barracks and the garrison church were hit with a loss of seven dead. The crew also claimed to have dropped smaller missiles near the Crystal Palace, then being used as a naval training centre. The explosives fell in nearby Beckenham, tearing up a park and some garden plots without causing human injury.

The raid petered out before midnight when the other three Giants failed to penetrate inland. Sixty British aeroplanes patrolled the skies between London and the coast, and saw nothing. But the British triumphed in an imaginative communiqué: 'Several of our pilots engaged the enemy. One of them fought an action over the Kent coast, and shortly afterward a large enemy machine was seen from the shore to crash into the sea.'[197]

Although all five Giants returned safely, one very nearly was lost that night. With three of their four engines dead, the crew of R.33 struggled desperately to keep their bomber in the air. Reaching the Belgian coast well under a thousand feet, the Giant landed without mishap at an emergency field. Bentivegni's airmen were evidently better at flying than they were at dropping bombs. But on the very next night, 17 February, the crew of R.25, commanded by Lieutenant Max Borchers, proved itself adept at both.

Attacking alone, the Giant reached London unmolested and passed through the gun defences from the south-east. Once beyond the zone of heavy fire, the Germans found the skies relatively free of flak. They could easily see the layout of the city. Thus favoured, the Staaken unhurriedly put on 'an exhibition of well-aimed bombing'. Borchers first released two trial bombs on the southern edge of the capital. These were followed by ten 110-pound bombs, all individually sighted at 'prominent objects' in the boroughs south of the Thames. One missile exploded on a lawn outside a sandbagged church at Hither Green in which nearly 200 people were sheltering. Another crashed through five stories of a building occupied by the Cambridge University Press without exploding.

A final salvo of six 110-pound bombs fell on and around St. Pancras Station. Booking offices, stores, and the first-class waiting room were wrecked. The stately Midland Hotel next door was damaged. A station archway sustained a direct hit. The concussion took a heavy toll among a group of people huddled underneath. One eyewitness recalled 'that the lanterns of the ambulance men, seeking in the dark for dead and injured, made a weird, unforgettable picture'.[198] Fifty-three Londoners were gathered up, twenty-one of whom were beyond all medical help.

Its work finished, R.25 recrossed the Thames. The barrage became lively as searchlights lit up the massive, slow-moving bomber. The fiery tracks across the sky were somewhat less frightening inside the enclosed cabin. Interior lights glowed softly behind their dark blue covers. Black curtains shaded the square glass panels further to reduce the glare. But for the gunner-mechanics in their small open cockpits between the wings, the flight over London was like looking down into the pits of hell from a box seat. Bracketing bursts splattered the Staaken with shell fragments. The propeller of the rear port engine was shattered, and it had to be stopped. Still the bomber flew on, sustained by the serene good fortune which never deserted the Giants over England.

R.25 evaded all but one of the sixty-nine British aeroplanes out hunting for what was believed to be at least half a dozen raiders. The fighter pilot, much excited at the sight of the flying monster, opened fire at close range. He swerved to avoid a collision, as the flashes of his gun blotted out the awesome outline. Before he could see clearly again, the Giant had disappeared like a phantom.

'An attack by a single R-plane is sufficient to alert the entire British defence system, and to cause the expenditure of vast quantities of ammunition,' Borchers gloated in his report. 'Seemingly from nervousness,' guns were observed to 'fire blindly into the air' as far away as twenty miles from the Giant's path.[199]

The British were suffering from a bad case of raid jitters. The following evening, 18 February, the Horse Guards was alerted that 'hostile aircraft crossed the coast shortly after 9 P.M. and headed for London'. Over fifty fighters searched the skies. The guns went again into action, some firing steadily for two hours. The Germans bombed Calais that night, but not England. Excitable observers had triggered off the phoney raid when the raiders flew within hearing distance of the Kent coast. Referring to the episode as 'something of a mystery night', the official British history commented that 'these alarms and excursions reveal how sensitive the nerves of the public, and some of these responsible for the protection of the public, had become'.[200]

Nearly three weeks passed before the Giants returned on 7 March. Except for Bentivegni's ambition to make a name for himself, it is hard to understand why he should have chosen that particular night for a raid. Squadron 501 had moved from Gontrode to its newly completed aerodrome at Scheldewindeke that same day. The hangars were not yet ready. Even under settled conditions, preparing the big Staakens for a flight was a difficult job. Each aircraft required a ground crew of forty men. The sky was moonless, swept by high winds, and it was bitterly cold. Yet, all six Giants were ordered to attack London for the first time. The bombers took off at ten-minute intervals beginning at 10 P.M.

'We approach the coast; the night is so dark that the coastline below is but a mere suggestion,' writes Captain Arthur Schoeller, the commander of R.27. 'Under us is a black abyss, no waves are seen, no lights of surface vessels flicker as we head for the Thames estuary at Margate. On our right, in the distant north, is our only light, the weak pulsating glow of the aurora borealis. . . . We have neither a weather report from the high seas, nor wind measurements to go by.'

R.27 climbed above 'continually thickening clouds'. Schoeller searched in vain for some glimmering light, some landmark, confirming that he was on course for London. 'Suddenly,' he continues, 'a breath of relief. Directly ahead the searchlights illuminate the sky. . . . Now we are certainly over England, but where? Because all surface lights are blacked out, it appears as if we are soaring over a dead land. But the enemy has heard us, therefore we are free to request wireless bearings. The operator sends a pre-arranged signal. . . . In a few minutes we receive a message giving our location at the time the signal was flashed. We are south-east of London.'[201]

Spotting a lighted airfield, Oberleutnant Günther Kamps dropped four bombs 'in return for the attacks on our aerodromes'. He reserved the rest for his assigned target, the docks along the Thames. The 'grey band' of the river appeared through a break in the clouds. The bombs fell in Battersea and beyond the river. Bentivegni aboard R.39 had already released a one-ton projectile over London. Another Giant arrived to blast the north-west suburbs, but the capital escaped the wrath of the other three raiders. One bomber strayed far to the north over Hertfordshire. Most of its explosives, and those of another which turned back in the face of the outer gun barrage, spent themselves in open fields. A sixth Staaken never reached England because of engine trouble. The attack killed twenty-three persons and injured thirty-nine. The only casualties in the air were also British. Two Royal Flying Corps captains died when their Sopwith Camels collided in the dark sky.

Bad luck awaited the Germans over Belgium where two of the Giants crash-landed. One of them was Schoeller's R.27. The Staaken, its fuel lines frozen owing to water-contaminated petrol, glided in from the sea close to the battle front with four dead engines. The Germans saw nothing but 'trenches and hollows', as they dropped flares for an emergency landing. Schoeller realized that the descent 'will end in a crash. . . . By pulling sharply on the controls, I stall the aircraft, letting it fall almost vertically. . . . The right landing gear collapses and the right wing shatters, but no crew member is injured'.[202] The airmen stumbled onto the command bunker of a German brigade, and notified their squadron. R.27 was later destroyed by Allied shellfire, but not before its engines and instruments had been salvaged.

As Schoeller and his crew were being comforted by their infantry comrades, the grim task of bringing aid and relief to the victims of the bombing was going on in London. Rescuers were still digging at dawn, and the work continued long into the day. Given up for dead, one man was brought out at midday with only a few scratches to show for his ordeal. A young woman was kept alive for five hours only to die as she was being freed. Many of those extricated had taken their pets with them down into the basements. One woman, whose life was saved by a heavy beam, emerged with her canary alive in its cage.

Warrington Crescent, Paddington, where Bentivegni's big bomb had struck, was the scene of all the horrors any blitz could bring to London. The street, one of fading Victorian elegance with its four-storey brick homes, was devastated. Possibly intended for Paddington Station, the huge bomb fell squarely on No. 67, and crashed through two floors before detonating. The house was pulverized; several others in the 'explosion funnel' collapsed. The top-floor occupant of one of these homes was playing the piano at the time.

He was killed when the walls were blown in and the floor gave way, plunging him down into the cellar. The sections of some houses were strangely left intact, as if struck by a freakish tornado. Picture frames could be seen hanging undisturbed in some of the exposed interior rooms. The street itself was heaped with masonry and broken furniture.

This demonstration of what a single bomb could do made a deep and lasting impression. The ravaged neighbourhood attracted 'great crowds from all parts of England'. Escorted by Lord French, the King and Queen and other high dignitaries came to extend their condolences and praise the 'heroic behaviour' of the survivors.

Lena Ford, an American widely known as the author of the words of 'Keep the Home Fires Burning', that popular English war song for which Ivor Novello wrote the music, was among the dead. Her body, and that of her son, were not found until four days later. The deaths, attributed 'to suffocation from the collapse of a house caused by explosion of bombs', led to some legal complications. A divorcée, Mrs Ford had left all her property to her late son. He, in turn, had willed his estate to his father. A court ruled that the husband was not entitled to anything unless it could be proven that Mrs Ford had died first. He lost his case when a physician testified that the son, judging from the density of the debris about his face and body, had expired before his mother.

The attack was particularly disconcerting because it was the first carried out by aeroplanes without a moon. Air raids, officials warned, could now be expected at any time of the month. They assumed that the raiders no longer required moonlight to guide them to England, but this was only true of the radio-equipped Staakens and the Zeppelins.

Five of the German Navy's newest airships attempted to bomb the English Midlands on the drizzly night of 12 March. Foiled by low clouds and erroneous radio bearings, the crews dropped most of their bombs over the sea or open country. A few houses were damaged in Hull where a woman, the only casualty, died of shock.

Three Zeppelins set out for England the following afternoon. Over the North Sea, they were recalled to their bases in north Germany because of high winds. Already within sight of the English coast, one airship commander defied the order. He waited offshore for forty minutes for complete darkness, and then attacked West

Hartlepool from above 16,000 feet. The unsuspecting town was brightly lighted. Many bombs found their mark, and nearly fifty people were killed or injured.

The England Squadron, revitalized by Brandenburg, was ready to resume the raids on London in mid-March, but OHL had more important plans. A gigantic offensive calculated to crush the Allies before effective American help could reach them was unleashed on 21 March. All available air squadrons were ordered to support the German advance. During a one-week period beginning on 20 March, the Gothas bombed Calais, Dunkirk, and Boulogne almost nightly.

The German armies exhausted themselves short of Amiens before the end of the month. OHL followed up with a body blow against Haig in Flanders in early April. The desperate drive to capture the Channel ports began. The Gothas and the Giants again took to the air to raid troop camps, ammunition dumps, and railways behind the British front. Only the Zeppelins could be spared for the raids on England.

On the night of 12 April five airships attacked in adverse weather. Three did not penetrate much beyond the coast, but the other two roamed blindly over a wide area. Explosives fell as far west as Wigan. Attracted there by the glow of 'blast furnaces', the airship commander mistook the well-lit town for Sheffield. The inhabitants had no warning until the bombs struck a suburb. Another Zeppelin ineffectively bombed the Birmingham area. Only one British aeroplane engaged the raider during its six-hour foray over the country. The fighter pilot was wounded in a brief duel, and forced down at Coventry.

Although the casualties (7 killed, 20 injured) and the damage were slight, this latest incursion revived British fears of the Zeppelin. Carrying a lethal load of three tons, the newer types could attack beyond the reach of the defences. A new combined command, the 'North Air Defences', was organized under Brigadier-General P. Maud for the protection of northern England.

The threat of the Giants was dramatically lessened on the night of 9 May, one of disaster for Squadron 501. That the England Squadron was spared a similar blow was largely due to Georgii's persuasiveness and experience as a meteorologist.

'Ii,' Brandenburg called out as the lieutenant walked into his office that afternoon, 'we shall fly tonight.'

The weather officer was a little surprised. The Gothas had bombed Dunkirk and Calais the night before. There had been no hint of another flight that evening. Brandenburg explained that the Giants were preparing for a raid on England. He would be a 'yellow dog' not to send his own bombers out with them. Georgii replied that he would be a 'dog' too, if he did not advise against the attack. A heavy fog was expected over England. Brandenburg finally agreed to keep the squadron grounded, adding that he would urge Bentivegni not to make the raid.[94]

Four Giants set out all the same to bomb Dover before the weather closed in. Soon after they left, German weather stations reported worsening conditions over the Channel. The crews were radioed to change course and bomb alternative targets on the French coast. Some time later the bombers were recalled altogether. A ground fog was now developing at Scheldewindeke. The crews would be unable to land unless they turned back at once.

Two Staakens, R.32 and R.39, had already bombed Dunkirk when this last order went out. The aircraft were the first to return to base. A terse, but unclear message was transmitted to them as they circled overhead: 'Cloud height 100 metres Brussels clear visibility.' The commanders of both aeroplanes nonetheless decided to attempt a landing at Scheldewindeke. The Giants had been aloft three hours, and the time was 1 A.M.

R.32, guided by searchlights visible through the fog as 'washed out circles of light', made several approaches. Each time, the pilot lost his bearings and he was forced to circle back again. After one final pass over the field, the Giant struck some trees and ploughed into a meadow half a mile away. An unreleased bomb exploded. Badly injured, one airman came stumbling out of the fog to inform the landing party that nearly all on board had been killed.

Bentivegni and the crew of R.39 owed their lives that night to Freiherr von Lenz, the first pilot. He knew exactly how the aerodrome was laid out with reference to the beacons. Dropping down out of the fog, the bomber made a perfect descent between the glowing lights at the edge of the field. The huge aeroplane rolled the length of the landing strip, and stopped only inches away from a ditch.

R.26 and R.29 had gone on to bomb Calais after the recall order because the target was not far away. By the time they arrived over

Scheldewindeke, the fog was too thick to permit them to come in. 'Landing impossible, clouds 100 metres high Ghistelles clear for landing,' beamed the base urgently. But the Giants continued to circle over the field. Twenty minutes later, another message ordered: 'Land at Ghistelles otherwise use parachute.'[203]

Ignoring both instructions, the crews chose to make a blind let-down at Scheldewindeke. R.26 flew straight into the ground and burst into flames. All were killed except for a mechanic. Seeking to avoid a similar fate, R.29 turned on its landing lights and went into a glide approach. Off course, the pilot spotted some tree tops straight ahead as he broke through the mist. He instantly gave the engines full throttle, but it was too late. A landing gear snagged the upper limbs, sending the mammoth machine careering through the trees. The wings crumpled and the fuel tanks burst. The quick-thinking pilot averted a fire by cutting off the ignition. Damaged beyond repair, the aircraft was later dismantled.

Bentivegni had the names of the places he raided painted on the nose of R.39. The notation for 9 May 1918 was 'Dover'. Embittered by the loss of their comrades, the surviving crews blamed the reck-lessness of their decoration-seeking commander for the fiasco. Much as he strove for the honour, Bentivegni was never awarded the Pour le Mérite. The Giants were neither first over London, nor did they ever succeed in striking some spectacular blow.

Major von Bülow concluded in his analysis of the raids that their development was a mistake: 'Although the R-bombers dropped a total of 27,190 kg. [60,000 lbs.] of bombs on England, this amount was not in proportion to the immense effort which went into their construction, and the vast apparatus required for the maintenance and servicing of these machines.'[127]

However disappointing the Giants may have been to the Germans, one can only marvel that they should have been used at all during the First World War. The London air defences never brought one down. And, except for the Zeppelins, nothing of larger dimensions has ever flown in anger over England.

CHAPTER TWENTY-ONE

Khaki and Blue: An Air Force is Born

The Giant bomber first came to official British attention just at the time the Smuts report on a separate air force was about to be shelved. The scorn Trenchard had shown for this 'planner's pipe dream' while in London in early October 1917 had not been without effect on the War Cabinet. Only Smuts kept pressing for action. On 5 October he again asked the Cabinet if a decision had been reached. Reluctant to precipitate a political crisis, Lloyd George replied that the time was 'not ripe' for any 'premature disclosure'.

Five days later Lord Cowdray of the Air Board revealed, in 'strictest confidence', that the proposed Air Ministry had been virtually ruled out. His confidant was Mark Kerr, a keen air-minded admiral of long experience. Becoming interested in aeroplanes as a counter-weapon to the submarine, he had qualified as a pilot in 1914. Flying, Kerr found, gave one the feeling of having had 'an extra glass of champagne'.

Cowdray's confidential remark really set the spirited admiral bubbling. A recent Admiralty addition to the Air Board, he had strongly disputed Haig's objections to raiding the German homeland. He ardently believed that 'whichever side got in first with their big bombers would win the war'. Disturbed over 'the extraordinary danger of delay', Kerr prepared a memorandum which became known among Air Board members as 'the Bomb Shell'.

The Germans, Kerr wrote, had a fearsome new bomber 'actually ready for use'. The aircraft, of which 'photographs had been taken,' was said to have six engines and to 'carry up to five tons of explosives'. Disclaiming any 'exaggeration in this', the admiral warned that 'Woolwich, Chatham, and all the factories in the London district will be laid flat, part of London wiped out, and workshops in the south-east of England will be destroyed'. He further indicated on the basis of Italian reports that 'the Germans are building 4,000 big bombing machines'. To beat them to the punch, Kerr urged the 'building of 2,000 big machines as a minimum. . . . To supply all this the Air must have a Ministry with executive power, and also priority of output for a while. . . .'[204]

The memorandum was addressed to the President of the Air Board. On receiving it, Cowdray immediately ordered his car and rushed off to see the Prime Minister. Within an hour he was back at the Hotel Cecil. 'Lloyd George read your memo,' Kerr quotes him as saying, 'and it is the first time I have ever seen him "with the wind up".'[204]

Hastily printed and distributed, the dire estimate received the speedy attention of the full War Cabinet. 'There was a great sending for Secret Service people and others to find out if the information . . . was correct,' Kerr recalled. He evidently was not disproven. On 16 October, Bonar Law informed the House of Commons that the Government had definitely decided to organize an Air Ministry.

The Air Force Bill, 'a landmark not only in the history of aviation, but in that of the Armed Forces of the Crown', was introduced in Parliament early in November. Pemberton-Billing, long a crusader for an 'Imperial Air Service', provided the only notable opposition. He derided the bill as 'merely a blind to keep the people quiet'. Objecting to 'Force', Pemberton-Billing insisted that 'Service' was 'infinitely better' because the 'aeroplane, even as it is today—the most punitive weapon ever placed in the hands of mankind—may eventually render war so horrible as to result in its abolition altogether'.[205]

William Joynson-Hicks (later Lord Brentford) 'thankfully welcomed' the bill. He reminded the House that he had for years 'pressed most strenuously for an independent strategic striking force in the air'. He had indeed. 'Jix' began preaching on 'the possibilities of aerial warfare' in 1912 with the publication of a tract on 'the Command of the Air'. Early in the war he had asked for 'continuous raids of some four or five hundred aeroplanes dropping bombs on the Rhine bridges and the giant Krupp factory at Essen'.[206] Now speaking with a sense of vindication, Joynson-Hicks observed that 'the rival armies have had three and a half years with guns and shells, trying to beat one another. . . . Many of us who have been called fanatics have felt that there is a chance of the war being decided in the air'.[205]

The debate brought out many points not otherwise clearly specified in the bill. More than a 'war measure', the Air Force it created
was to continue in 'time of peace'. The transfer of the existing air
services was to be 'complete and absolute'. The Bill easily passed
both Houses, and the royal assent needed to make it law was
given on 29 November 1917.

Britain, recognizing that 'supremacy in the air is as essential to
our national existence as supremacy at sea', thus became the first
nation to have an autonomous Air Force. The swiftness of this
unprecedented step is best illustrated by comparing it to the
American experience. The United States did not see fit to organize
a distinct and fully-fledged Air Force until thirty years and one
world war later.

The British, a proud people, are more prone to credit their foresight than their fears for the birth of the Royal Air Force. James M.
Spaight, a formidable authority on the subject, wrote a decade later
that Britain's 'claim to be regarded as the founder of air power
cannot be questioned, it has titles manifold'.[207]

Early in World War II, C. G. Grey also published a history of the
Air Ministry. He traced its origins to the 1916 'murder charge'
Pemberton-Billing had made about inferior British aeroplanes at the
front, 'which brought about the appointment of the Air Enquiry
Committee, which in turn produced the Air Board, which again
produced the Air Ministry'.[208] No mention was made of Smuts, or
his recommendations inspired by the Gothas over London.

Grey evidently forgot that he had pointed to 'the writing on the
walls of Folkestone and the City of London' in June 1917. 'Captain
Brandenburg,' he had written then with unabashed admiration,
'deserves some signal mark of recognition from this country for
convincing so many thousands of people that an aerial invasion of
enemy territory must be an important part of our war policy in this
or any future war. . . .'

Grey had even suggested replacing 'those idiotic Landseer Lions
from Nelson's pillar' in Trafalgar Square with the statues of four
notable Germans. One was the Kaiser, 'who found our Imperial
soul for us'. Another was Hindenburg, 'who forced us to raise an
an Army worthy of our position in the world'. A third was Count
von Zeppelin, 'who awoke us to the need for an Air Fleet'. And,
lastly, Brandenburg, 'who showed us how it should be used'.[209]

Kerr certainly felt that some similar honour was due to him for having stirred up the Cabinet. Cowdray fully expected that he would become the first Air Minister, as did everyone else. A first-rate organizer, he had done a prodigious job in speeding up aircraft production. But all he got was the back of Lloyd George's hand. Unbeknown to Cowdray, the Prime Minister offered the post to the whimsical Northcliffe over a quiet lunch at 10 Downing Street. The press lord had long been a booster of aeronautics; but it was really his sway over the public mind which made him preferable politically.

Lloyd George's 'repeated invitations' were rejected the next day, not in a personal communication, but in the pages of Northcliffe's leading newspaper, *The Times*. Denouncing the Prime Minister's Government as 'quite unworthy of the people of Britain', Northcliffe informed Lloyd George in an open letter that he did not want to be 'gagged by a loyalty I do not feel towards the whole of your administration'.[210]

Cowdray promptly sent in his resignation as President of the Air Board. Wanting his own letter published, he had to write a second draft because the first one was 'unprintable'. Lloyd George, bemoaning Northcliffe's 'passion for the startling gesture', asked Cowdray to stay on for the time being. He refused rather than 'weaken my protest'.

The Prime Minister's turnabout to Northcliffe's public taunts amazed everyone. He next offered the Air Ministry to his detractor's younger brother, Lord Rothermere. A well-fed man with a walrus moustache, Rothermere made his home in London's finest hotels, periodically moving from one to another. A better administrator than his brother, he too owned a chain of newspapers. At the time he was in charge of the Army's clothing supplies.

Rothermere asked that Trenchard be made the Chief of the Air Staff. Smuts had already arranged that Henderson should be appointed, at least for the first six months. Haig was on record as saying: 'I cannot spare Trenchard.' But Lloyd George backed his minister, and Trenchard was summarily recalled in mid-December for an interview. This time, he made the trip by destroyer.

The general arrived at Rothermere's private suite at the Ritz in Piccadilly at three o'clock in the afternoon. The hearty welcome he received failed to soften his hostility to the idea of a separate Air Force, or the job of heading it. He flatly refused, in fact, when the conversation turned to an attack on Haig and his strategy. Trenchard had no intention of fighting 'the Army and Navy during the war'.

The two men were also at odds on the 'big aerial offensive' that was being planned against Germany. Rothermere had strong views on the matter of 'air reprisals'. He insisted that they should be carried out 'on a scale which, in point of thoroughness and terror, had not hitherto been dreamed of'. For 'every raid on London' he intended to 'absolutely wipe out one or two large German towns. . . .' Rothermere anticipated retaliation raids of '100 to 150 aeroplanes and carrying bombs enough to lay the place attacked level with the ground in the course of a few hours'.[211]

Trenchard had no qualms about bombing anybody, but he was frankly sceptical about the means for such raids. He reminded Northcliffe, who was also present, 'that it was easier to bomb Berlin in headlines than from the cockpit of any machine likely to be constructed for years'. The exchange became 'hotter and more unpleasant' as it dragged on late into the night and the early morning hours. Trenchard, feeling exhausted, finally agreed to become Chief of the Air Staff. He did so to 'head off' Rothermere, believing strongly that 'the expansion of the air service' should not 'jeopardise the whole of the Western Front'.[212]

Returning to France, the perplexed general consulted with his Commander-in-Chief. According to Haig, Trenchard 'stated that the Air Board are quite off their heads as to the future possibilities of aeronautics for ending the war'.[213] Haig's own concern was to keep Trenchard in command at the front. He appealed to Lord Derby to have the air general serve in a dual capacity, because 'the coming four months will probably be the most critical of the whole war in France'. Derby concurred, as did Rothermere, but the War Cabinet turned down the double appointment in January.

Trenchard was a fighter who based his battle creed on 'the will and power to attack the enemy, to force him to fight and defeat him'. His return home was a definite bonus to the Germans in their air diversion campaign against England. As for the work of unifying the air services, no combination could have been more incongruous than that of this brusque, wilful general with the civilian novice who was not above political intrigue. 'Don't forget,' Trenchard had warned Rothermere, 'I'm not the man you think I am.'

The first Air Council was established on 2 January 1918. In

addition to Rothermere and Trenchard, Kerr was named as Deputy
Chief of the Air Staff. A place was found for Henderson as 'additional Member and Vice-President'. The Hotel Cecil, long the
object of public wrath, depending on the frequency of the air raids,
hardly seemed suitable for the new body. When it was announced
that the British Museum would be requisitioned to house the Air
Ministry, the cry of 'vandalism' was heard from the press and 'the
learned section of the community'. The Germans, it was feared,
would bomb the 'sacred edifice', if it were so used. The Museum
had the largest roof in London. The Government backed down, and
the Air Ministry remained at the 'aesthetically damned' hotel
through 1918.

Various departments of the Ministry had to be organized prior
to the actual unification of the two air services. The Royal Naval
Air Service, often treated as a stepchild after Churchill left the
Admiralty, was happy enough to break away from the Navy. But
the *esprit de corps* Trenchard had infused into the Army's air arm
died hard. 'Practically every soul in the R.F.C. is against the combination Air Force,' reported C. G. Grey. 'Officers and men alike
are proud to belong to the British Army. . . . They have no desire to
be pushed into an aerial wilderness. . . .'[214] The pilots of one Home
Defence Squadron protested that they did not want any 'bell-
bottomed buggers' sent to their unit.

For the Army airmen the crowning insult was the new service
uniform—'The final prostitution of the Royal Flying Corps to the
amorous advances of the sailor!'[215] The original dress was a pale
blue with stripes of gold lace, and an elaborate cap device with a
spray of gold leaves which was likened to 'a bunch of bananas'. Since
the old uniforms could still be worn, many rejected the ridiculed
garb. The men of the early R.A.F. were a motley sight, sometimes
wearing khaki and sometimes blue, and even khaki with naval rank
stripes.

The date on which the Royal Air Force officially came into being,
1 April 1918, struck some as 'perversely chosen'. To Trenchard, it
seemed appropriate enough that 'the child of Smuts' should be born
on All Fools' Day. Only Rothermere's cajoling had kept him on as
Chief of the Air Staff. Trenchard, who had once advised Henderson
that 'you cannot resign in war', had done just that twelve days before
the ceremonial occasion.

'I was filled with profound anxiety,' Rothermere wrote the general after the fusion, 'lest your resignation might become public and rumour with its thousand tongues might allege you had resigned to protest against some policy of mine which would be disastrous to the interests of the 25,000 officers and 140,000 men who were just going to become the Royal Air Force. . . .'[216]

As early as January, when Trenchard made a visit to France, Haig noted that his former R.F.C. commander 'thinks that the Air Service cannot last as an independent Ministry, and that Air Units must again return to the Army and Navy. . . .'[217] The Chief of the Air Staff's obvious lack of enthusiasm rankled Rothermere from the beginning, and they were soon bickering over the smallest triviality. The Air Minister, on receiving a letter from some citizen stating he had heard an aeroplane fly loudly over his house during an air raid, passed it on for comment. Trenchard replied that 'it was no more easy to hear than to smell a particular type of aeroplane'. Rothermere, in turn, peevishly informed the Chief of the Air Staff that 'the matter was referred to the Home Defence Authorities, who stated that it was quite easy to detect by hearing certain types of aeroplanes. A certain number of young practical airmen were asked, who returned exactly the same reply. . . .'[218]

The Air Minister's practice of consulting flying officers home on leave, often junior in rank, infuriated Trenchard. He insisted on being 'the only adviser . . . on the carrying out of aerial operations'. Rothermere, very much mindful of his ministerial prerogatives, rebutted that 'You . . . are my principal, not necessarily my sole adviser. . . .'[219]

The conflict 'as to the proper use of air-power' was more significant in bringing about a break. 'I should be the recipient—at not infrequent intervals—of all kinds of plans for the employment of aeroplanes, strategically and otherwise. These I am hoping to receive,' Rothermere prodded his Chief of the Air Staff.[220]

'In getting rid of Trenchard I flatter myself . . .' Rothermere further unburdened himself to Bonar Law after it was all over. 'With his dull unimaginative mind and his attitude of "Je sais tout" he would within twelve months have brought death and damnation to the Air Force. As it was, he was insisting on the ordering of large numbers of machines for out-of-date purposes.'[221]

Lloyd George, concerned over the possible repercussions of the

feud, had asked Smuts to investigate. The South African predictably ruled against Trenchard, and his standing resignation was
accepted. Major-General Frederick H. Sykes became Chief of the
Air Staff. Twice passed over, Henderson was greatly upset at having
to serve under Sykes, once a subordinate he had come to dislike.
Unwilling to become 'a focus of discontent and opposition', Henderson chose to sever his last tie with the air arm he had organized in
1912. Kerr was already out as Deputy Chief, having run foul of
Trenchard 'on matters of strategy'.

The turmoil over the sudden departure of Trenchard, 'already
then a legend and an inspiration', first broke out in the press.
Rothermere, in 'great terror of newspaper criticism', issued a long
statement of explanation. When the debate reached the House of
Commons, he added his own resignation to the list on 25 April. The
Air Minister was on the edge of nervous collapse, a condition
aggravated by the recent loss of a son, the second to be killed in the
war.

Encouraged by Rothermere's downfall, Trenchard's supporters in
Parliament began to agitate for his return to the Air Ministry. The
move was skilfully blocked by Lloyd George. He agreed that
Trenchard had qualities 'of the Nelson type', but that his services
should be used 'where they can be of more advantage to the air
force'. Haig came through with the command of an infantry brigade,
an offer which the unemployed general was quite willing to accept.

No matter how troubled the waters, the force of Trenchard's
personality was such that he came bobbing to the surface like a cork.
Lloyd George instructed the new Air Minister, Sir William Weir
(later Lord Weir of Eastwood), to find him another job. Thanks to
Weir's own plans to hit back at the Germans in a big way, the
remarkable Trenchard would soon have another chance to become
'the patron saint of modern air power', so canonized by General
Carl Spaatz, an American admirer.

End of a Round

... to the German air forces, to the air forces that came into existence during the war, that grew and increased to an enormous power, that to the last day did their work, far away in the countries of the enemy, unvanquished, feared and admired ... a threatening cloud, a sharp eye and a sure shield on every frontier, to the air forces that once upon a time existed but are no more.... Still ... the tap-root is still alive and the day is bound to come, when the tree will grow again.... That will be the time when the German air fleet reawakens to the honour and the protection of the entire German people.

General Ernst von Hoeppner (1921)

CHAPTER TWENTY-TWO

The Biggest Raid—and the Last

The uproar over Trenchard's departure from the Air Ministry was heightened by the coinciding crisis at the front. His resignation was made public on 15 April, the same day that Haig's famous last ditch order was published: 'With our backs to the wall . . . each one of us must fight to the end.' If there was ever a time when the British spirit could have been broken, it was in April 1918, the very month that neither the Giants nor the Gothas ventured over England.

Some of the 'mistakes made by the German High Command' are suggested in the official British air history of the war: 'The Germans . . . should have accumulated their bombing forces and prepared, with the same acumen as they gave their other preparations, for a campaign against England timed to exert its maximum effort when it would best help the military offensive in France.' An aerial onslaught against London at this time 'might have had results leading to a popular clamour which the Government might have found themselves unable to withstand'.[222]

OHL, while willing to experiment with strategic bombing, did not differ greatly from Haig and Trenchard in its views of air-power. The first task of the German bombing squadrons was to support the Army at the front. That much had been decided with the disapproval of Kleine's plans for large-scale raids on Britain in the autumn of 1917. Only one concession was made to the England Squadron's dual role after that. When, at the end of 1917, the six-flight Kagohls were reorganized for greater mobility into three-flight Bogohls (Bombengeschwader OHL), the permanently based Ghent Squadron was kept intact with six flights.

A raid on London in May 1918, the largest of the war, was more a consequence of Brandenburg's drive than OHL policy, not to mention the endurance of his crews. They flew on four of six nights, beginning on the evening of the 14th. On one night alone the

Gothas dumped over twenty tons of explosives on British installations along the front. All the while, the Staffeln were under alert for a flight to England.

Brandenburg had not been to London for nearly a year. Determined to make the raid one to be remembered, he assembled thirty-eight Gothas and two single-engined aeroplanes. The smaller aircraft were to be sent ahead to observe the weather. What few bombs they could carry were to be dropped on Dover. That town would be the target if the capital could not be reached. Bentivegni, still crushed by the losses of 9 May, prepared his three remaining Giants. Forty-three aeroplanes, sixteen more than had ever been sent against England before, were poised to strike against London. As the weekend approached, the biggest raid waited only on the weather to be flown.

On Whit-Sunday evening, 19 May, an aircraft was heard circling off the North Foreland on the Kent coast. British observers were puzzled as it hovered in the moonlit sky without flying inland. The mysterious machine left a flare burning brightly over the sea, and its drone faded away. The lull was brief, for German bombers were already winging their way towards England. The flickering light was a signal telling them that the weather to the west was clear.

The first warning reached London at 10.42 P.M. From that hour, German aircraft kept coming in at five-minute intervals until long past midnight. Hundreds of observer reports jammed the telephone lines to the defence sub-commands and the Horse Guards. An ominous roar filled the warm night air throughout Kent and Essex. The bombers' courses crossed and recrossed as some passed out to sea, and still more came in.

Unlike other nights, when the raids had been made by only a few elusive Giants, British airmen found the skies swarming with Germans. Captain Brand, one of the pilots who had made the first night flight in a Sopwith Camel with Murlis-Green, came across one incoming Gotha. He was patrolling out of Throwley aerodrome when he was attracted by searchlights, probing between Canterbury and Faversham.

'I arrived over this vicinity still climbing . . .' Brand wrote in his report. 'I turned to engage the enemy aircraft. . . . His rear gunner opened fire. I immediately returned his fire, and a subsequent burst apparently put his starboard engine out of order.

'The aircraft did a rapid turn with nose well down, and passed beneath me. He was going downwards rapidly. Soon after my opening fire the aircraft burst into flames, which also enveloped my own machine for an instant. The aircraft fell to earth in pieces over the south-east side of the Isle of Sheppey.'[223]

Another Gotha flew a 'perfect course' up the Thames to London, eluding the Sheerness defences and some searchlights at Tilbury. After unloading on Rotherhithe and Peckham, the raider was set upon by Major F. Sowrey, the commander of 143 Squadron. He fired two drums of tracers before his guns jammed. The bomber flew on, but with the pilot wounded. A Bristol Fighter from 141 Squadron later attacked the same Gotha. Blazing away at close quarters, the two crews engaged each other in furious combat. The German pilot sideslipped sharply, seeking to upset the fighter with his slipstream. He again managed to break away, this time with a shot-up engine.

The limping Gotha had nearly reached the coast when it turned back. Flying low over the aerodrome at Harrietsham, the Germans fired distress signals. They attempted to land and crashed. Only the rear-gunner survived. Nursing a broken arm, the sergeant told his captors that a large fire was raging in London.

The prisoner also settled the counterclaims for the victory. He confirmed that it was the 'Brisfit' which had made the fatal attack. Lieutenant Edward E. Turner was given one of the Gotha's machine-guns, and his observer, Lieutenant Henry B. Barwise, a propeller. Both airmen received the D.F.C. and a black cross from the downed bomber was tacked up in the squadron mess. The 'kill' was the first for Biggin Hill aerodrome. The squadrons stationed there during World War II destroyed some 1,400 German aircraft, a record unequalled by any other fighter station.

The guns along the coast had excellent shooting that May evening. One Gotha was ringed with shells after it flew in near Great Wakering, Essex. The Germans were weaving desperately when they received a direct hit. Blazing brightly in the clear night sky, the aircraft plunged into the sea near Maplin Sands with its full load of bombs. Another raider fell victim to the batteries defending the Dover–Folkestone area. It was found floating off the Knuckle Light the next morning, but only one body was recovered. The guns dropped a third bomber off Foreness Point. Signal flares were seen, but a search yielded no trace of the aeroplane or its crew.

Although the guns fired over 30,000 shells, a fighter brought down the only Gotha to come to grief near London. Driven off course by the outer gun defences, the German bomber was first attacked by a Sopwith Camel from 78 Squadron. The British pilot gave up the fight after exhausting his ammunition. The Gotha's glowing exhausts were later spotted over Hainault Forest by Lieutenant A. J. Arkwell and Air Mechanic A. T. C. Stagg, patrolling in a Bristol Fighter from 39 Squadron. As the bomber flew into the barrage, the guns in the immediate vicinity stopped firing to allow the fighter to close in.

The Gotha dived down from 10,000 feet to shake off the 'Brisfit'. At 1,500 feet, the pursuing airmen riddled one of its fuel tanks. Residents of East Ham heard the rattle high in the sky, and saw 'a point of light which rapidly grew into a red glare'. Two Germans jumped without parachutes, but the third rode the flaming craft to his death. Spectators cheered as it crashed into a cabbage patch near Roman Road. Ignoring the falling shrapnel, hundreds of people ran through the streets. On reaching the crash site, they saw 'a little compact heap of wreckage not more than a dozen yards square'.[224]

Another wild quest was set off by calls pouring in that a 'Hun' aeroplane had 'fallen in flames' in Epping Forest. The search ended several days later when a young pilot admitted that he was to blame for the false reports. British aeroplanes had flares mounted on their wing tips which could be ignited electrically to light up the ground for an emergency landing. The pilot had unknowingly tripped the switch. Thinking that his aircraft was on fire, he had gone into a dive and landed in a clearing.

Bombs struck at scattered points. Sydenham in South London was hit. A dairy in Sydenham Road was demolished; the owner, his wife, and three daughters were killed. Four people died in a bakery next door. Nearby, a group of soldiers were standing outside some empty shops which had been requisitioned as troop billets. On seeing one of the raiders snared by the searchlights, one of them shouted scornfully: 'Go to it, Jerry!' Seconds later he was blown to bits.[225]

The nurses of one large hospital led the patients in prayers and hymn singing. Voices were raised in 'Praise God from Whom All Blessings Flow', as a salvo of bombs exploded dangerously close by.

Another explosion did little harm, except to the shrubbery, when it blasted a park. Only one Giant reached London. The other two, including R.39 carrying a one-ton bomb, reported bombing Chelmsford, but that town was not mentioned as having been attacked.

The British estimated that eleven tons of explosives had been dropped on London and various other places in Kent and Essex. Over a thousand houses and business premises were destroyed or damaged. Most of the 226 victims, including all forty-nine dead, were Londoners. Casualties would have been much greater had it not been for the pleasant weather and the Whitsuntide holidays. Central London was practically deserted. Holidaymakers, their festive mood broken by the news of the raid, rushed back from the country and seaside resorts to check on their homes and relatives.

In contrast to their frequent jeers in the past, the newspapers loudly praised the pilots and the gunners for their work on a night when German bombers had streamed across the south of England for nearly three hours. A few days later the 'few' were officially recognized by the 'many' in a message Ashmore received from the Lord Mayor:

> The citizens of London are filled with admiration and gratitude for the splendid defensive measures taken by the Air Services against the enemy's attack, and will be glad if their appreciation and thanks may be conveyed to those who gallantly and successfully protected the capital on that occasion.[226]

Londoners had no way of knowing, but the big raid was also the last of the war against their city. The assault actually seemed to signal the start of large-scale attacks. On land and in the air, the Germans were striking out with a vigour which belied their desperate situation. Fearing the worst, Ashmore estimated that 'the 3rd Hun bombing squadron is at full strength'. He confided that the Germans had 'some special aeroplanes' which 'would enable them to overcome his blanket defence'.[227]

Work continued throughout the summer on a rapid, two-way communications net. Telephone lines for exclusive military use were laid from the L.A.D.A. headquarters in London to twenty-five sub-controls in the south of England. Each sub-control was linked in

turn with the gun batteries, searchlight companies, balloon squadrons, aerodromes, and observer posts in its area. This system became
operative at noon on 12 September 1918. Ashmore could hardly wait
to try it out. Three hours later, he called on British aircraft to fly a
practice 'raid'. Warnings came in so swiftly that the odds on interception were estimated to have been bettered fourfold.

'I sat overlooking the map from a raised gallery,' described the
L.A.D.A. commander. 'In effect, I could follow the course of all
aircraft flying over the country as the counters crept across the map.
The system worked very rapidly. From the time an observer at one
of the stations in the country saw a machine over him, to the time
when the counter representing it appeared on my map, was not, as a
rule, more than half a minute. In front of me a row of switches
enabled me to cut into the plotters' lines, and talk to any subordinate
commanders at the sub-controls.'[228]

Seated next to Ashmore at Warning Control was a Scotland Yard
representative. He relayed information to the police and fire brigade.
Higgins was another gallery occupant. Now a brigadier-general, he
directed fighter operations as the commander of VI Brigade. The
ground-to-air 'wireless telephone', urged by Henderson after the
first Gotha raid, had finally come into general use in June 1918.

During daylight hours, Higgins exercised immediate control of
fighter formations through a direct line to a long-range transmitter
erected near Biggin Hill. At night, when interception was more
difficult, each squadron commander ordered his own aircraft on the
basis of broad instructions from Higgins. Individual aerodromes
were equipped with short-range transmitters for night operations.
This vital defence arrangement was completed too late to be tested
by German bombers in 1918. But, 'in all essentials', it was 'the fore-
runner of the sector control system that played so decisive a role in
the Battle of Britain'.[229]

Five Zeppelins, aerial lemmings bent on suicidal fulfilment under
the fanatical leadership of Fregattenkapitän Peter Strasser, made
one final attempt to bomb England on the night of 5 August 1918.
Piloting a D.H.4, Major Egbert Cadbury sighted three of the airships
off the Norfolk coast. Attacking head-on above 16,000 feet, Cadbury
and his observer, Captain Robert Leckie, set the lead ship on fire
with tracer bullets. In less than one minute the huge craft became 'a
roaring furnace from end to end'.

A disintegrating mass, the airship broke in two as it plunged seawards. The luckless ship was L.70, the newest of the German super-Zeppelins. Strasser had boasted that this latest type was virtually immune from British fighters. He was killed with all his crew, dying 'as he would have wished it, while fighting at the head of his men in a last battle'.[230]

Shaken by the fiery fall of their chief, the commanders of the other airships carried out a hasty and futile attack. They reported bombing towns and gun batteries along the coast, but no explosives fell on land. Although the effects were nil, this last abortive raid sufficed to keep the British on the alert until the Armistice.

In October, when the Germans were in full retreat all along the Western Front, the Air Council reviewed the forces frozen in England for air defence. North and south, sixteen squadrons waited in idleness for the bombers which never returned. Five squadrons could be spared, the Council decided, 'in view of the heavy casualties and material damage caused by the enemy bombing of our back areas' in France.[231] Only one of these arrived in France before the war ended.

Haig appealed urgently for 150 anti-aircraft guns, and a like number of searchlights that same month. The equipment was needed to defend some 2,000 square miles of territory recently overrun by British troops. The request was still being considered when hostilities ceased. The Germans were thus able to maintain their primary objective of pinning down sizeable forces in England until the very end.

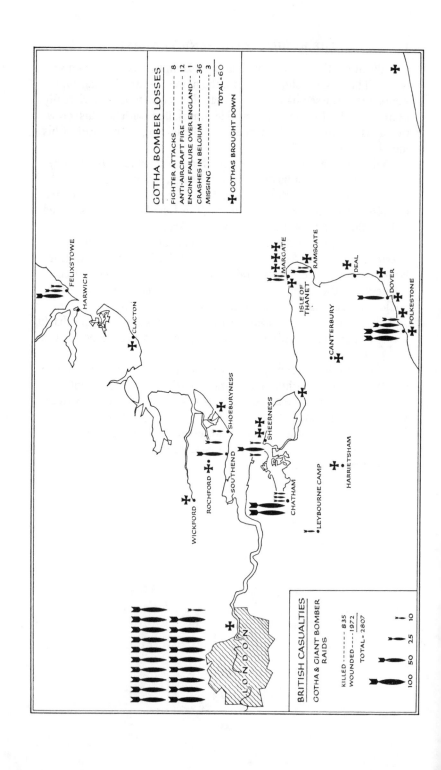

GOTHA BOMBER LOSSES

FIGHTER ATTACKS -------- 8
ANTI-AIRCRAFT FIRE ------- 12
ENGINE FAILURE OVER ENGLAND --- 1
CRASHES IN BELGIUM -------- 36
MISSING --------------- 3

TOTAL-60

✚ GOTHAS BROUGHT DOWN

FELIXSTOWE
HARWICH
CLACTON
SHOEBURYNESS
SOUTHEND
ROCHFORD
WICKFORD
SHEERNESS
ISLE OF THANET
MARGATE
RAMSGATE
DEAL
DOVER
FOLKESTONE
CANTERBURY
HARRIETSHAM
CHATHAM
LEYBOURNE CAMP
LONDON

BRITISH CASUALTIES

GOTHA & GIANT BOMBER
RAIDS

KILLED -------- 835
WOUNDED ----1972

TOTAL = 2807

100   50   25   10

CHAPTER TWENTY-THREE

Retreat to Oblivion

The England Squadron's biggest raid on London in May 1918 was also its worst defeat. Six Gothas failed to return and another crashed near its aerodrome on the way home. The Germans, some accounts suggest, were so badly beaten that they never dared fly over England again. Had OHL calculated that the results were worth the losses, the Gothas would certainly have continued the raids.

Brandenburg, for one, planned further attacks on London. But after this last raid his squadron was unrelentingly committed to supporting the Army. On 27 May, OHL launched an offensive on the Aisne. As the German divisions reached the Marne near Château-Thierry, the Gothas bombed St. Omer on three successive nights. The Giants were attacking Abbeville and other targets. Even after the drive began to slacken, the bombers kept pounding Dunkirk, Calais, and Boulogne.

Good weather over the North Sea coincided with a period of relative quiet at the front in late June. The Gothas were made ready for a flight to England on 1 July. The raid was called off only a short time before they were to start. The OHL approval Brandenburg had counted on was withheld at the last minute. Another such attack was planned for the last night of the month.

Aschoff, now leader of Staffel 17, returned from leave in Germany that afternoon. His Gotha was being overhauled, and a spare bomber he flew had been damaged in a ground collision. Kollberg, his pilot, had not yet returned from leave. After several calls Aschoff learned that a crew at Oostakker needed an observer. He hurriedly packed his flying gear and rushed out to that airfield. The Gothas were loaded and about to take off when the flight to England was cancelled. Without explanation, the airmen were ordered to attack Etaples on the French coast instead.

Although Paris was bombed as late as September, the OHL virtually abandoned long-range air attacks with its decision not to use the

Elektron incendiary bomb. For the Gotha crews, it was already quite evident by early August that the cross-Channel flights were over. Some of the Staffeln began receiving Halberstadt two-seater aeroplanes. The role of Brandenburg's airmen was being reversed. When not out bombing themselves, they were sent up on patrols against the Handley Pages flying almost nightly over Belgium. Within a week, the Gotha airmen shot down two of the British bombers.

One afternoon early in September, Aschoff arrived at the quarters of his Staffeln, a large mansion at Lendonck, to find the crews hushed and sad-faced. Kollberg, he was told, had just been killed at Gontrode. Stunned and unbelieving, Aschoff rode wildly out to the field. A mechanic told him that Kollberg and another pilot had gone up on a short flight in a Halberstadt. They were doing aerobatics when, suddenly, a wing ripped away. The Halberstadt spun in and plunged straight to the ground. 'It had never occurred to us,' Aschoff wrote, 'that one of the crew would die alone without the others. We always thought that, if we were to die, we would all do so together, and at least while flying against the enemy.'[232]

The grieving flight leader was off on another trip to Germany. This time, he journeyed to Königsberg in East Prussia to take Kollberg's body home for burial. Aschoff was all the more depressed on his return. His airmen were confused and disheartened by the worsening turn in the war. While new aeroplanes and replacements were still coming in, German troops were steadily giving ground at the front. Aschoff flew with various crews until he was assigned another pilot. The night raids continued.

The targets seemed small and insignificant. Called upon to substitute for artillery, the Gothas were now dropping bombs on British troops, gun emplacements, and even truck convoys. Georgii recalls the 'utterly incomprehensible orders of the Kommandeur der Flieger of the Fourth Army', directing the squadron to strafe British infantry positions with the Halberstadts. 'The bomber crews, starting at night and inexperienced in the ways of the front, understandably suffered their heaviest losses on these missions.'[94] The flights became shorter as the battle lines drew closer to Ghent. Weather permitting, the crews were now making two and three attacks a night. 'We fly and fly,' Aschoff wrote in his diary, 'but no one has any hope of victory.'

The Allied advance in Flanders forced the evacuation of the Ghent bases in October. The England Squadron was ordered to fall back to Evere, near Brussels. Immediately needed items were hauled away in lorries, while bombs and other supplies were heaped on barges for shipment by canal. The unused Elektron incendiaries were dumped into the river Schelde. Low clouds were drifting over Gontrode, as the Gothas took off for the last time.

'We fly low over the castle where we lived,' observes Aschoff. 'Our eyes take in once more the picture of the old city, the streets and church towers, and finally all sinks away in the mist.'[233] The deserted airfields were taken over by German fighter squadrons.

Evere aerodrome, to which many other squadrons were relocated, was already a scene of chaos. Hundreds of aircraft of all types jammed the field. The Gothas were assigned to a Zeppelin hangar, already occupied by other units. The crews found quarters in the city, and the flights against the advancing British were half heartedly resumed. On 30 October, Aschoff made his last two raids, on a British supply depot at Menin.

Rumours were rampant that the German Government was seeking a 'provisional suspension of arms'. Fearful of a hostile population, the crews moved out of Brussels to cramped but safer lodgings near the aerodrome. Officers were no longer able to maintain discipline in some squadrons. The airmen vented their frustration on their aircraft, and looting broke out.

With the signing of the Armistice, one final bitter task remained for Brandenburg. The terms specifically listed 'all night-bombing aeroplanes' among those weapons to be surrendered 'in the first place' and 'in good condition'. Within forty-eight hours, the Gothas were turned over to a commission of British officers. 'Outwardly, they looked perfect,' mused Aschoff, 'but our mechanics would have never allowed us to fly those machines.'[234]

Stripped of their bombers, Brandenburg and his airmen left Evere by truck convoy. After a forlorn eight-day journey across hostile Belgium and their revolt-torn Fatherland, they finally arrived at their last destination, Frankfurt-an-der-Oder. The squadron was demobilized by the end of November.

Squadron 501, which was disbanded in Düsseldorf early in 1919, fared somewhat better. A few Staakens were smashed and abandoned in Belgium, but those fit for flight returned to Germany. The indestructible R.12, whose combat service was longer than that of any other Giant, was shown to 'awed crowds' in Kassel and other German cities. For the benefit of spectators, the proud crew chalked the targets they had attacked and the total weight of the bombs dropped, nearly thirty tons, on the side of the huge bomber's box-like fuselage.

Bentivegni's own aircraft, R.39, also returned with twenty raids to its credit, including three over London. Converted into a transport, R.39 was finally destroyed in August 1919. The Staaken was shot down over Silesia while flying to the Ukraine to help in the fight against the Bolsheviks. Bentivegni was no longer its commander, but it was on another trip to distant Russia, one he made quite unwillingly more than twenty-five years later, that he met his death.

A business executive between wars, Bentivegni fell into the hands of the Russians in 1945. Someone by that name, it appears, was on a list of Germans wanted for war crimes. Nearly sixty, he was led away with other prisoners on a forced march to Russia. Eventually, Bentivegni reached Tiflis where he was made to work in the streets. Relatives in Germany were later informed that he had died in captivity early in 1946.

Squadron 501 lost no aircraft over England. Brandenburg, in his final report, listed the losses of Bogohl 3 as 137 dead, 88 missing, and over 200 wounded. Casualties suffered on the raids at the front were included in these totals. Sixty Gothas were lost on the flights to England alone. Twenty-four were shot down by the British, or else disappeared over the sea. The remaining thirty-six bombers were destroyed in crashes. These statistics hardly reflect the raw courage that was required to challenge the North Sea and the defences of London with extremely unreliable aircraft. Considering its strength, the England Squadron was wiped out nearly twice over during its year of operations against Britain.

If for no other reason than the weighty consequences of their raids, these early German airmen do not merit being consigned to a limbo in aviation history. Some fifty years later, it is still not widely recognized that 'Long-range bombardment techniques were pioneered, not by Douhet, Trenchard, or Mitchell, but by German airmen, flying two hundred sorties in Zeppelins and twice as many sorties in Gotha bomber planes over England alone from German bases'.[235]

Whatever debt the Germans owed the British for the pain and anxiety of this pioneering effort, it was to be repaid a thousandfold a quarter of a century later.

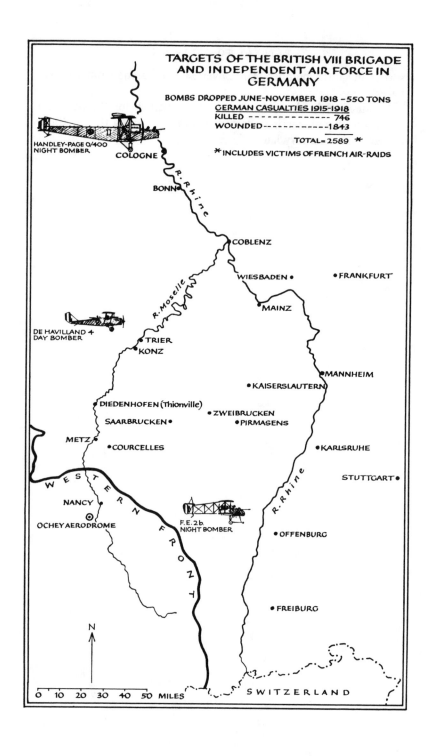

TARGETS OF THE BRITISH VIII BRIGADE
AND INDEPENDENT AIR FORCE IN
GERMANY

BOMBS DROPPED JUNE-NOVEMBER 1918 – 550 TONS

GERMAN CASUALTIES 1915-1918
KILLED -------------- 746
WOUNDED ------------ 1843

TOTAL = 2589 ✱

✱INCLUDES VICTIMS OF FRENCH AIR-RAIDS

HANDLEY-PAGE O/400
NIGHT BOMBER

COLOGNE

R. Rhine

BONN

COBLENZ

R. Moselle

WIESBADEN

FRANKFURT

MAINZ

DE HAVILLAND 4
DAY BOMBER

TRIER
KONZ

MANNHEIM

KAISERSLAUTERN

DIEDENHOFEN (Thionville)

ZWEIBRUCKEN
PIRMASENS

SAARBRUCKEN

METZ

COURCELLES

KARLSRUHE

STUTTGART

W
E
S
T
E
R
N

NANCY

OCHEY AERODROME

F
R
O
N
T

F.E. 2 b.
NIGHT BOMBER

R. Rhine

OFFENBURG

FREIBURG

N

FREIBURG

0 10 20 30 40 50 MILES

S W I T Z E R L A N D

CHAPTER TWENTY-FOUR

The First Bomber Command

'The German bombing squadrons,' runs one British comment on the diversion of forces caused by the Gotha raids, 'needed only to make sufficient attacks on England to keep the threat alive; they could be mainly employed against objectives on the Western front.'[236] Yet, the British largely denied themselves that very flexibility in organizing their Independent Air Force in 1918.

The I.A.F., as its name proclaimed, was intended to operate completely independently of Haig's armies. Truly an anachronism in its day, this first Bomber Command amply demonstrates the singlemindedness, if not vindictiveness, with which the British undertook to even the score in the last year of the war. Its creation was as portentous as that of the Royal Air Force itself.

Weir's enthusiasm for long-range bombing antedated the Gotha raids. Nearly a year before Smuts wrote his report, the testy little Scotsman had stressed the economy of such warfare. He maintained that 'bombing aeroplanes will drop more high explosives behind the German lines, for the same cost and at a longer range than howitzers, since a bomb needs less steel than a shell, and petrol is cheaper than cordite'.[237] Now Air Minister, he gave first priority to the activation of the I.A.F.

Trenchard was offered the new command. Weir assured him that the invitation was not being extended 'on any ground of quelling of what you call "the agitation".' The general, however, was not satisfied that the job was 'of value'. Independent air operations, in fact, struck him as a 'great waste'.

'I cannot conceive,' he replied, 'why any officer in London should think he is in a better position or more capable to say which particular town should be bombed at which particular moment. It would be fatal in my opinion to direct the actual carrying out of orders from London. . . .'[238] Trenchard further reminded the Air Minister that 'one of the best generals in the air service, Newall, is already in charge of this bombing.' Now a brigadier, Newall commanded the five squadrons at Ochey which had expanded into VIII Brigade.

'I am trying to interrupt the main railway lines feeding the present battle . . .' he reported in March 1918. 'There is no doubt the Huns have had to draw back a lot of machines for the defence of the Fatherland, and I trust that their aviation is as annoyed . . . as we were when two [fighter] squadrons had to be sent home to protect London. . . .'[239]

Newall's raids, though limited, were certainly distressing to German civilians. Early in February a delegation of Rhineland mayors journeyed to OHL headquarters. The mayors, much concerned about the 'monuments and relics' in their localities, pleaded with Hindenburg and Ludendorff to stop the bombing of Allied towns. Such attacks only invited reprisals, they argued, a threat which would greatly increase with the arrival of American squadrons in France. The delegation also warned of serious unrest and strikes if the killing of German citizens continued.

Hindenburg, his impatience bordering on anger, wasted little time with his alarmed visitors. The effects of air raids, he told them curtly, had been greatly exaggerated on both sides. He disagreed that the Rhineland was in serious danger. Informed that the war in the air would go on as before, the mayors were sent packing.

In April the Chamber of the Grand Duchy of Baden voted a resolution urging Berlin to negotiate with the Allies for 'the cessation of hostile air raids on places outside the zone of military operations'. Bavaria and Hesse also joined in the appeal. A similar agreement was advocated in the Reichstag by Herr Geck, a socialist member. OHL retorted that the hardships of the German populace did not even begin to compare with what the people in some Allied cities 'had been enduring for three years with remarkable courage'. Berlin was advised to say nothing about the air raids until some specific proposal was received from the Allied camp.

The British War Cabinet was not about to make any such overtures in the face of public insistence on retaliations. The *Daily Mail* pointed out that it would be the 'greatest mistake' for the Allies not to use their superiority in the air to the 'fullest measure'. The *Daily Graphic* cited the outcry in Germany as the 'proof of the efficiency of our fliers. The Germans consider anything which is to their advantage as being proper, but when one pays them back with the same money, they begin to cry'.[240]

The French were more inclined to come to some understanding, especially after the Germans announced that Paris would suffer the consequences of British as well as French raids on their cities. The French capital was closer than London, and much less strongly defended. Making Paris the scapegoat for British forays over Germany was also not likely to endear the British to the French. In consulting with London, French leaders found that their ally was 'hostile' to the idea of giving up air raids. There was no more talk about the slaughter of innocent women and children. The 'Huns' had started this game, and as far as the British were now concerned, they would finish it.

Trenchard was not immediately inclined to help out. Doffing his uniform, he sought peace and quiet in London's Green Park. Weir, trying to place the general where his 'experience may contribute to the success of the Royal Air Force', became exasperated after nearly a month of coaxing. In a sharply worded letter he finally told the ex-Chief of the Air Staff 'that I will not create a position specially for you. . . . If there are any points not clear in the above, I shall be available for half an hour between nine-thirty and ten tonight'.[241]

Trenchard stubbornly ignored the ultimatum, but a chance conversation he overheard one day, as he was settling down to his reading in the park, stung his pride. Two passing naval officers were intently discussing his resignation 'at the height of the battle'. They agreed that they would 'have him shot'. Disturbed, Trenchard went home to his bachelor flat in Berkeley Street, and wrote Weir that he would take over the Independent Air Force. While still questioning its merits, he promised to 'do my best to make it a success as far as possible'.[242] Weir was satisfied, if not relieved. Bonar Law hastened to end the debate on Trenchard by announcing in the House of Commons that the general was to command 'a very important part of the British Air Force in France'.

The I.A.F. officially came into being on 5 June 1918, 'for direct action against the heart of the German industrial system'. With Newall as his deputy, Trenchard quickly set out to instil an offensive spirit into the Ochey squadrons. In speaking to the brigade, wing, and squadron commanders, he called for 'cloud flying' because 'we can't always do fine weather bombing'. He insisted that the crews 'must fly long distances on dark nights without a moon as long as it's clear'.

Trenchard also emphasized 'the importance of keeping in friendly touch with the French and Americans'.[243] This last point was important to Weir. Not content with the I.A.F., the Air Minister proposed an inter-Allied bomber fleet of some sixty squadrons. This force, he told Trenchard, would be a 'big command, particularly if associated with America'. But Marshal Foch was no less hostile than Haig had been at having large strategic air forces operating independently of the armies.

The Allied Commander-in-Chief even refused to recognize the I.A.F., 'an irregular air force' controlled from London. The dispute was referred to a sub-committee of the Supreme War Council at Versailles. 'Independent of what? Of God?' questioned General Duval, the Chief of the French Air Service. 'The committee is being asked to say that the primary object is to bomb Germany and the secondary one merely to defeat the enemy in the field. We need unification of effort, not dissipation.'[244]

The deadlock stymied Weir's plans. Lack of French co-operation also complicated Trenchard's supply problems. Ochey was far from British depots. Relying on his talents as an improviser, he succeeded in persuading local French Army commanders to support his isolated squadrons. Trenchard was equally crafty in his dealings with Weir, usually by-passing Sykes, his successor as Chief of the Air Staff.

Major-General John Salmond, Trenchard's successor as Haig's air commander, was put out by the 'serious' diversion of men and equipment to the I.A.F. 'This force,' recorded one inside observer, 'profits by Trenchard's strong individuality and enthusiasm. . . . Consequently, it is the pet child, and this independence of all control by Foch, Haig or Salmond is naturally resented as it is against common sense.'[245]

Trenchard struck a more responsive chord with the Americans. 'Billy' Mitchell was keen on learning from the British. 'He's a man after my own heart,' Trenchard remarked of the young colonel commanding the air squadrons of the U.S. First Army. 'If only he can break his habit of trying to convert opponents by killing them, he'll go far.'[246]

Trenchard took it upon himself to train American aircrews located east of Rheims, and to supply them with Handley Page and de Havilland bombers. He also felt that some of the U.S. squadrons in England should be trained in long-range bombing. 'It is of the most vital importance to them and me,' he wrote Weir. The Armistice ended this budding partnership before the Americans could join in the raids of the I.A.F. But the germ of a new way of war had been lastingly transmitted.

Visiting Trenchard at his headquarters at Autigny-la-Tour early in September, an admiring military correspondent found him 'the same as ever, brilliant, full of ideas, alert, combative and a mine of information. He has 120 aeroplanes, mainly Handley Pages, for long-range bombing, and the squadrons are scattered round partly concealed in the woods. . . . He declares that he has not changed his views that bombing is necessary. . . .'247

The bomb tonnage dumped on the Germans rose from over seventy in June to more than a hundred in August. Weir followed this progress with intense interest. 'I would very much like if you could start up a really big fire in one of the German towns,' he told Trenchard in September. The Air Minister was confident of spectacular results, if incendiaries were scattered in the older districts with few 'good, permanent, modern buildings'. From Behncke's 1914 master plan for fire raids on the 'soft goods quarter' of London, the bombing game had now gone full circle.

'If I were you,' Weir suggested on another occasion, 'I would not be too exacting as regards accuracy in bombing railway stations. . . . The German is susceptible to bloodiness, and I would not mind a few accidents due to inaccuracy.'

'I do not think you need be anxious,' reassured Trenchard. 'The accuracy is not great at present, and all the pilots drop their eggs well into the middle of town generally.'248

Marshal Foch finally agreed, after much wrangling, to the formation of an inter-Allied Air Force. Trenchard was appointed commander-in-chief on 26 October 1918. French, American and Italian bomber squadrons were placed under him, but none flew raids as part of the new command. Had the war continued into 1919, a large-scale air offensive would have been launched against Germany.

A prototype of the Handley Page V/1500, the British counterpart of the German Giant aeroplane, had been flown in May. The four-engined bomber could carry a bombload of 7,500 pounds, and stay aloft for over twelve hours. Three of the big aircraft were delivered to a flight at Bircham Newton, Norfolk, early in November. The machines were fuelled and loaded for the first raid on Berlin when the Armistice silenced all the guns and grounded all the bombers.

Trenchard wired Foch that same day for authority to return the I.A.F. to Haig's command. The squadrons were promptly transferred, and by mid-November Trenchard was on his way home. Salmond, on whom the units of the I.A.F. were unloaded, was riled by the general's eagerness 'to pass on an unwanted baby and clear out with all speed'. Air Chief Marshal Sir Philip Joubert has written that Trenchard, at the time, was apparently 'not completely converted to the view that the strategic role was important'. Otherwise, 'he might have wished to establish an embryo Bomber Command in the years of peace'.[249]

Weir was more mindful of the future. He instructed Trenchard to 'keep your final dispatch educational'. Since June, the I.A.F. had dropped 550 tons of bombs on German targets, roughly double the amount which had fallen on England during the entire war. Half this tonnage, however, had been directed against aerodromes because of the stiff German fighter opposition to Trenchard's bombers.

This fateful beginning is recalled with pride in British air history. To quote Joubert again: 'The bomber squadrons of the Independent Air Force (within the R.A.F.) were the first to start attacking German industrial targets beyond the Rhine. This was the first strategic use of air power—the first step which started us along the road to where we are today.'[250]

'Strategic bombing was born with this British scheme,' confirms a U.S. Air Force general.[251] Such unqualified acclaim of Britain as the fountainhead of air-power is justified only in an organizational sense. Conceptually, British insight was acquired at the receiving end of German bombs. To react in kind was a spirited and understandable response, but still only a response. The decision 'to carry the war into Germany', comments Air Vice-Marshal E. J. Kingston-McCloughry, was 'for retaliation rather than as a result of a greater conception of air strategy'.[252]

Most of the credit for this irrevocable turn is ironically given to Trenchard, the 'man of vision'. One still reads today that the I.A.F. was formed because he 'went to Parliament' over the heads of the

Army and the Navy. Mitchell, needing support for his own embattled stand on air-power, perpetuated this myth in the 'Twenties.[253]

Trenchard was practical and hardheaded, qualities which explain his durability and achievements. Undoubtedly one of the outstanding high-ranking air commanders of 1914–18, he concentrated on fighting that war, not the next one. Trenchard himself would be satisfied with this unvarnished tribute. Never, in his long life, did he ever claim any other. He particularly disliked being called 'the Father of the Royal Air Force'.

Following the swift dissolution of the I.A.F., the fate of the Royal Air Force itself rested in the hands of Winston Churchill. In a reshuffle of the Cabinet, he became Minister for War and Air early in 1919. Acting on an 'inspired impulse', he chose to deviate from Lloyd George's policy not to keep the Air Force 'as a separate Department'.

'The integrity, the unity, the independence of the Royal Air Force will be sedulously and carefully maintained,' Churchill announced in February.[254] He was much influenced by Weir, who had asked to be relieved as Air Minister. Weir further counselled his successor that Trenchard was 'your best man' as Chief of the Air Staff.

'You must come back and I won't hear of any refusal,' Churchill told the general.[255] Trenchard, with his winning instinct, now joined wholeheartedly in the political manœuvring required to preserve the R.A.F. against the inroads of the Army and Navy. The burden of that struggle was largely his after Churchill left the Air Ministry with the downfall of the Lloyd George Government in 1922.

The intervening years of peace were as lean for the R.A.F. financially as they were for Churchill politically. But both came through to fight and win their greatest battle less than two decades later, when the survival of Britain, and much more, hung in the balance.

A Fearsome Legacy

The Fighters are our salvation, but the Bombers alone provide the means of victory.

Winston Churchill (September 1940)

CHAPTER TWENTY-FIVE

Only a Beginning

The first Battle of Britain was no Armageddon. The number of German air attacks may seem surprisingly high—fifty-one by airships and fifty-two by aeroplanes. But the casualties averaged slightly less than forty-seven per raid. Altogether, 1,414 persons were killed and 3,416 were injured. The Gotha and Giant raids accounted for nearly 60% of these casualties. Although the damage totalled nearly three million pounds, the military effect must be weighed in terms of the British forces diverted to air defence. While not inconsiderable, this factor was in no way decisive. As a sideshow to the slaughter of the Western Front, the German raids were dismissed after the war as being of 'no real consequence'. But in the light of still another World War, these early 'air invasions' of England take on an almost awesome significance.

Captain Liddell Hart, writing in 1937 of the fear of war then gripping Europe, observed that the people's 'thoughts instinctively fly upwards—and their imagination flies faster. Memory of air attacks in the last war is as much the propellant as any knowledge of air developments since'. He went on:

> To anyone who analyses the comparatively slight material results of air raids in 1914–18, it is remarkable to find what a profound psychological impression they made, and have left. . . . The effects have not disappeared with the cessation of the cause: they are traceable in the general tendency among the public, whenever they think of war, for the thought to be associated immediately with the idea of being bombed from the air. And from this apprehension springs a natural exaggeration.[256]

'I shall be specially careful not to exaggerate,' Churchill had told the House of Commons in 1934, in one of his many speeches about the 'rearmament of Germany in the air'. Citing fire raids as 'the most dangerous form of air attack', he vividly described how the Germans had planned 'a dreadful act of power and terror' with the Elektron bomb in the summer of 1918. Mindful of the unrest one week of Gotha raids had caused among Londoners, Churchill continued:

> We must expect that under pressure of continuous air attacks upon London at least three or four million people would be driven out into the open country. . . . This vast mass of human beings . . . without shelter and without food, without sanitation and without special provision for the maintenance of order, would confront the Government of the day with an administrative problem of the first magnitude. . . .
>
> It is just as well to confront those facts while time remains. . . .[257]

The Gothas and the Giants were kept flying in a barrage of books and articles appearing after 1935. Sir Malcolm Campbell, a wartime pilot, wrote that, 'in a single day and night', an enemy could drop 1,000 tons of bombs, 'four times the weight that fell on the whole country during four years of war'. Campbell was far from certain that the British capital would stand up under such a blow, as he recalled 'how nearly to cracking the morale of London came' during 1917–18:

> The 'stop the war' cry was heard far more frequently than was pleasant or flattering to our belief in the sticking-to-it qualities of our people. Who that lived or spent any time in London during the time when air raids were fairly frequent will ever forget the scenes of panic terror to be seen immediately the warning maroons were exploded? People rushing in their thousands to take refuge in the tube railways, in the churches and public buildings. . . .[258]

Another author carefully analysed the destruction done by the one-ton bomb dropped on Paddington in March 1918. He concluded that if a bomb twice its size should 'fall in Parliament Square and another, say on the Horse Guards Parade, there would, necessarily, be very little of Administrative London left standing'.[259] The horrors of possible gas warfare were added to the memories of the 1914–18 raids. Britons were reminded that 'one-third of our population lives in fifteen cities', and that 'we may lose the next war in twelve hours'.

Working from the World War I experience, the Air Staff estimated that in a future war, bombing casualties would be fifty per ton of explosives dropped on Britain. The 1940–1 raids on London would show this figure to have been over-estimated fourteen-fold. As the Air Staff saw it, the Gotha and Giant night raids had inflicted casualties at the rate of fifty-two per ton. The daylight attack of June 1917 had caused 121 dead or wounded per ton.

By 1938, the Germans were believed capable of delivering 3,500 tons on the first day of war, and 600 tons every twenty-four hours thereafter. And these figures were constantly being revised upwards. Using the Air Staff estimates, the Ministry of Health came up with some rather chilling statistics: 600,000 killed and 1,200,000 wounded during the first few months of war. Half a million homes would be destroyed or made uninhabitable. Panic on a wide scale was feared. Londoners, it was believed, would flock into the Underground and 'refuse to come out'.[260]

'I was soon to know for the first time the meaning of fear,' Marshal of the Royal Air Force Sir John Slessor recalls of the summer of 1937. 'I do not mean physical fear . . . but the gnawing dread of national shame and disaster that curdles the tummy and wakes one up at three in the morning. . . .'[261] For many of his countrymen, the fear was physical as well.

The 'very deep impression' the raids of 1914–18 produced on the 'popular mind' has been described as amounting 'almost to a trauma. This trauma, in its turn, was to have profound effects on the policies of the democracies, and was in due course to be ruthlessly exploited by the dictators. . . . Those critics who still speak so glibly of Chamberlain's moral cowardice in the autumn of 1938 should remember what, to him, seemed the alternative. . . .'[262]

The British Prime Minister had some vivid recollections of that 'trauma'. As Lord Mayor of Birmingham in 1916, he had presided over an 'air-raid conference' of alarmed officials, hastily convened after a Zeppelin attack on the Midlands. Chamberlain's urgent mission then had been one to London to plead for the protection of the region against the raiders.

The 'betrayal of the Czechs' is usually considered only within the context of the contemporary situation—the revival of German air-power, the 'horrible examples' of Barcelona and Guernica in the Spanish Civil War, and British unpreparedness. These immediate factors were overriding at Munich. But the underlying fear which magnified the German air threat out of all proportion to what it would prove to be was something on which the British had been feeding for twenty years.

The Prime Minister had asked the British Chiefs of Staff in March 1938, when the Germans marched into Austria, for a report on the 'military implications' of going to war in defence of Czechoslovakia. They replied categorically 'that any involvement in war with Germany at this stage could well lead to an ultimate defeat....' Lieutenant-Commander P. K. Kemp, an Admiralty historian, writes that the Chiefs of Staff were 'most alarmed' at the weakness of the country in the air. 'Intensive propaganda in the years between the wars had raised an unholy fear of the bomber and its power of destruction.' Citing the estimate as the 'true background of Munich', Kemp adds that Chamberlain was placed 'in a position from which there was no escape. . . .'[263]

Field-Marshal Lord Ironside, who became the Chief of the Imperial General Staff at the outbreak of war, wrote in late 1937 that the Cabinet 'are terrified now of a war being finished in a few weeks by the annihilation of Great Britain. They can see no other kind of danger than air attack and discount all other dangers. . . .[264]

And at the height of the Czech Crisis, he recorded:

I am now told that all the authorities have insisted upon the parcelling out of troops all over London during air raids. . . . They want the sight of uniforms to quieten the people. . . . It is a curious ending to a Field Army and it seems stupid that we should go through the motions of training these men for anything other than these new police-duties. For these we are completely untrained.[265]

A few days later, 'an exciting few days' which 'have ended with one of the greatest humiliations we could have suffered', Ironside himself conceded that '*we cannot expose ourselves now to a German attack. We simply commit suicide if we do. . . .* At no time could we stand up against German air bombing. . . . What a mess we are in.'[266]

Paris, too, had been bombed regularly in 1918. But, at the time of the worst raids, the city was also being shelled by German long-range guns. Air attacks, however disturbing, added little to the very real concern over land invasion. After the war, the French trained and equipped their Air Force for 'close support of land operations. . . . They had no belief in the offensive power of air forces acting independently, and no intention of creating a long-range bomber force'.[267]

The French gambled their security on the Maginot Line. Though it was to fail them, they at least were right in their anticipations of the German blow of 1940. The British, on the other hand, let their Army deteriorate to the point that it 'was far less ready for a continental war than it had been in 1914'.

There were only two divisions of 'fully trained troops in England' in 1939.[268] Pioneers of tank warfare, the British could not muster one complete armoured division. This incredible nakedness was a consequence of Government rearmament policies dating back to 1934, attuned to the 'limits of financial stability'. Officials were certain that 'the main danger' in a war with Germany 'would lie in bombardment from the air'; hence, in rearming, 'full priority need only be given to the Royal Air Force'.[269]

The Navy, while less affected than the Army by budgetary restrictions, found its 'fighting efficiency' greatly impaired as a result of the 'political decision' to establish an independent Air Force in 1918. For a time, all shipborne aircraft of the Fleet were those provided and manned by the 'non-nautical airmen' of the R.A.F. No naval officers were trained as pilots until 1925. True integration between sea and air was delayed until 1937, when administrative control of the Fleet Air Arm was restored to the Admiralty. Even then, the Air Ministry retained the responsibility for the design and production of all aircraft, although the Naval Staff was 'consulted'. Because of the reluctance to abandon the 'tried and tested biplane formula', the Fleet went to war in 1939 with such aircraft as the Sea Gladiator and the Fairey Swordfish, sterling aeroplanes of another era complete with struts and bracing wires.[270]

'Founders of air-power', the British had no tactical air arm to support the Army divisions that were sent to face the tanks of the

German Wehrmacht. 'A real row has now developed,' Ironside wrote in the first months of World War II. 'The Air Ministry say that they cannot allot any machines to the Army because they are short themselves. . . . It seems ridiculous that we should be fighting these quarrels internally just before we enter the worst battle of our history.'[271]

The British might have taken a more realistic view of what awaited them, had they been less mesmerized by the bomber. The debacle of 1940 was not inevitable, but the Battle of Britain was after Dunkirk. Peter Fleming, in his book *Operation Sea Lion*, states that absolutely no thought was given to the danger of invasion 'at any time before the middle of May 1940'. Finding this 'scarcely capable of a rational explanation', he nonetheless attempts one, writing in part:

> . . . as war approached, people at all levels became increasingly obsessed with the part which air power, and the bombers in particular, would play in it; had it been advanced, the idea that the coasts might need defending would have seemed obsolete and irrelevant while shelters were being hastily excavated in Hyde Park. . . . Few, in their hearts, ruled out the possibility of Britain's defeat. . . .[272]

The country was partitioned under Twelve Regional Controllers who were to govern 'if Whitehall and Westminster were wiped out'. Over two hundred and fifty thousand hospital beds were readied for the casualties. A million and a half women and children were evacuated to provincial towns and seaside resorts. And on the day war came, 3 September 1939, an estimated two million more Londoners took flight in private cars and taxis. The sirens wailed in a city 'keyed up for instant horrors', but the alarm was false. No bombs fell on London that Sunday, nor would they for nearly another year.

Pompous Hermann Göring, playing on old fears, voiced a boastful threat in the last days of 1939. 'Once again,' he blustered in a New Year's message, 'as the German Zeppelins did twenty-five years ago, German squadrons will unleash air-raid alarms over London. . . .

All that is needed in the Führer's command. . . . The German Air Force will strike at Britain with an onslaught such as has never been known in the history of the world. . . .'[273]

The onslaught, when it finally came, did live up to that promise. But it was far from the 'knock-out blow' the British fully expected within hours after the war began. Falling for a bluff, they had grossly misjudged the Germans' true intentions and strategy. Göring, on his side, completely underestimated what he was up against. Twenty-two years after the Giants had raided London, the Germans had no four-engined bombers to send to Britain.

Apart from the strong impulse to retaliate, long-range bombing had appealed to the British as a means of striking over the heads of the opposing armies. The German response to the problem of the solid front was lightning war—the Blitzkrieg. A swift, crushing advance would make air blows on rear areas unnecessary. That the Germans were more advanced in their thinking seemed undeniable until their panzer divisions were halted by the Channel. Once the plans for invasion were abandoned, whatever chances the Germans had of bringing the British to concede defeat were even less without a powerful strategic air force.

German neglect of the heavy bomber may seem a paradox after the enterprising efforts of 1914–18. But, because they had been made too soon, the Zeppelin, Gotha and Giant raids had been less than inspiring. Not only was the material damage negligible, but the psychological effects were hardly those which had been anticipated.

German disenchantment is quite clear in Major von Bülow's post-war study. The bomb tonnage the Gothas and the Giants tried to deliver was considerably greater than what the British were able to trace. Bülow's detailed analysis was published in 1927. Had the British Air Staff heeded it, they might have come up with far less frightening estimates of what was going to happen in the next war. Seen from the German side, the Gotha and Giant effort produced less than twenty-three casualties per ton.

Even if the Germans had been satisfied, any continuity in their strategic air doctrine was very unlikely after the break-up of the Luftstreitkräfte in 1919. Reorganization of the military forces became a problem for the General Staff headed by General von Seeckt. Seeckt, 'the midwife of German air strategy between the World Wars', was an infantry soldier. The generals dismissed the

Douhet concept as 'pseudo-strategy'. The result was a German Air Force whose purpose and capabilities were geared to the tactical support of the Army.

The Luftwaffe, reborn officially in 1935, was inherited by the German 'aces' of the First World War, notably Göring and Udet. Their influence was quite different from that of Trenchard and Mitchell on Anglo-American air-power. Though 'entranced by the ideas of Douhet', Göring 'had no concept whatsoever of strategic air warfare or of up-to-date technical requirements'.[274] Technical matters were left to Udet. His chief contribution was the dive-bombing 'Stuka madness'. When an order was issued that 'all aircraft must be able to dive', German designers were hard put to satisfy the requirement with four-engined aeroplanes.

General Max von Wever, the first Chief of the German Air Staff, nonetheless planned a large force of heavy bombers capable of reaching targets from Scotland to the Urals. Prototypes were built in 1936, and they could have flown against England in 1940. The project was abandoned after von Wever was killed in an air crash. 'The Führer will not ask how big the bombers are,' Göring remarked, 'but how many there are.'[275] Later efforts to rectify this mistake were spectacularly unsuccessful.

Brandenburg's little known post-war career was no less ironic. Since Germany was denied an air force by the victorious Allies, Seeckt set out to develop one under the cloak of civil aviation. Hand-picked by Seeckt, Brandenburg became the head of that department under the Transport Ministry in 1924. Under his capable direction, the agency became the womb of the future Luftwaffe. Army officers were secretly enrolled in commercial pilot training schools. The innocuous civil air branch sponsored the research and development of aircraft and equipment needed for the embryo air force. In all, 27 million marks were channelled to the Reichswehr for military aviation through Brandenburg's office. The lame ex-commander of the England Squadron also cajoled German airlines into one 'state-controlled instrument', known as Lufthansa, in 1926. Some years later, Göring extolled Lufthansa as 'the stronghold of the Luftwaffe spirit during the years of darkness'.

But Brandenburg went into eclipse soon after the Nazis came into power. His last important function was as a delegate to the 1932–4 Geneva Disarmament Conference, where he passionately pleaded

Germany's cause. Since she could not have an air force, he argued, other countries should 'abolish their entire military aviation'. The threat to 'the disarmed people' was to be bombed 'into rubble and ashes'. Having already done much to rearm Germany in the air, Brandenburg was to live to see his fears come true.

While at Geneva he learned that Erhard Milch, the director of Lufthansa, had superseded him at home. Göring had chosen Milch as his deputy, and made him Reichskommissar for Air. On his return, Brandenburg resigned from all ties with German aviation. He was in charge of Roads and Autobahns for a time, but he was forced to withdraw from this post as well. 'An ingenious man ruined by the National Socialist régime,' he spent his last years on a meagre pension. Brandenburg died, much embittered, in 1952.

Hitler's bombers, Spaight wrote smugly after the storm of the Battle of Britain and the Blitz had passed, 'were the weapons of an *ersatz* air power. We had the true armoury'.[276] The indomitable British had indeed. But, in a real sense, it was the Germans themselves who had set off, in 1917, the chain of events which led to their first decisive setback in World War II.

The pilots who battled the Zeppelins and the Gothas have been credited with laying 'the foundation of a tradition on which the Luftwaffe broke in 1940'.[277] That tradition was very much alive at the time of the Battle of Britain. Captain Brand, the pilot who shot down a Gotha on the last raid on London in 1918, was in 1940 Air Vice-Marshal Sir Christopher J. Q. Brand, commanding No. 10 Group of Fighter Command. Also serving in No. 10 Group was Murlis-Green, who, with Brand, had made the first night flight in a Sopwith Camel. Murlis-Green had gone to France in the summer of 1918 and finished the war with thirty-two victories to his credit. A Group Captain in 1940, he commanded Aston Down aerodrome.

But Britain defeated the Luftwaffe with more than a tradition. The Gotha raids, lasting an entire year, by day and by night, had confronted the British with most of the defence problems which had to be overcome when survival itself was at stake. Except for differences of scope and speed, the lessons of the first Battle of Britain still applied. Smuts's 'recommendations regarding home defence', writes Air Chief Marshal Joubert, 'were to have an influence that extended throughout the First World War, through the years of peace and into the dark periods of the bombings of London during the Second World War. The general lay-out of the air defences that he envisaged, though subject to continued modification ... remained basically the same until 1945. . . .'[278]

The British began to reorganize their air defences in earnest in 1938. The 'system', as they called it, was but an updated version of 'Ashmore's Shield' of 1918, with its anti-aircraft guns, barrage balloons, and 'counters creeping across the map' at Warning Control. In the mid-twenties, Ashmore himself had set up 'the basic organization of the Observer Corps which later operated in the Battle of Britain'.[279]

Some of the air defence marvels of World War II, such as radar and the eight-gun Spitfire, 'the best defensive fighter of the world', were fostered by a frame of mind, a sense of insecurity, born of the Gotha raids. Without that unsettling intrusion, the genius which made these devices and weapons possible might well have remained dormant. Sir Robert Watson-Watt, who developed the first operational radar system for air defence, seems to hint at such inspiration by denying it, writing: 'History never repeats itself in detail; World War II was, in any case, the first air war in all history.'[280]

The creation of the Royal Air Force, then, was quite a stroke of prevision. Sir Robert would probably agree with C. G. Grey's opinion that 'the Royal Air Force was formed parthenogenetically. That is to say it sprang fully armed from the collective brain of the House of Commons as Minerva sprang fully armed from the brain of Jove.'[281] At any rate, he does admit to its influence. 'I am certain,' writes Watson-Watt, 'that the existence of a separate Air Ministry and a separate Royal Air Force was of great importance to our rapid evolution of radar. The comparative calendars of radar in the three services speak.'[282]

Radar aside, the truly redemptive feature of the Royal Air Force's independent development was its all-round qualitative superiority in the Battle of Britain. Unlike the American Army Air Forces, which went to war without first-rate fighters, or the Luftwaffe unpossessed of heavy bombers, the Royal Air Force had both when they were needed. As Air Minister back in 1921, Churchill had expounded on this very point with an uncanny grasp of things to come:

We are sure that if, after a prolonged spell of peace, war on a great scale suddenly broke out again, the Power which had made the most intensive study of aerial warfare would start with an enormous initial advantage, and the Power that neglected this form of active defence might well find itself fatally situated.

Proceeding on this assumption, we contend that the British policy is to develop the independent conception of the air as an art, an arm and a service; and that this method alone will secure that qualitative ascendancy and superiority which the safety of the country requires.[283]

Spaight, writing from hindsight, explains why England did not 'find itself fatally situated' in 1940:

It is not to strain the probabilities of the case to trace a direct connection between what happened in 1940 and what happened in 1918. The Battle of Britain was won because the Royal Air Force had better pilots and better machines. . . . They might not have been better if the system had been still that which was in existence in 1917.[284]

Since the Battle of Britain was a tactical struggle for control of the air, not an all-out bomber assault on London, it is all the more ironic that the British should have given the fighter weapon no priority until 1938. This nearly disastrous policy was also an outgrowth of the 1917–18 experience. Convinced that there was no effective defence against the bomber, the British relied on retaliation to deter attack. As early as 1925, Trenchard was programming three bomber squadrons for every one of fighters. Except for its salutary effects on 'the morale of city dwellers', he dismissed the fighter as being of little value.

Very nearly at the eleventh hour, the introduction of radar restored British faith in an active defence system. Even so, the legendary Spitfires were too 'few' to have anything but a secondary role in 1940. Slessor records that the aircraft available to Fighter Command (mostly Hurricanes) 'proved just adequate against a scale of attack which proved less intensive than we had anticipated'.[285]

CHAPTER TWENTY-SIX

The Sky on Fire

The strategic Independent Air Force the British created in 1918, in their leap from the emotional springboard of the Gotha raids, was as momentous for the future as the formation of the Royal Air Force. Much of the sincere but blatant advocacy of air-power as 'the golden road to victory' between wars was due to 'the lead which Britain gave'.

This development in warfare is most often attributed to the doctrines of Douhet. 'First to advance a full-scale theory of air-power', the controversial Italian general is widely accepted as the inventor of strategic aerial warfare, and the original exponent of the 'independent air arm'. Douhet's books were certainly read and debated by the military staffs of all the leading powers during the inter-war period. His writings served as a peg on which lesser 'air prophets' could anchor their own arguments. But, officially, the air arms of the various nations developed along more traditional lines.

Douhet was too radical to be followed in the uncertain game of war. No country, even the most air-minded, 'staked everything on the aeroplane' in World War II. Trenchard, who wrote little and published less, was undoubtedly of greater practical influence. Even 'official Italian air doctrine came from Britain and the British development of an independent air service'.[286] Before 1945, only the British and the Americans looked upon the big bomber as an indispensable weapon. They alone used it on a massive scale as an integral part of their strategy. 'The view,' writes Liddell Hart, 'that the bomber would be the decisive factor in any future war, and would suffice in itself to produce a decision ... had actually been a primary article in the R.A.F. creed before Douhet's theory had gained currency.'[287]

A first-hand experience, such as the British had in 1917–18, is much more likely to be acted upon than a mere theory, however formalized or vividly expounded. Their phobia over attack from the air—that 'this great city of London could be totally destroyed'—was revived as early as 1922. Rid of the Germans for the time being, the British became alarmed over the French whose air force was seen as 'the strongest and best-equipped on earth'. Trenchard, by this time, was preaching his belief in the bomber with the fanaticism of a convert. As Chief of the Air Staff, he stated, in 1923, the policy to be followed 'in a single-handed war against France':

It is on the bomber offensive that we must rely for defence. It is on the destruction of enemy industries and, above all, on the lowering of morale of enemy nationals caused by bombing that ultimate victory rests. . . .[288]

The 'above all' of that policy was the old German idea of 'frightfulness', something which harked back to the burning of Belgian villages in 1914. Such murky origins of a way of war, now British, may be denied. They were certainly obscured by what came to be accepted as 'strategic bombing'. But they became more apparent with their telling influence on the conduct of World War II. At the Casablanca Conference of 1943, the Combined Chiefs of Staff spelled out the objectives of the Anglo-American air offensive against Germany. The directive read:

Your primary objective will be the progressive destruction of the German military, industrial, and economic system, and the undermining of morale of the German people to a point where their armed resistance is fatally weakened.[289]

Britain was evidently still giving 'the lead'. Yet, the American version of air-power varied very definitely from the British concept. The big-bomber ideas Mitchell had brought home in 1919 had no traumatic strings attached. U.S. air doctrine, as it developed at the Air Corps Tactical School, held that 'the real target was industry itself, not national morale'.[290] American airmen were trained to hit the 'pickle-barrel'. Daylight precision bombing was stubbornly adhered to, despite heavy losses, over Europe for the better part of the war. The Americans finally changed their tactics to ones of indiscriminate fire raids over the cities of Japan. While made for practical reasons, the switch was not entirely unrelated, even if only subconsciously, to the events of 7 December 1941.

Trenchard, writes his biographer, 'did not dwell on the cumulative savagery of unrestricted bombing'. Undoubtedly, his considerations were purely military just as they had been when he opposed the practice in 1917. But the commitment to the 'bomber offensive' was anything but unemotional at Cabinet level. In an often quoted address to the House of Commons in 1932, Prime Minister Stanley Baldwin said:

> I think it well . . . for the man in the street to realize there is no power on earth that can protect him from bombing, whatever people may tell him. The bomber will always get through. . . .
>
> The only defence is in offence, which means you have got to kill more women and children quicker than the enemy if you want to save yourselves. I mention that so people may realize what is waiting for them when the next war comes.[291]

The black despair of this strategy was the very thing weighing Baldwin down at the time. The Geneva Disarmament Conference, then in session, was making no progress on the limitation of aerial bombing. France insisted on denying Germany's claims to 'equality of status' in the air. The Conference petered out without agreement after Brandenburg and his delegation walked out in 1933.

Bomber Command came into being with the reorganization of the Royal Air Force in 1936. The following year, Sir Cyril Newall became Chief of the Air Staff. 'If Newall had no other claim to fame,' Slessor writes, 'his reputation would rest secure on his having sponsored the programme which ultimately gave us Bomber Command as it developed in the later years of the war.'[292] Newall, it will be recalled, was the lieutenant-colonel who had gone to Ochey to launch the first of Lloyd George's reprisal raids in October 1917.

Sponsored in 1938, the 'programme' provided for 'a striking force of 1,360 first-line aircraft with about 300 per cent reserves, all of which were ultimately to be heavy bombers'. By 1939, the Air Staff was thinking in terms of 3,500 heavy bombers. The British 'finished the war with just over 1,700 heavies', far short of their production goals.[292] But with considerable American help, Bomber Command had enough. Before the Armistice in 1918, Handley Page had been able to deliver only three four-engined bombers, out of an order for 255. During World War II, four out of every ten heavy bombers built in England were Halifaxes, a Handley Page product. The Halifaxes alone dropped 225,000 tons by 1945.

Recalling the pre-war prophecies of swift and certain doom, Spaight calls it a 'curious thing' that they 'dwelt always on what was going to happen to *our* cities. . . . Bomber Command was, somehow, overlooked. The fact that here in Britain, while we dithered about our own safety, we were all the time creating a tremendous engine of offensive war, that the bases were taking shape in eastern England . . . was simply not mentioned in polite society in the years 1936–39. The English are a queer race.'[293]

A critic of bomber warfare, Admiral Sir Gerald Dickens, testifies that the 'strategic principle' was adopted 'many years before the war and so was not merely a forced reaction to the policy of destruction from the air pursued by the Germans. We find therefore a clash in policies, a divergence in principles, at a time when there were no alarums and excursions to interfere with the process of clear reasoning. . . . The tendency to bomb towns . . . first showed itself towards the end of the 1914–18 war, when Handley-Page bombers were being assembled . . . to bomb Berlin'.[294]

Dickens did not go back quite far enough. Their centuries-old sense of island security turned topsy-turvy in 1917, the British emerged not only as big-bomber enthusiasts, but also as the first apostles of 'massive retaliation'. 'It had always been an article of faith with the Air Staff,' Slessor notes, 'that the counter-offensive was the most important element in our defence.'[295]

Just as air-power was 'a two-edged sword which cuts both ways', so were the over-estimations of its capabilities. Air Vice-Marshal Kingston-McCloughry, in commenting on the years between wars, writes that 'the Air Force High Command, which at that time was not provided with many particularly intelligent personalities, badly overstated their claims. . . . These claims were based partly on faulty deductions from the First World War that the morale of the civil population would not be able to withstand the strain of air bombardments. The Air Force High Command over-assessed the material damage which could be inflicted . . . at that time; and they scarcely appreciated the measures to which an enemy is prepared to resort in order to continue the struggle. . . . Nor did they appreciate the difficulties of selecting the best targets, and of accurate bombing, as well as counter-measures. . . .'[296]

The Air Staff's conviction that a country could be demoralized into defeat from the air was based largely on the reaction of Londoners to the Gotha raids. Until 1940, there was little else to go on. In Slessor's words, 'we really did not know anything about air warfare on a major scale'.[297] The miscalculations resulting from the unnerving but limited experience of 1917–18 are understandable. But, oddly enough, the Air Staff estimate of civilian morale was not one of the illusions shattered by the Blitz. If anything, the theory of the 'knock-out blow', as applied to the Germans, seemed to flourish in its wake.

General Sir Alan Brooke, who was soon to become Chief of the Imperial General Staff, recalls the spring of 1941 as 'a time when the . . . attitude was growing fast that the war could best be won by a vast bombing effort. . . . The Air Ministry looked upon the re-entry of the Army on to the Continent as most improbable and quite unnecessary'.[298] Trenchard, now nearly seventy, staunchly supported this view. His personal recipe for winning 'the war in a reasonable time', one he put forth in a 'powerful paper' to Churchill after the Dieppe Raid of August 1942, was to 'avoid entanglement in land campaigns on the mainland of Europe and instead put everything into air-power (British and American) against the enemy's vital spots. If we can put such force into attack from the air, German morale and ability to continue the war will be broken. . . .'[299]

'Opinions are divided,' Churchill acknowledged well into World War II, 'as to whether the use of air-power could by itself bring about a collapse in Germany and Italy. Well, there is certainly no harm in trying.'[300] There was a certain consistency in Churchill's cheerful but non-committal statement. 'The government of a great nation,' he had said in October 1917, was not likely to surrender as a result of 'any terrorization of the civil population which could be achieved by air attack. . . . Familiarity with bombardment, a good system of dugouts or shelters, a strong control by police and military authorities', would suffice to keep 'the national fighting power unimpaired'.

Churchill may have contradicted himself years later in his warning speeches to Parliament. But the strengthening factors he outlined in 1917 were precisely those Nazi Germany was best capable of developing in World War II. Indeed, in 1917, he had gone on to say: 'Nothing we have learned of the capacity of the German population to endure suffering justifies us in assuming that they could be cowed into submission by such methods. . . .'[301] But, in World War II, Churchill was all for 'trying', or as he is reported to have said: 'To make the enemy burn and bleed in every way.'[302]

The British thus had long before the Battle of Britain and the Blitz, and even the war, an air strategy which the Germans themselves had first tried and rejected except when it would directly and immediately assist their Army in battle. That strategy, though nourished by the 'enthusiasm of the specialist', did not suit all the British in the opening phase of the war. 'Whatever be the length to which others might go,' Chamberlain told the House of Commons early in 1940, 'the Government will never resort to blackguardly attacks on women and other civilians for purposes of mere terrorism.'[303]

Bomber Command, for the first eight months, was confined to attacking only 'legitimate military objectives . . . capable of identification'. The restriction, a consequence of Government policy which held that 'deliberate attack on the civilian population' were 'against international law', ironically dated back to 1938, the year that the Air Staff initiated its big-bomber programme. The Government was also much concerned about neutral public opinion, particularly in the United States. The Cabinet insisted on 'incontrovertible evidence' that the Germans had first resorted to bombing civilians. Perhaps because no bombs had fallen on British cities, Warsaw was overlooked.

'We never had the least doubt that sooner or later the gloves would come off,' Slessor recalls of the Air Staff position during that period when Britain drifted from peace into the strange lull known as the 'Phoney War'.[304] 'There was an eager desire to find an excuse, or even provoke an occasion,' writes Liddell Hart, 'for trying out the British air theory of destroying the enemy's sources of war production. The effort was initiated almost immediately after the German Army's offensive in the West opened in May 1940.'[305]

On 10 May, the day the German panzers rolled, Churchill became Prime Minister. That night, two months before the start of the Battle of Britain, Bomber Command made its first raid against the German mainland. Thirty-six bombers attacked the outskirts of

München-Gladbach. 'Germany did begin it in the first world war but not in the second,' confirms Spaight.[306]

On the night after the blasting of Rotterdam, 15 May, the first large-scale British raid, one of nearly a hundred bombers, was carried out against Germany. Air Chief Marshal Sir Hugh Dowding, much alarmed over the frittering away of his Fighter Command in France, 'had urged a bombing raid on the Ruhr in order to draw reprisals upon this country. This was highly logical . . . but the Germans firmly kept their eyes on the main battle and did not take the bait.'[307]

Although Bomber Command attacked Hamburg, Bremen, Essen, and a score of other German cities during the summer of 1940, the Luftwaffe ignored London. Then, on the night of 24 August, a dozen German aircraft, seeking to bomb oil tanks at Thameshaven and Rochester, dropped their explosives on central London, the first since 1918. The bombing was due to a navigational error. With the Battle of Britain entering a critical phase, the British quickly rose to the occasion. The 'bait', this time, was a raid on Berlin in 'reprisal' for the bombing of London. Bomber Command kept up its attacks for a week.

Hitler was now faced with much the same situation which had confronted Lloyd George after a week of Gotha raids in late September 1917. 'The Berliners are stunned,' wrote William L. Shirer in his diary. 'They did not think it could ever happen.'[308] On 4 September 1940, Hitler announced to a wildly emotional crowd that 'such attacks on our cities' would be met by 'razing their cities to the ground'. He had a lot more to lose than Lloyd George.

The Luftwaffe turned from the sector control stations and airfields of Fighter Command for what the British welcomed as 'the less dangerous bombing of London'. On 7 September, over three hundred escorted bombers struck at the city in daylight. The assault was continued into the night by 'a continuous stream of bombers'. The toll on this, the twenty-fifth anniversary of the first big Zeppelin raid on London, was over 1,600 casualties.

Göring's boast had been fulfilled. At the same time, the British had diverted the Luftwaffe from winning the Battle of Britain by 'offering London as a sacrifice'. In 1934, Churchill had prophetically referred to the exposed city as 'a tremendous fat cow, a valuable fat cow, tied up to attract the beasts of prey'.[309]

The British had also precipitated the Blitz. That the Germans were provoked into 'strategic' bombing, something they did not foresee, and for which they were ill-equipped, there can be no doubt. Of the spasmodic and savage blows rained on Britain that fiery autumn and dark winter of 1940, Fleming writes:

> Had there existed . . . a plan for the systematic reduction of England by bombing it would be possible to argue that the three Air Fleets, poised in a great arc to pave the way for *Sea Lion*, had all the time an ulterior role. . . . The air offensive against London and other cities was not planned as an insurance against invasion proving impossible. In fact it was not planned in advance at all.[310]

For the Germans, bombing 'was in no sense an alternative strategy'. The British, however, were too weak at this time to challenge the enemy in any other way. It was inevitable that their 'air theory', fermented by fear for over two decades, should prevail with total fury.

Bomber Command, much to its chagrin, had discovered early in the war that daylight attacks on small, strictly military targets were dangerous and costly; by night, they were discouragingly unrewarding. The latest object lesson learned at the hands of the Germans, the raid on Coventry, was closely studied. The tactics of 'area bombing', a euphemism for city-killing, were adopted. What followed was, in the words of Liddell Hart, 'the most uncivilizing means of warfare that the world has known since the Mongol devastations'.[311]

The first thousand-bomber raid was made on Cologne in May 1942. The massive attack was carefully planned to 'capture the imagination of the British people and impress the government'.[312] On both scores, it was a 'colossal' success. Cologne was made to glow with the light of 12,000 fires. The horrors of *Operation Gomorrah*, the multiple fire raids on Hamburg in July 1943, may have convinced many Germans that the war was lost. But they were still fighting when the ancient city of Dresden, never before attacked, was destroyed by fire in February 1945.

The 'fantastic glow' guided the bombers from two hundred miles away. The pilot of a Lancaster, the last to leave the city, estimated that the 'sea of fire' below him covered 'some forty square miles. . . . The sky was vivid in hues of scarlet and white, and the light inside the aircraft was that of an eerie autumn sunset. We were so aghast . . . that we flew around in a stand-off position for many minutes before turning for home. . . .'[313]

An estimated 135,000 people died in the awesome fire-storm of Dresden. This toll is more than double the number of civilians killed in Britain by German air action in all six years of the war. In human lives, even the atomic bombing of Hiroshima and Nagasaki do not equal it. Churchill felt that the 'bombing of German cities simply for the sake of increasing the terror, though under other pretexts', had gone far enough. 'We shall come into control of an utterly ruined land,' he warned the British Chiefs of Staff. In Parliament, the attack was denounced 'as an eternal "blot on the escutcheon" of the British Government'.[314]

'I am still not satisfied that I fully understand why it happened,' Air Marshal Sir Robert Saundby, the war-time Deputy-Commander of Bomber Command, wrote nearly twenty years afterward.[315] Seeking the 'precedents' of this frightful holocaust, the author of a well documented account begins by saying: 'Air historians trace the earliest roots of the area offensive against Germany to the events of 10th May 1940.'[316]

Liddell Hart goes as far back as the sixteenth century. He reasons that, historically, this 'strategy of devastation from the air' was 'in the natural line of descent from Britain's traditional strategy'. A 'naval-type strategy', Liddell Hart explains, had always been 'inherently more "barbarous"' than the military-type strategy of Clausewitzian and Continental practice'. The 'starvation blockade' and 'destructive raids' on coastal places, such as the burning of Washington, are cited as examples.[317]

'Our belief in the bomber, in fact, was intuitive—a matter of faith,' states Slessor.[318] An 'act of faith' is also what Spaight calls the creation of the Royal Air Force. C. P. Snow, who strongly disapproves of wars run on 'gusts of emotions', nonetheless indicates that 'bombing had become a matter of faith'.[319]

For all that fateful faith, it would still seem that the true genesis of the British bombing strategy, and its excess in World War II, was more psychological than it was mystical, or even nautical. The destruction of Germany's cities in the Second World War was a legacy of the First, one which began with the spectacle of 'little silver specks' creeping across the London sky on a sunny day in June in that pandoric year of 1917.

That legacy, with all the human fears and fallibility which made it possible, is still ours today. Only the adversaries, and the weapons, have changed.

An Afterword

by

Marshal of the Royal Air Force

Sir John Slessor

G.C.B., D.S.O., M.C.

The Sky on Fire is a fascinating book and one that badly needed writing. Major Fredette has clearly taken great pains to get at the facts, and the result is intensely interesting.

After reading the author's most readable account of the first Battle of Britain fifty years ago, few will deny to the Germans the credit for being pioneers of what we now call 'strategic' air warfare—and perhaps fewer will be disposed to grudge them that dubious distinction! It is the more astonishing—and for us in Britain extremely fortunate—that little more than twenty years later they should have been so bad at it.

But the main interest in this book is its relevance to what the author calls 'only the beginning'—the beginning of the evolution of strategic thinking on a new dimension of warfare. And here I think Major Fredette has been rather less than fair to Lord Trenchard. I say that—not merely out of affection and respect for old 'Boom', under whom and with whom I served in varying degrees of intimacy for some forty years—but because I think he was absolutely right in his attitude towards the formation of an independent Air Force *at that time and in those circumstances.*

Trenchard was very inarticulate—his mind always worked quicker than his tongue; he was almost physically incapable of expressing his thoughts on paper—his handwriting had to be seen to be believed, his dictating was a nightmare to his stenographers, and his instructions were often a cause of puzzlement (and sometimes amusement) to his Staff officers. His closest friends (or worst enemies) could hardly accuse him of being an intellectual type of officer. But he had a flair, an instinct, for getting at the really essential core of a problem. He was never one to set much store by the codified principles of war as set out in the Manuals—indeed I doubt whether at that time he had ever read them; but he had an unerring instinct for that one which I think is the absolutely vital one for airmen, wielding as they do an essentially flexible (and therefore easily divertible) instrument of war—I mean the principle of concentration of force on that task or objective which is the really critical, the potentially decisive one *at the moment*.

Major Fredette sums up Trenchard's attitude in 1918 in one short sentence—'he concentrated on fighting that war, not the next one'. Who shall say he was wrong? Consider the background against which he was working. He had been at Haig's side throughout the desperate battles of 1916 and 1917, and had seen at first hand the near-collapse of the French Army after the failure of the Nivelle offensive. He was manifestly right in his conviction that, with the primitive short-range aircraft of the day, there was not the remotest possibility of winning that war by independent 'strategic' action against Germany in the air; but he believed that the proper application of air power could be invaluable in making sure that the Army won it in France on the ground. Indeed, while the Independent Force was being formed and the R.A.F. being born, it was not so much a question of how we could win the war as whether there was not still a real possibility of our losing it before the Americans could make their weight felt. 'Remember again the military situation on the battle-front' I wrote in a book published in 1936.* 'No sooner had one terrific German offensive been brought to a standstill on one part of the front, with a loss of hundreds of square miles of ground, than another was launched elsewhere; and the Allied Armies were literally gasping for breath. Invalids, "C 3 men", labour battalions, airmen of balloon sections, cooks and batmen were taking their places in the line, and the Allied resources in men and material were strained almost to breaking point. Among these resources not the least formidable were the bombing aircraft, which in the opinion of many officers at the time were capable of making a contribution of the utmost importance to the defeat of a hostile offensive by interfering with the enemy's communications serving the front of attack.' And I concluded then that 'the employment of the Independent Force against objectives in Germany *at this time* was an entirely unjustified diversion of effort'.

1914–18 was essentially a land war, and the only possible means of winning it was the defeat of the German armies in the field.

---

* *Air Power and Armies*. Oxford University Press, p. 76.

That was the one vitally critical, the only decisive, task and Trenchard was perfectly right in opposing any diversion from it.

Nevertheless, it was as well for Britain that the vision and determination of Smuts, the fear-stricken state of public opinion and what Major Fredette quotes C. G. Grey as calling the 'Parthenogenetic' initiative of the House of Commons did call the R.A.F. into existence before the Armistice. That would certainly not have happened once the war was over and the air threat to British cities ceased to hang over us. And it is ironic to recall that, but for Trenchard, the war-time decision would almost certainly have been reversed in the early years of the uneasy peace—and that might well have resulted in our defeat in World War II. Then was the time to start thinking about how to win the next war; and Trenchard did so with the vision and singleness of purpose that had characterized his attitude towards winning the last one.

The relevant point today, as the author reminds us, is that the German air attacks of 1915 to 1918 were the beginning of a new conception of war. It was not only the so-called 'Air Enthusiasts', Trenchard and the Air Staff in those early days, who held that bombardment from the air could be decisive in war. Major Fredette quotes others, not airmen at all, such as Smuts and Churchill, Cowdray and Weir, who foresaw that possibility before there was such a thing as an Air Staff. Even Marshal Foch (reflecting, I always suspect, the views of his brilliant Staff officer, Weygand) is on record as saying that the moral effect of air action might in future prove decisive in forcing a Government to sue for peace.

What in fact did the claim of the 'Air Enthusiasts' amount to? Answer—that explosive delivered from the air could be decisive, without the intervention of armies or navies, in destroying the will and capacity of a nation to resist. Will anyone today, in an age of inter-continental missiles with multi-megaton nuclear war-heads, argue that they were wrong? Of course not—they were perfectly right, beyond their own wildest dreams. Where we were very wrong in 1939 (as I am on record as frankly admitting*) was in a gross under-estimate of the weight of explosive and the technical efficiency of the means of delivery necessary to achieve decisive results; and in an almost equally serious under-estimate of the capacity of civilian populations to stand up to the scale of attack available

* *The Central Blue.* Cassell, 1956. Chapter IX.

before the advent of nuclear explosive. So I think it relevant to reflect for a moment on just how wide of the mark we actually were in that first misjudgment, and whether we had not a pretty valid reason for the second. I do not intend this as an apologia for the Air Staff before and during World War II, but as an attempt to look fairly and objectively at the facts and possibilities as they existed— or anyway as we saw them—as a guide to the future. And let the reader remember that we did not then enjoy many advantages of hindsight, that our actual experience of 'strategic' air warfare was confined to the German raids which Major Fredette describes so ably, the very limited operations of the Independent Force in 1918 (a total of 550 tons of bombs aimed at German cities) and a few alarming stories of the Spanish Civil War.

Consider first our misjudgment, before the outbreak of Hitler's war, of the probable effect of German air attack on our own population. Read Major Fredette's accounts of the near-panic reactions of the populace in London, Southend, Ramsgate, etc., to the Gotha and 'Giant' raids. Sir Malcolm Campbell, in the passage quoted on page 232, did not exaggerate in writing that 'the "stop the war" cry was heard far more frequently than was pleasant or flattering to our belief in the sticking-to-it qualities of our people'. Liddell Hart (quoted on page 231) wrote in 1937 of 'the general tendency among the public, whenever they think of war, for the thought to be associated immediately with the idea of being bombed from the air' and he went on, quite rightly, to say that 'from this apprehension springs a natural exaggeration'.

I know my own feelings in 1939 as Director of Plans on the Air Staff when events were moving inexorably towards war, were coloured by a personal memory of one evening in 1915 when I was a very young officer; I had a minor crash trying to land in fog after pursuing a Zeppelin over London on the night of 23 October; returning next evening with the spares necessary to repair the damage, from Farnborough through the East End of London (which had taken a few bombs the night before) with headlights on to help us to get back quickly to our airfield, I and my little party were mobbed and had to get a policeman to stand on each running board of the tender to get us through a crowd which it is no exaggeration to describe as panic-stricken. I remember in 1939 my old friend Colonel H. L. Ismay (as he then was), with whom I was associated on the Rae Committee on the evacuation of Government departments from London, saying to me: 'You know, Jack, I really shudder to think of the effect on our easy-going, peaceable people of being subjected to this sort of thing.' In the light of my boyhood experience, I could not agree with him more; if a few small bombs had that effect on an East End crowd twenty-four years earlier, how would people react to the scale of attack we were then anticipating? It was an immense relief—and a proud surprise to me—to find how gallantly those same people, and their sons and daughters, stood up to terrible punishment when the time came.

In the light of wisdom after the event it is easy, and indeed justifiable up to a point, to criticize us for gross exaggeration of what was coming to us, both the scale of attack and its results (incidentally, it was by no means only the Air Staff who took that unduly alarmist view). But we and our civilian colleagues could only do our imperfect best—in the light of our own experience and the limited, and in some respects misleading, information available to us—to make as reasonable an estimate as possible of what the results might be. It was surely better—indeed in the circumstances it was inevitable—that we should over-estimate rather than the reverse. It was our duty to present what we honestly regarded as the worst case; we should have been culpable indeed if in the event we had proved to have under-estimated, and hence failed to order enough of the necessary counter-measures—shelters, evacuation, hospital beds and so on.

No one before the war could possibly have foreseen what civilian populations turned out to be able to endure in the way of air bombardment. I always think the resistance of the populations in places like Berlin, Hamburg and the Ruhr to what must have been almost intolerable pressure was little short of miraculous. Experience of, for instance, London in the renewed blitzes of April 1941, and of Liverpool in the following month, sometimes makes me wonder rather uneasily whether citizens of a free Democracy would ever stand up to the same scale of punishment as subjects of an iron-regimented totalitarian dictatorship did—no doubt had to do, whether they liked it or not.

However—that is now ancient history and entirely different from an age when total war would mean the complete obliteration of whole cities in a matter of minutes. But it is not irrelevant to consideration of the influence of public opinion on decision-making in any future crisis.

Now—how badly wrong were the 'Air Enthusiasts' who thought that even in Hitler's war 'strategic' air action could be decisive? It would be silly to pretend that at the beginning of the war we did not enormously under-estimate the bomber strength and efficiency necessary to get decisive results; but is anyone quite sure that two or three years later, and especially when the U.S. bomber force was building up at our side, we were never within practical reach of getting them if we had chosen to deploy our resources with that in view? Major Fredette quotes Trenchard as telling Churchill in 1942 after the Dieppe Raid that, if we avoided entanglement in land campaigns in Europe and 'put everything into air-power (British and American) against the enemy's vital spots. If we can put such force into attack from the air German morale and ability to continue the war will be broken.'

Was he wrong? Of course, no one can possibly be sure—this is now all a matter of sheer speculation. In any event, by that time the course of the war had progressed to a point where there was no practical possiblity of the old man's advice being accepted. If it could have been, then my own bet (for what it is worth) would be that Trenchard would have been proved right. Consider the incendiary attacks on Hamburg in July 1943—about 42,000 deaths in the resulting firestorms; Albert Speer, a level-headed character, said of that in evidence at Nürnberg: 'I reported for the first time orally to the Führer that if these aerial attacks continued, a rapid end to the war might be the consequence.' Suppose we had possessed the resources in 1942 to follow up quickly the first thousand-bomber raid on Cologne in May by a dozen more on selected German cities (and remember by that time Bomber Command had been continually milked to find squadrons for other theatres—seventeen of them to Coastal Command alone); is it not at least a tenable assumption that the war might have been brought to an end in 1943? I don't know—obviously no one does. I think at least we should be very chary of asserting that even in Hitler's war, before the coming of nuclear weapons, air power could not have been decisive in itself if it had received the necessary priorities.

Said Churchill in the House of Commons in 1943: 'As between the different Services, while avoiding invidious comparisons, I should certainly say that the outlook of the Royal Air Force upon this war was more closely attuned to the circumstances and conditions as they emerged by painful experience than those of either of the other two Services.' I have already admitted our shortcomings and misjudgements in relation to the numerical strength and technical efficiency required. But I make so bold as to claim for the Air Staff that the really astonishing thing was, not how wrong we were, but how right in the long run we turned out to be. We were certainly absolutely right in adopting the heavy four-engined bomber programme when we did, before the war; Major Fredette rightly criticizes the Germans for not following up in that line their astonishing technical achievements in World War I. We probably could not have achieved when we did the necessary tactical and technical efficiency—the radio and radar aids to navigation and bomb-aiming in particular—without the bitterly costly experience in actual operations during the earlier years of the war. It is no good bemoaning now our inability to concentrate sooner on the build-up of our bomber strength; these diversions of effort to other theatres were inevitable in the circumstances—especially those designed to help avert defeat in the Battle of the Atlantic. The same is true of the priority afforded to the build-up of our defensive fighter strength. Incidentally our failure to make adequate provision for fighters in all but the last of the pre-war expansion schemes stemmed largely from our experience in the days of which Major Fredette writes so well; we were probably not quick enough to appreciate fully the enormous, the revolutionary implications of radar; in the background of our minds was the experience of the days before radar, when the numbers of fighters required to give any chance of even partially effective defence were so prohibitively colossal, that perhaps naturally we attached undue importance to the bomber counter-offensive as a means of defence.

But consider these facts—in the words of the official U.S. Bombing Survey Report: 'Of the tonnage dropped on Germany proper, in the neighbourhood of 85% was subsequent to January 1st 1944. Perhaps even more significant is the fact that of all the tonnage dropped on Germany, 72% was after July 1st 1944. If the bombing of Germany had little effect on production prior to July '44, it is not only because she had idle resources upon which to draw, but because the major weight of the air offensive against her had not been brought to bear. After the air war against Germany was launched on its full scale, the effect was immediate.'

It seems to me impossible to resist the conclusion that if, when the Americans entered the war, our Governments had allocated the necessary priority in man-power, material and scientific effort to the bomber offensive, German resistance would have been broken, as Trenchard said, well before it was, and a relatively small army could have gone into Germany before June 1944, on a march-table instead of the operation order that hurled them against the Normandy beaches.

All this is now only a matter of conjecture and of history—and, in this nuclear age, most of the history of past great wars is wholly irrelevant to the future. But we can still learn something from it in one critically important field—that of political reactions and human behaviour under the threat of imminent war. World War II was the first war of which it was clear in advance that death and destruction would not be confined to the military forces in the field, but would have a direct and immediate impact on civilian populations at home. Those in Britain and France today who talk about independent national nuclear deterrents, which imply (if they mean anything) the willingness in the last resort to engage in a bilateral nuclear exchange with Soviet Russia without the support of the United States, would do well to read Major Fredette's story of the first Battle of Britain of fifty years ago, and ponder its impact on the minds of responsible leaders twenty years later, facing the imminence of a war of which the implications were incomparably less catastrophic than they would be today or tomorrow.

Tables

BRITISH AIR DEFENCES IN 1918

London Air Defence Area	Guns	Searchlights	Balloon Aprons	Fighter Squadrons*
January	249	323	4	8
November	304	415	10	11
Northern Air Defence Area				
November	176	291	0	5
Total at the Armistice	480	706	10	16

* Authorized 24 aircraft each

HOME DEFENCE SQUADRONS OF THE LONDON AIR DEFENCE AREA IN NOVEMBER 1918

	Squadron	Aircraft Type	Aerodromes
47th Wing	No. 51	F.E.2b	Mattishall, Norfolk Tydd St. Mary, Lincs. Marham, Norfolk
49th Wing	No. 39	Bristol Fighter	North Weald Bassett, Essex
	No. 44	Sopwith Camel	Hainault Farm, Essex
	No. 78	Sopwith Camel	Sutton's Farm, Essex
	No. 141	Bristol Fighter	Biggin Hill, Kent
50th Wing	No. 37	Sopwith Camel	Stow Maries, Essex Goldhanger, Essex
	No. 61	Sopwith Camel	Rochford, Essex
	No. 75	Avro	Hadleigh, Suffolk Elmswell, Suffolk
53rd Wing	No. 50	Sopwith Camel	Bekesbourne, Kent
	No. 112	Sopwith Camel	Throwley, Kent
	No. 143	Sopwith Camel	Detling, Kent

BRITISH AIR RAID CASUALTIES, 1915-1918

(See also map on page 214)

Gotha and Giant Raids, 1917–1918	*Killed*	*Injured*	*Total*
London and Environs	488	1,437	1,925*
Folkestone (incl. Shorncliffe Camp)	89	184	273
Chatham (incl. the Naval Barracks)	132	96	228
Harwich–Felixstowe (incl. the Naval Air Station) ..	27	56	83
Southend–Shoeburyness (incl. Rochford Aerodrome)..	34	47	81
Sheerness	17	51	68
Dover	12	36	48†
Margate	15	24	39
Ramsgate	10	23	33
Kent (incl. Leybourne Camp)	8	25	33
Essex (various places)	1	3	4
Suffolk (various places)	3	—	3
Total	836	1,982	2,818

Raids by single-engined aeroplanes, 1915–1917 ..	21	76	97
Airship Raids, 1915–1918	557	1,358	1,915
Total	1,414	3,416	4,830‡

* The London casualties include 24 killed and 196 injured by British anti-aircraft fire; also 14 killed and 14 injured in air-raid shelter stampedes.

† The Dover casualties include 1 killed and 10 injured inflicted by German aircraft not belonging to Kagohl 3 on the night of 2 September 1917.

‡ Overall total includes the following military casualties: 354 killed, 642 wounded.

SUMMARY OF THE GOTHA AND GIANT RAIDS ON ENGLAND

Date	Bomber force Started / Attacked	Places raided	Bombs dropped (kgs.)	British casualties and damage	Aircraft losses
25 May 1917	23/21 Gothas	Folkestone, Shorncliffe Camp	5,200	95 killed 195 injured £19,405	1 Gotha lost over Channel 1 Gotha crashed
5 June 1917	22/22 Gothas	Sheerness; Shoeburyness	5,000	13 killed 34 injured £5,003	1 Gotha shot down
13 June 1917	20/17 Gothas	London; Margate	4,400	162 killed 432 injured £129,498	No German losses 1 British aircraft forced down
4 July 1917	25/18 Gothas	Harwich; Naval Air Station, Felixstowe	4,400	17 killed 30 injured £2,065	No German losses 1 British aircraft forced down
7 July 1917	24/22 Gothas	London	4,475	57 killed 193 injured £205,622	1 Gotha shot down 4 Gothas crashed on landing 2 British aircraft shot down 1 British aircraft forced down
22 July 1917	23/21 Gothas	Harwich; Felixstowe	5,225	13 killed 26 injured £2,780	1 Gotha crashed on landing
12 Aug. 1917	13/11 Gothas	Southend; Shoeburyness; Margate	2,125	32 killed 46 injured £9,600	1 Gotha shot down 4 Gothas crashed on landing
22 Aug. 1917	15/10 Gothas	Margate; Ramsgate; Dover	1,900	12 killed 27 injured £17,145	3 Gothas shot down

Date	Bomber force Started/Attacked	Places raided	Bombs dropped (kgs.)	British casualties and damage	Aircraft losses
3–4 Sep. 1917	5/4 Gothas	Chatham Naval Barracks; Sheerness; Margate	1,315	132 killed 96 injured £3,993	None
4–5 Sep. 1917	11/9 Gothas	London; Margate; Dover	3,060	19 killed 71 injured £46,047	1 Gotha missing
24 Sep. 1917	16/13 Gothas	London; Dover, Leybourne Camp	4,285	21 killed 70 injured £30,818	1 Gotha crashed on return 1 British aircraft crashed
25 Sep. 1917	15/14 Gothas	London; East Kent	4,000	9 killed 23 injured £16,394	1 Gotha missing 2 British aircraft crashed
28 Sep. 1917	25/3 Gothas 2/2 Giants	Coastal areas in Suffolk, Kent, Essex	3,100	No casualties £129	3 Gothas shot down 6 Gothas crashed on landing 1 British aircraft crashed
29 Sep. 1917	7/4 Gothas 3/3 Giants	London; Sheerness	3,375	14 killed 87 injured £23,154	1 Gotha shot down 1 Gotha forced down in Holland
30 Sep. 1917	11/10 Gothas 1/1 Single-engined aircraft	London; Margate; Dover	3,690	14 killed 38 injured £21,482	None
1–2 Oct. 1917	18/11 Gothas	London; Kent; Essex	3,705	11 killed 41 injured £45,570	No reports available

Date	Bomber force Started/Attacked	Places raided	Bombs dropped (kgs.)	British casualties and damage	Aircraft losses
29 Oct. 1917	3/1 Gothas	Essex coast	450	None	1 British aircraft crashed
31 Oct.–1 Nov. 1917	22/22 Gothas	London; Ramsgate; Dover	5,815	10 killed 22 injured £22,822	5 Gothas crashed on landing 2 British aircraft crashed
6 Dec. 1917	19/16 Gothas 2/2 Giants	London; Sheerness; Margate; Dover	7,770	8 killed 28 injured £103,408	2 Gothas brought down by gunfire 1 Gotha missing 1 Gotha crashed on landing
18 Dec. 1917	15/13 Gothas 1/1 Giant	London; Margate	5,125	14 killed 83 injured £238,861	1 Gotha shot down 1 Gotha crashed on return 6 Gothas crashed on landing
22 Dec. 1917	2/2 Giants	Kent coast	2,000	None	None
28–29 Jan. 1918	13/7 Gothas 1/1 Giant	London; Sheerness; Margate; Ramsgate	3,700	67 killed 166 injured £187,350	1 Gotha shot down 4 Gothas crashed on landing 1 British aircraft forced down
29–30 Jan. 1918	4/3 Giants	London Essex coast	3,000	10 killed 10 injured £8,968	None
16 Feb. 1918	5/5 Giants*	London; Dover	4,250	12 killed 6 injured £19,264	None
17 Feb. 1918	1/1 Giant	London	1,000	21 killed 32 injured £38,922	1 British aircraft crashed

* Based on German records; according to the British only 3 Giants attacked.

Date	Bomber force Started/Attacked	Places raided	Bombs dropped (kgs.)	British casualties and damage	Aircraft losses
7–8 Mar. 1918	6/5 Giants	London; Herne Bay	5,020	23 killed 39 injured £42,655	2 Giants crash-landed on return flight 2 British aircraft collided and crashed
19–20 May 1918	38/28 Gothas 3/3 Giants 2/2 Single-engined aircraft	London; Faversham; Dover	14,550	49 killed 177 injured £177,317	1 Gotha forced down in England 5 Gothas shot down 1 Gotha crashed on return flight
8 Daylight Raids 19 Night Raids ___ 27 Total	383/297 Gothas 30/28 Giants		111,935 kgs.	835 killed 1,972 injured £1,418,272	24 Gothas shot down or missing 36 Gothas lost or damaged in crashes 2 Giants lost in crashes ___ 62 Total 6 British aircraft forced or shot down* 10 British aircraft lost or damaged in crashes ___ 16 Total

* German bomber crews claimed 10 victories.

Bibliographies

Bibliographies

All references in the text and in the sources are to the first-named edition or title of any book.

I. SELECTED BIBLIOGRAPHY

OFFICIAL HISTORIES AND PUBLICATIONS

Jones, Henry A. *The War in the Air*, vol. ii–vi (Oxford: Clarendon Press, 1928–37).

Der Kommandierende General. *Nachrichtenblatt der Luftstreitkräfte*, 1917–18.

THE RAIDS ON ENGLAND

Aschoff, Walter. *Londonflüge 1917* (Potsdam: Ludwig Voggenreiter Verlag, 1940).

Ashmore, Edward B. *Air Defence* (London: Longmans, Green, 1929).

von Bülow, Hilmer. 'Die Angriffe des Bombengeschwader 3 auf England' in *Die Luftwacht*, 1927.

Charlton, L. E. O. *War Over England* (London: Longmans, Green, 1936).

von Eberhardt, Generalleutnant a. D. Walter. *Unsere Luftstreitkraefte 1914–18* (Berlin: Vaterländischer Verlag C. A. Weller, 1930).

Haddow, G. W. and Grosz, Peter M. *The German Giants* (London: Putnam, 1962).

Lewis, Cecil. *Sagittarius Rising* (New York: Harcourt, Brace. London: Peter Davies. 1936).

MacDonagh, Michael. *In London During the Great War* (London: Eyre & Spottiswoode, 1935).

Morison, Frank (Albert H. Ross). *War on Great Cities* (London: Faber & Faber, 1937).

Morris, Joseph. *The German Air Raids on Great Britain* (London: Sampson Low, Marston, 1920).

Rawlinson, A. *The Defence of London 1915–1918* (London: Andrew Melrose, 1923).

Robinson, Douglas H. *The Zeppelin in Combat* (London: G. T. Foulis, 1962).

THE ROYAL AIR FORCE

Beaverbrook, Lord. *Men and Power* (London: Hutchinson, 1956).

Boyle, Andrew. *Trenchard* (New York: W. W. Norton. London: Collins, 1962).

Grey, Charles G. *A History of the Air Ministry* (London: Allen & Unwin, 1940).

Joubert, Sir Philip. *The Third Service* (London: Thames & Hudson, 1955).

Spaight, James M. *The Beginnings of Organised Air Power* (London: Longmans, Green, 1927).

2. OTHER BOOKS REFERRED TO IN THE TEXT

Bowman, Gerald. *War in the Air* (London: Pan, 1958. Evans, 1956).

Bryant, Sir Arthur. *The Turn of the Tide* (*The Alanbrooke Diaries*) (Garden City: Doubleday. London: Collins, 1957).

Campbell, Sir Malcolm. *The Peril from the Air* (London: Hutchinson, 1937).

Chamier, J. A. *The Birth of the Royal Air Force* (London: Isaac Pitman, 1943).

Churchill, Winston S. *While England Slept* (New York: Putnam's, 1938).

Coxon, Stanley W. *Dover During the Dark Days* (London: John Lane, The Bodley Head, 1919).

Cuneo, John R. *Winged Mars*, vol. i–ii (Harrisburg: Military Service Publishing Co., 1942, 1947).

Dickens, Gerald. *Bombing and Strategy* (London: Sampson Low, Marston, 1946).

Drew, George A. *Canada's Fighting Airmen* (Toronto: Maclean, 1930).

Emme, Eugene M. *The Impact of Air Power* (Princeton: D. Van Nostrand, 1959).

FitzGibbon, Constantine. *The Winter of the Bombs* (New York: Norton, 1957). *The Blitz* (London: Wingate, 1957).

Fitzroy, Almeric. *Memoirs* (London: Hutchinson, 1925).

Fleming, Peter. *Operation Sea Lion* (New York: Simon and Schuster. London: Hart-Davies, 1957).

Fuller, J. F. C. *The Conduct of War* (New Brunswick: Rutgers University Press. London: Eyre & Spottiswoode, 1961).

Hancock, W. Keith. *Smuts*, vol. i *The Sanguine Years, 1870–1919* (Cambridge University Press, 1962).

Hermann, Hauptmann. *The Rise and Fall of the Luftwaffe* (New York: G. P. Putnam's, 1943. London: Long, 1944).

von Hoeppner, Ernst. *Deutschlands Krieg in der Luft* (Leipzig: von Hase & Köhler, 1921).

Ironside, Lord (ed. Macleod, Kelly). *Time Unguarded* (New York: David McKay, 1962). *The Ironside Diaries* (London: Constable, 1962).

Irving, David. *The Destruction of Dresden* (New York: Holt, Rinehart & Winston. London: Kimber, 1963).

Joynson-Hicks, William. *The Command of the Air* (London: Nisbet, 1916).

Kemp, P. K. *Key to Victory* (Boston: Little, Brown, 1957). *Victory at Sea* (London: Muller, 1958).

Kerr, Mark. *Land, Sea, and Air* (London: Longmans, Green, 1927).

Kingston-McCloughry, E. J. *The Direction of War* (London: Jonathan Cape, 1955).

Kraus, René. *Winston Churchill* (New York: J. B. Lippincott, 1940).

Liddell Hart, B. H. *Europe in Arms* (New York: Random House. London: Faber, 1937).

Liddell Hart, B. H. *The Revolution in Warfare* (New Haven: Yale University Press, 1947. London: Faber, 1946).

Lloyd George, David. *War Memoirs* (London: Ivor Nicholson & Watson, 1933–6).

Ludendorff, Erich. *The General Staff and Its Problems* (London: Ludendorff, Erich. *Ludendorff's Own Story* (New York: Harper, 1919).

Mitchell, William: *Memoirs of World War I* (New York: Random House, 1960).

Moore, Samuel Taylor. *U.S. Air Power* (New York: Greenberg, 1958).

Poolman, Kenneth. *Zeppelins Against London* (New York: John Day, 1961). *Zeppelins Over London* (London: Evans Bros., 1960).

Pound, Reginald, and Harmsworth, Geoffrey. *Northcliffe* (London: Cassell, 1959. New York: Praeger, 1960).

Repington, C. à Court. *The First World War* (Boston: Houghton, Mifflin, 1920. London: Constable, 1920).

Reynolds, Quentin. *They Fought for the Sky* (London: Cassell, 1958. New York: Bantam, 1958).

Robertson, Sir William. *Soldiers and Statesmen* (London: Cassell, 1926).

Robinson, Douglas H. *The Zeppelin in Combat* (London: G. T. Foulis, 1962).

Ropp, Theodore. *War in the Modern World* (New York: Collier, 1962. London: Cambridge University Press, 1960).

Saundby, Sir Robert. *Air Bombardment* (New York: Harper. London: Chatto & Windus, 1961).

Shirer, William L. *The Rise and Fall of the Third Reich* (New York: Simon & Schuster, 1960. London: Secker & Warburg, 1963).

Slessor, Sir John. *The Central Blue* (London: Cassell, 1956).

Smith, Dale O. *U.S. Military Doctrine* (New York: Duell, Sloan and Pearce, 1955).

Snow, C. P. *Science and Government* (Cambridge, Mass.: Harvard University Press. London: Oxford University Press, 1961).

Snowden Gamble, C. F. *The Air Weapon*, vol. i (London: Oxford University Press, 1931).

Spaight, James M. *Air Power and War Rights* (London: Longmans, Green, 1947).

Spaight, James M. *Bombing Vindicated* (London: Bles, 1944).

Spender, John A. *Weetman Pearson, First Viscount Cowdray 1856–1927* (London: Cassell, 1930).

Sutton, H. T. *Raiders Approach!* (Aldershot: Gale & Polden, 1956).

von Tirpitz, Alfred. *My Memoirs* (New York: Dodd, Mead, 1919. London: Hurst & Blackett, 1919).

Wallace, Graham. *R.A.F. Biggin Hill* (London: Putnam, 1957).

Watson-Watt, Robert. *The Pulse of Radar* (New York: Dial, 1959).

Wood, Derek, and Dempster, Derek. *The Narrow Margin* (New York: McGraw-Hill. London: Hutchinson, 1961).

Wrench, John E. *Struggle 1914–1920* (London: Ivor Nicholson & Watson, 1935).

Zuerl, Walter. *Pour le Mérite Flieger* (Munich: Curt Pechstein Verlag, 1938).

Sources

*All references in the text and in the sources are to the
first-named edition or title of the book.*

1. Charlton. *War Over England*, p. 134.
2. Pound & Harmsworth, *Northcliffe*, p. 301.
3. *The Times*, 29 November 1916.
4. *The Aeroplane*, vol. xi, No. 23, 6 December 1916, pp. 1079–1081.
5. *Flight*, vol. ix, No. 29, 19 July 1917.
6. Chamier. *The Birth of the Royal Air Force*, p. 2.
7. Cuneo. *Winged Mars*, p. 134.
8. Boyle. *Trenchard*, p. 100.
9. Cuneo. *Winged Mars*, p. 105.
10. Kraus. *Winston Churchill*. p. 183.
11. Emme. *The Impact of Air Power*, pp. 27–9.
12. Boyle. *Trenchard*, p. 107.
13. Jones. *The War in the Air*, vol. ii, p. 182.
14. Cuneo. *The Air Weapon 1914–1916* (vol. ii of *Winged Mars*), p. 268.
15. Jones. *The War in the Air*, vol. v, p. 12.
16. Jones. *The War in the Air*, vol. v, p. 8.
17. *The Times*, 8 May 1917.
18. Coxon. *Dover During the Dark Days*, p. 195.
19. Jones. *The War in the Air*, vol. v, p. 21.
20. Coxon. *Dover During the Dark Days*, pp. 194–5.
21. *The New York Times*, 18 June 1917.
22. Coxon. *Dover During the Dark Days*, pp. 192–4.
23. Jones, *The War in the Air*, vol. v, p. 22.
24. Snowden Gamble. *The Air Weapon*, vol. i, p. 263.
25. Jones. *The War in the Air*, vol. v, pp. 24–5.
26. *Flight*, vol. ix, No. 23, 7 June 1917, p. 597.
27. *The Times*, 25 July 1917.
28. *The Times*, 15 January 1916.
29. *The Aeroplane*, vol. xii, No. 14, 4 April 1917, p. 846.
30. *Flight*, vol. ix, No. 23, 7 June 1917, pp. 596–7.
31. *The Times*, 4 June 1917.
32. *The Times*, 28 May 1917.
33. Poolman. *Zeppelins Against London*, p. 150.
34. *The Times*, 4 February 1916.
35. Robinson. *The Zeppelin in Combat*, p. 50.
36. Robinson. *The Zeppelin in Combat*, p. 65.
37. Poolman. *Zeppelins Against London*, p. 36.
38. Robinson. *The Zeppelin in Combat*, pp. 95–6.

39. Reynolds. *They Fought for the Sky*, pp. 37–8.
40. *Der Frontsoldat*, No. 10, 1937, p. 305.
41. von Bülow. In *Die Luftwacht*, No. 5, May 1927, p. 262.
42. von Bülow. In *Die Luftwacht*, No. 6, June 1927, p. 331.
43. Letter, Kurt Küppers to the author, 2 May 1965.
44. *The New York Times*, 2 July 1917.
45. *The New York Times*, 14 June 1917.
46. *The New York Times*, 2 July 1917.
47. von Bülow. 'Die Angriffe des Bombengeschwader 3 auf England' in *Die Luftwacht*, No. 6, June 1927, p. 337.
48. Kogenluft, *Nachrichtenblatt der Luftstreitkräfte*, No. 7070 B., 21 June 1917, p. 34.
49. von Hoeppner. *Deutschlands Krieg in der Luft*, pp. 111–12.
50. *Flight*, vol. ix, No. 25, 26 June 1917, p. 622.
51. *The Times*, 15 June 1917.
52. Robertson. *Soldiers and Statesmen*, vol. ii, pp. 16–17.
53. Jones. *The War in the Air*, vol. iv, p. 134.
54. Lewis. *Sagittarius Rising*, p. 167.
55. *The New York Times*, 26 June 1917.
56. Robertson. *Soldiers and Statesmen*, vol. ii, pp. 243–7.
57. *The Aeroplane*, vol. xiii, No. 1, 4 July 1917, p. 12.
58. *The Times*, 9 March 1916.
59. Ludendorff. *The General Staff and Its Problems*, vol. ii, pp. 449–52.
60. *The New York Times*, 22 June 1917.
61. Ludendorff. *The General Staff and Its Problems*, pp. 453–8.
62. MacDonagh. *In London During the Great War*, p. 198.
63. MacDonagh. *In London During the Great War*, pp. 199–200.
64. *Flight*, vol. ix, No. 28, 12 July 1917, p. 704.
65. *The Aeroplane*, vol. xiii, No. 3, 18 July 1917, p. 190.
66. *Flight*, vol. ix, No. 28, 12 July 1917, p. 703.
67. *Flight*, vol. ix, No. 28, 12 July 1917, p. 702.
68. *The New York Times*, 9 July 1917.
69. MacDonagh. *In London During the Great War*, p. 203.
70. Jones. *The War in the Air*, vol. v, p. 40.
71. Robertson. *Soldiers and Statesmen*, vol. ii, p. 17.
72. *The Times*, 14 July 1917.
73. Jones. *The War in the Air*, vol. v, pp. 38–9.
74. Jones. *The War in the Air*, vol. iv, p. 154.
75. *The Times*, 9 July 1917.
76. *Flight*, vol. ix, No. 29, 19 July 1917, p. 731.
77. Lloyd George. *War Memoirs*, vol. iv, p. 1863.
78. *Flight*, vol. ix, No. 29, 19 July 1917, p. 730.
79. *The New York Times*, 21 August 1917.

80. Jones. *The War in the Air,* vol. v, pp. 487–91.
81. Ashmore. *Air Defence,* p. 40.
82. Jones. *The War in the Air,* vol. v, p. 44.
83. Lewis. *Sagittarius Rising,* pp. 181–2.
84. Letter, Walter Georgii to the author, 14 September 1963.
85. Kurt Delang. 'Bomben über England' in *Der Frontsoldat,* No. 14, 1937, p. 435.
86. Ashmore. *Air Defence,* p. 43.
87. Delang. In *Der Frontsoldat,* No. 14, p. 436.
88. *The New York Times,* 14 August 1917.
89. *The Aeroplane,* vol. xiii, No. 8, 22 August 1917, p. 552.
90. *Flight,* vol. ix, No. 34, 23 August 1917, p. 865.
91. *The Times.* 'The Air Arm: Last War Years' in *History and Encyclopædia of the War,* Part 242, vol. 19, 8 April 1919, p. 264.
92. Letter, Kurt Küppers to the author, 11 September 1963.
93. *La Gazette de Hollande,* 28 August 1917.
94. Letter, Walter Georgii to the author, 12 July 1963.
95. *Flight,* vol. ix, No. 35, 30 August 1917, p. 903.
96. *Morning Post,* 6 October 1917.
97. *The Aeroplane,* vol. xiii, No. 9, 29 August 1917, p. 626.
98. *The Times,* 8 February 1916.
99. Emme. *The Impact of Air Power,* pp. 33–7.
100. *The Times,* 15 February 1916.

101. *The Times,* 17 February 1916.
102. Jones. *The War in the Air,* vol. iii, p. 270.
103. *The Times,* 25 May 1916.
104. *The Times,* 16 May 1916.
105. Jones. *The War in the Air,* vol. iii, p. 271.
106. *The Times,* 18 May 1916.
107. Jones. *The War in the Air,* vol. iii, 1931, p. 276.
108. Jones. *The War in the Air,* vol. iii, pp. 277–8.
109. Spaight. *The Beginnings of Organised Air Power,* p. 119.
110. *The Times,* 3 January 1917.
111. *The Times,* 5 April 1917.
112. Beaverbrook. *Men and Power,* p. 220.
113. Beaverbrook. *Men and Power,* p. 219.
114. Joubert. *The Third Service,* p. 19.
115. Boyle. *Trenchard,* p. 34.
116. Boyle. *Trenchard,* pp. 232–3.
117. Haig, Sir Douglas. 'Views on a Separate Air Service' in *The Air Power Historian,* vol. iii, No. 3, July 1956, pp. 153–7.
118. *The New York Times,* 6 September 1917.
119. Lewis. *Sagittarius Rising,* pp. 182–3.
120. Ashmore. *Air Defence,* p. 53.
121. Lewis. *Sagittarius Rising,* p. 183.
122. von Eberhardt. *Unsere Luftstreitkräfte 1914–18,* p. 142.
123. Kogenluft, *Nachrichtenblatt der Luftstreitkräfte,* No. 10000 B., 20 September 1917, p. 236.

124. Ashmore. *Air Defence*, p. 57.
125. Lewis. *Sagittarius Rising*, pp. 191–3.
126. von Bülow. In *Die Luftwacht*, No. 6, June 1927, p. 338.
127. von Bülow. In *Die Luftwacht*, No. 6, June 1927, p. 332.
128. von Bülow. In *Die Luftwacht*, No. 6, June 1927, p. 339.
129. *The Aeroplane*, vol. xiii, No. 15, 10 October 1917, p. 1066.
130. Jones. *The War in the Air*, vol. v, 1935, p. 78.
131. *The New York Times*, 12 September 1917.
132. Lewis. *Sagittarius Rising*, p. 190.
133. *The New York Times*, 27 September 1917.
134. von Eberhardt. *Unsere Luftstreitkräfte 1914–18*, pp. 222–4.
135. Kogenluft. *Nachrichtenblatt der Luftstreitkräfte*, No. 10800 B., 11 October 1917, p. 290.
136. *The New York Times*, 1 October 1917.
137. Morison (Ross). *War on Great Cities*, pp. 142–3.
138. Jones. *The War in the Air*, vol. v, 1935, p. 90.
139. *The Aeroplane*, vol. xiii, No. 17, 24 October 1917, p. 1222.
140. Rawlinson. *The Defence of London 1914–1918*, p. 204.
141. Rawlinson. *The Defence of London 1914–1918*, p. 209.
142. Hancock. *Smuts*, vol. i *The Sanguine Years 1870–1919*, p. 442.
143. Wrench. *Struggle 1914–1920*, p. 251.
144. Jones. *The War in the Air*, vol. v, 1935, p. 86.
145. Spender. *Weetman Pearson: First Viscount Cowdray 1856–1927*, p. 234.
146. *The New York Times*, 4 October 1917.
147. Jones. *The War in the Air*, vol. v, p. 88.
148. *The Aeroplane*, vol. xiii, No. 15, 10 October 1917, p. 1072.
149. *The Aeroplane*, vol. xiii, No. 15, 10 October 1917, p. 1007.
150. *The Aeroplane*, vol. xii, No. 26, 27 June 1917, pp. 1645–6.
151. *The Times*, 18 June 1917.
152. *The Times*, 22 June 1917.
153. *The Times*, 27 June 1917.
154. Jones. *The War in the Air*, vol. v, p. 31.
155. Jones. *The War in the Air*, vol. v, p. 39.
156. *The Times*, 24 July 1917.
157. *The Aeroplane*, vol. xiii, No. 9, 29 August 1917, p. 568.
158. *The New York Times*, 5 October 1917.
159. Boyle. *Trenchard*, p. 235.
160. Repington. *The First World War*, vol. ii, p. 64.
161. Repington. *The First World War*, vol. ii, p. 97.
162. Joubert. *The Third Service*, p. 38.
163. Boyle. *Trenchard*, p. 204.
164. Boyle. *Trenchard*, p. 219.
165. Haig. 'Views on a Separate Air Service' in *The Air Power Historian*, vol. iii, No. 3, July 1956, pp. 154–5.

166. *The Aeroplane*, vol. xiii, No. 17, 24 October 1917, p. 1226.
167. von Tirpitz. *My Memoirs*, vol. ii, pp. 271–2.
168. Robinson. *The Zeppelin in Combat*, pp. 66–7.
169. Jones. *The War in the Air*, vol. v, 1935, p. 102.
170. *The New York Times*, 2 November 1917.
171. *Flight*, vol. ix, No. 45, 8 November 1917, p. 1174.
172. *The Aeroplane*, vol. xiii, No. 18, 13 October 1917, p. 1304.
173. *The Aeroplane*, vol. xiii, No. 23, 5 December 1917, pp. 1637–8.
174. Lewis. *Sagittarius Rising*, pp. 203–4.
175. Lewis. *Sagittarius Rising*, pp. 205–6.
176. Morison. *War on Great Cities*, p. 153.
177. Lewis. *Sagittarius Rising*, pp. 208–9.
178. von Bülow. In *Die Luftwacht*, No. 6, June 1927, p. 334.
179. von Ludendorff. *Ludendorff's Own Story*, vol. ii, pp. 351–2.
180. Hermann. *The Rise and Fall of the Luftwaffe*, pp. 3–4.
181. von Bülow. In *Die Luftwacht*, No. 7, July 1927, pp. 381–2.
182. Zuerl. *Pour le Mérite Flieger*, pp. 274–5.
183. Drew. *Canada's Fighting Airmen*, pp. 238–45.
184. Kogenluft, *Nachrichtenblatt der Luftstreitkräfte*, No. 13300 B., 20 December 1917, p. 463.

185. MacDonagh. *In London During the Great War*, pp. 238–9.
186. Jones. *The War in the Air*, vol. v, pp. 109–10.
187. *The Aeroplane*, vol. xiii, No. 23, 5 December 1917, p. 1644.
188. Ashmore. *Air Defence*, p. 76.
189. *Flight*, vol. ix, No. 49. 6 December 1917, p. 1281.
190. Morison. *War on Great Cities*, p. 157.
191. Rawlinson. *The Defence of London*, p. 238.
192. *The New York Times*, 31 January 1918.
193. *The Times*. 'The Air Arm: Last War Years' in *History and Encyclopædia of the War*, Part 242, vol. ii, 8 April 1919, p. 271.
194. Rawlinson. *The Defence of London*, p. 240.
195. *The New York Times*, 11 March 1918.
196. Haddow and Grosz. *The German Giants*, p. 32.
197. *The New York Times*, 18 February 1918.
198. Morison, *War on Great Cities*, p. 164.
199. Haddow and Grosz. *The German Giants*, p. 33.
200. Jones. *The War in the Air*, vol. v, p. 119.
201. Eberhardt. *Unsere Luftstreitkräfte 1914–1918*, pp. 442–3.
202. Eberhardt. *Unsere Luftstreitkräfte 1914–1918*, pp. 443–4.
203. Haddow and Grosz. *The German Giants*, p. 45.
204. Kerr. *Land, Sea, And Air*, pp. 290–1.

205. *Flight*, vol. ix, No. 46, 15 November 1917, p. 1206.
206. Joynson-Hicks. *The Command of the Air*, p. 114.
207. Spaight. *The Beginnings of Organised Air Power*, p. 16.
208. Grey. *A History of the Air Ministry*, p. 82.
209. *The Aeroplane*, vol. xiii, No. 1, 4 July 1917, p. 9.
210. Boyle. *Trenchard*, p. 246.
211. Fitzroy. *Memoirs*, vol. ii, p. 667.
212. Boyle. *Trenchard*, p. 254.
213. Beaverbrook. *Men and Power*, p. 220.
214. *The Aeroplane*, vol. xiv, No. 2, 9 January 1918, p. 172.
215. Wallace. *R.A.F. Biggin Hill*, p. 47.
216. Boyle. *Trenchard*, p. 271.
217. Beaverbrook. *Men and Power*, p. 221.
218. Boyle. *Trenchard*, pp. 266-7.
219. Boyle. *Trenchard*, p. 268
220. Boyle. *Trenchard*, p. 269
221. Beaverbrook. *Men and Power*, p. 236.
222. Jones. *The War in the Air*, vol. v, pp. 156-7.
223. Ashmore. *Air Defence*, p. 87.
224. *The New York Times*, 21 May 1918.
225. Morison. *War on Great Cities*, p. 168.
226. Wallace. *R.A.F. Biggin Hill*, p. 51.
227. Repington. *The First World War*, p. 336.
228. Ashmore. *Air Defence*, p. 93.
229. Wallace. *R.A.F. Biggin Hill*, p. 44.
230. Robinson. *The Zeppelin in Combat*, p. 332.
231. Jones. *The War in the Air*, vol. v, p. 151.
232. Aschoff. *Londonflüge 1917*, p. 131.
233. Aschoff. *Londonflüge 1917*, pp. 134-5.
234. Aschoff. *Londonflüge 1917*, p. 138.
235. Moore. *U.S. Air Power*, p. ix.
236. Jones. *The War in the Air*, vol. iv, p. 155.
237. Boyle. *Trenchard*, p. 289.
238. Boyle. *Trenchard*, p. 285.
239. Boyle. *Trenchard*, p. 274.
240. von Bülow. In *Die Luftwacht*, No. 7, July 1927, p. 387.
241. Boyle. *Trenchard*, p. 287.
242. Boyle. *Trenchard*, p. 288.
243. Boyle. *Trenchard*, p. 303.
244. Boyle. *Trenchard*, p. 293.
245. Repington. *The First World War*, vol. ii, p. 361.
246. Boyle. *Trenchard*, p. 299.
247. Repington. *The First World War*, p. 389.
248. Boyle. *Trenchard*, p. 312.
249. Joubert. *The Third Service*, p. 69.
250. Bowman. *War in the Air*, p. 13.
251. Smith. *U.S. Military Doctrine*, p. 122.
252. Kingston-McCloughry. *The Direction of War*, p. 72.
253. Mitchell. *Memoirs of World War I*, pp. 109-11.
254. Spaight. *The Beginnings of Organised Air Power*, p. 206.
255. Boyle. *Trenchard*, p. 330.

256. Liddell Hart. *Europe in Arms*, p. 24.
257. Churchill. *While England Slept*, pp. 142–3.
258. Campbell. *The Peril From the Air*, pp. 64–5.
259. Morison. *War on Great Cities*, p. 194.
260. FitzGibbon. *The Winter of the Bombs*, pp. 7–8.
261. Slessor. *The Central Blue*, pp. 153–4.
262. FitzGibbon. *The Winter of the Bombs*, p. 4 and p. 9.
263. Kemp. *Key to Victory*, p. 26.
264. Ironside. *Time Unguarded* (*The Ironside Diaries*), pp. 42–3.
265. Ironside. *Time Unguarded* (*The Ironside Diaries*), p. 61.
266. Ironside. *Time Unguarded* (*The Ironside Diaries*), p. 62.
267. Saundby. *Air Bombardment*, p. 63.
268. Bryant. *The Turn of the Tide*, pp. 31–3.
269. Kemp. *Key to Victory*, p. 18 and pp. 20–1.
270. See Donald Macintyre, 'Point of No Return' in U.S. Naval Institute Proceedings, vol. 90. No. 2, February 1964, pp. 36–43.
271. Ironside. *Time Unguarded* (*The Ironside Diaries*), p. 144.
272. Fleming. *Operation Sea Lion*, pp. 33–4.
273. Spaight, *Bombing Vindicated*, p. 55.
274. Wood and Dempster. *The Narrow Margin*, p. 44.
275. Wood and Dempster. *The Narrow Margin*, p. 45.
276. Spaight. *Bombing Vindicated*, p. 144.
277. Sutton. *Raiders Approach!* preface.
278. Joubert. *The Third Service*, p. 49.
279. Wood and Dempster. *The Narrow Margin*, p. 150.
280. Watson-Watt. *The Pulse of Radar*, p. 12.
281. Grey. *A History of the Air Ministry*, p. 78.
282. Watson-Watt. *The Pulse of Radar*, p. 105.
283. Boyle. *Trenchard*, p. 408.
284. Spaight. *Bombing Vindicated*, p. 37.
285. Slessor. *The Central Blue*, p. 180.
286. Ropp. *War in the Modern World*, p. 294.
287. Liddell Hart. *The Revolution in Warfare*, p. 10.
288. Boyle. *Trenchard*, p. 470.
289. Saundby. *Air Bombardment*, p. 103.
290. Emme. *The Impact of Air Power*, p. 189.
291. Emme. *The Impact of Air Power*, pp. 51–2.
292. Slessor. *The Central Blue*, p. 181.
293. Spaight. *Air Power and War Rights*, pp. 31–2.
294. Dickens. *Bombing and Strategy*, p. 3.
295. Slessor. *The Central Blue*, p. 166.
296. Kingston-McCloughry. *The Direction of War*, p. 75.
297. Slessor. *The Central Blue*, p. 150.

298. Bryant. *The Turn of the Tide*, p. 189.
299. Boyle. *Trenchard*, p. 727.
300. Spaight. *Air Power and War Rights*, p. 38.
301. Fuller. *The Conduct of War*, pp. 279–80.
302. Fuller. *The Conduct of War*, p. 286.
303. Fuller. *The Conduct of War*, p. 280.
304. Slessor. *The Central Blue*, p. 214.
305. Liddell Hart. *The Revolution in Warfare*, p. 93.
306. Spaight. *Air Power and War Rights*, p. 267n.
307. FitzGibbon. *The Winter of the Bombs*, p. 40.
308. Shirer. *The Rise and Fall of the Third Reich*, p. 778.
309. Spaight. *Air Power and War Rights*, p. 31.
310. Fleming. *Operation Sea Lion*, pp. 238–9.
311. Liddell Hart. *The Revolution in Warfare*, p. 95.
312. Saundby. *Air Bombardment*, p. 128.
313. Irving. *The Destruction of Dresden*, p. 146.
314. Irving. *The Destruction of Dresden*, pp. 229–30.
315. Irving. *The Destruction of Dresden*, p. 9.
316. Irving. *The Destruction of Dresden*, p. 19.
317. Liddell Hart. *The Revolution in Warfare*, p. 94.
318. Slessor. *The Central Blue*, p. 204.
319. Snow. *Science and Government*, p. 50.

Index

Aircraft are arranged under their names, or letters and numbers; squadrons (numbered) under 'Squadrons'.